STEPPIN' OUT WITH ATTITUDE

OTHER BOOKS BY ANITA BUNKLEY

Balancing Act
Sisters
Starlight Passage
Wild Embers
Black Gold
Emily, the Yellow Rose

STEPPIN' OUT WITH ATTITUDE

Sister, Sell Your Dream!

ANITA BUNKLEY

 HarperPerennial
A Division of HarperCollins*Publishers*

HarperCollins books may be purchased for educational, business, or sales promotional use. For information please write: Special Markets Department, HarperCollins Publishers, Inc., 10 East 53rd Street, New York, NY 10022.

FIRST EDITION

Designed by Nancy Singer Olaguera

Library of Congress Cataloging-in-Publication Data
Bunkley, Anita R. (Anita Richmond)
    Steppin' out with attitude : Sister, sell your dream! / Anita Bunkley. —
1st ed.
      p. cm.
    Includes index.
    ISBN 0-06-095288-1
    1. Success—Psychological aspects. 2. Success in business—Psychological aspects. 3. Afro-American women—Psychology. I. Title.
BF637.S8B765   1998
650. 1—dc21   98-23754

98 99 00 01 02 ❖/RRD 10 9 8 7 6 5 4 3 2 1

With love and appreciation to my mother, Virginia Richmond, who always stepped out and showed me the way

Maximize
the potential
hidden behind routine.
Fly!
Although your wings may be
tender
young
bitter
torn.
A realistic attitude
will cast away darkness
tears of lost hope
to welcome the sunshine.
Sister, you are not alone.

RAMONA SUSANE NICHOLAS

Contents

Acknowledgments

This book could not have been written without the support, inspiration, love, advice, assistance, and trust of these sisters: Virginia, Linda, Maria, Vickie, Angela, Tracey, Tracie, Martha, Bonnie, Carol, Karen, Barbara, Debra, Rita, Sharon, Terrie, Elaine, Kathryn, Cathy, Susan, Sara, Toni, Gloria, Joanne, Janis, Janice, Kim, Dianna, Sibyl, Aubrey, Carolyn, Sally, Ramona, Audrey, Helen, Faye, Gwyn, Mary, Adrienne, Denise, Rosalie, Julia, Darleane, Jackie, Cheryl, Megan, Elma, Jacqueline, Elizabeth, Emma, Donna, Nancy, Mignon, Pat, Reva, Lisa, Raquel, Suzette, Vanesse, Tiwoni, Geri, Angle, and LaNita.

Introduction

Speaking with confidence about an ability to do something well should be an honest expression of the faith we have in our skills, expertise, and experience. But telling the world how talented and wonderful we are is not easily done—at least not for most of us. We don't want to be thought of as boastful, vain, egotistical, or conceited, and we fear ridicule, criticism, and expressions of envy from those who are closest to us.

The manner in which we convey this sense of inner trust reflects the value we place on ourselves. A glory hound brags. An egotist boasts. A selfish person gloats. But a savvy sister with a mission has no trouble sharing information about herself with those who can help her meet specific goals.

Yes, it takes a great deal of courage and confidence to sell others on our dreams, and the process can become extremely problematic. This book, written for all of my sisters—black, white, Hispanic, Asian—is designed to help generate the enthusiastic support needed to launch a project, start a business, move up the corporate ladder, or affect change within an audience of importance.

The insightful tips and inspirational stories you will read in this book come from myself, as well as a wide range of women who accepted the challenge to step out and raise their visibility within the workplace, the marketplace, or the community at large. For us, approaching the commitment to stand out from the crowd means accepting the highs and the lows that come along with standing in the spotlight. By valuing our talents, studying our markets, and understanding our clients' needs, we have been able to live out our dreams. Achieving this took patience, confidence, and above all, the right attitude.

ATTITUDE PLAYS A MORE IMPORTANT ROLE IN SUCCESS THAN TALENT, CONNECTIONS, OR MONEY.

Too many of my sisters hold back at staff meetings and planning sessions, in social situations and at networking events, reluctant to talk about their ideas or reveal a skill they have quietly been developing. Too many of my talented sisters are hesitant about blowing their own horns, reluctant to tell the world about their expertise or creative ideas. Increasing awareness of our services, products, and talent should be thought of as a strategy to meet the needs of others while serving a specific audience (one person or a multitude). This combination shifts the concept of self-promotion far beyond egotistical indulgence, allowing sisters to charter a path toward the success they desire.

Ten years ago, as an aspiring author with little more than a dream, a manuscript, and a great deal of faith, I stepped out into the marketplace, determined to find the women I believed were hungering for the stories I wanted to write. Along the way to becoming a published author, I learned very quickly that I had to sell more than a manuscript to a publisher or a book to a reader. I had to sell myself.

In the late 1980's, I wrote, published and marketed my first novel, *Emily, The Yellow Rose, A Texas Legend,* my African-American romantic tale set during the Texas Revolution. It focused on the story of the wartime capture and escape of a beautiful mulatto woman who, according to music historians, may have inspired the song "The Yellow Rose of Texas."

Mainstream publishers and distributors refused to handle it, thinking there was no market for my novel. Chain bookstores locked me out because the book was self-published. But I never considered giving up. I knew there was a large African-American female audience that would embrace my novel, if only I could reach them, and I also knew that it was a market not yet recognized or tapped by major players in the publishing industry.

I became determined to prove the skeptics wrong. I knew there were hundreds of thousands of black women who were avid readers of women's fiction and would love to take a break from popular writers like Danielle Steele and Nora Roberts to embrace a sister's work—if only the same types of women's stories could be made available to them. Providing an alternative to readers like this became my ultimate objective as I focused on serving the needs of my target audience while making myself known to them.

Faced with the reality of the publishing industry at that time, I began to examine the complex mix of public relations, publicity, advertising, target marketing, and promotion that would provide the best chance of reaching my readers while fulfilling my personal and professional goals. Confident that I could sell my books, I set out to do just that.

Having worked as a teacher in both public and private schools, and as a director with two international nonprofit organizations, I was not intimidated about the prospect of speaking before large audiences and I had acquired a great deal of experience dealing with the media. Eagerly, I jumped into the spotlight to tell everyone about my novel, but a part of me still felt somewhat uncomfortable about tooting my own horn. I wanted to sell booksellers and readers on my publication, but I didn't want to come off as boastful and vain. While a little voice in my head said, "Go for it, girl," another said, "Slow down, be cautious, hold back." What was going on? Why was I feeling guilty about stepping out and speaking up?

I began talking to other sisters about their visions for the future and how they felt about taking charge of selling their dreams. We discussed our feelings about self-promotion and the need for us to orchestrate our own visibility to make our talents, services, and products better known. We soon found that we had a lot in common.

Some sisters told stories of holding back because the success they envisioned frightened them too much. They could not bring themselves to even contemplate the changes that would take place in their lives if their long-held dreams came true. There were conversations with artists, educators, technicians, managers, entrepreneurs, and community activists whose careers, projects, and businesses remained underdeveloped because they could not effectively tell the world what they were doing. Why? Because they were unclear about what to say and to whom. They needed a starting point as they struggled to overcome the words of caution that swam through their heads. They remembered their mother's and grandmother's stern admonishment about drawing attention to themselves. *Go along with the program* and *Don't rock the boat* were familiar messages given to many of us. In other words, if we played it safe and didn't dare stand out, we could avoid getting hurt.

At one time, such culturally based warnings were necessary—offered in the spirit of survival advice to protect young black children from those who would do them harm or take advantage of them. But over the years, such warnings may have affected our ability to take risks, undermining our self-confidence about moving too far too fast.

Another roadblock to stepping out that surfaced quite often was the fear of upsetting the gender balance in a marriage or a committed relationship. Sensitive, supportive sisters told stories of backing off from going out into the marketplace, of putting their dreams on the back burner in order to reassure the men in their lives that they were still in control. It can be difficult to balance the demands of the moment with a vision for the future when loyalties are divided and allegiances are tested.

The difficulties that result from being the only or the first woman of color to achieve a certain status were also discussed in many conversations. Minority women are most often judged by standards set by white men, affecting feelings of self-esteem and self-worth. Black women, in particular, have had cultural burdens to deal with that negatively impact their ability to adapt to a variety of professional and social environments. We must remove race-based obstacles by continuing to learn and grow, .moving forward to repair and overcome insecurities that stem from less than positive cultural, educational, social, and/or economic experiences.

The negative stereotypes and misinformation that have distorted African-American women's perception of themselves, and mainstream society's perception of them, remain major hurdles to conquer. By courageously entering new social and professional circles to let others know who we are and what we can do, we will help shatter such limiting stereotypes.

Talented women told me that they sometimes feared not being taken seriously because they were female and black. So they began questioning the merit of their input and their value to their companies.

Surprisingly, many of the women I talked to had uncomfortable feelings about wealth, having been brainwashed to believe that poverty is a virtue. It isn't. What is virtuous is using our God-given talent in the right way, living safely, comfortably, and enjoying the fruits of our labor. As long as we commit to enriching our brothers and sisters with our contributions to the economic growth of society, our wealth will be measured in more ways than dollars and cents.

Through discussions, interviews, and observations of hundreds of women of all races and cultural backgrounds, I have witnessed the promise that goes unfulfilled. I want to help all of my sisters banish their fears and better understand the cultural and race-based issues underlying their hesitancy to step forward and tell the world about themselves. Black women, especially, must be courageous, focused, and in touch with their heritage to accomplish this. They must also understand the importance of adopting a mission to serve.

The harsh reality is that African-American women will

always have to deal with issues of racism, sexism, and age-biased prejudices. But we cannot get stuck in the negatives and become blinded to the good that is going on around us.

Growing up in Columbus, Ohio, in a close-knit, two-parent, middle-class African-American household allowed me to observe firsthand the types of role models that many young black girls don't have access to today. I know how fortunate I was. My mother, a beautiful, creative entrepreneur who was deeply involved in our church and neighborhood activities, was always surrounded by active, socially conscious women. She spoke up and stepped out on many occasions, allowing me to witness the kinds of results that self-confidence and courage could produce.

Unafraid to showcase her intelligence and her talent, my mother worked as a couturier, dressing the high-profile women of our city—black and white—at a time when few black women would have been welcome in the elegant salons along High Street. Mother would create dresses for my four sisters and me, then coach us on how to stand, walk, and turn in order to show off her newest creations to audiences of all races, at hotels, churches, or in our home. It was fun. It was exciting. But most of all, these experiences were lessons in moving through life. My mother must have known what she was doing, because participating in her fashion shows gave me the sense of confidence and ease, even when on stage, that have served me well throughout my life.

A childhood love of reading and books inspired me to become a published author. When I was young, Saturday mornings meant trips to the neighborhood library, where I could check out enough books to last until the next visit. I always finished my supply by midweek, then began scrounging around for more books to read. My teachers granted me extra time in the library, loaned me books from their personal libraries, and encouraged my love for great stories. Later, with a degree in Spanish and French from Mount Union College, a small college in central Ohio, I entered the classroom to encourage other students to fall in love with words and language.

It was not until much later, when my own daughters were entering their teens, that I sat down at a typewriter and began writing my first novel. One of my closely held goals was to have books with my name on the spine sitting on the shelves of the same library I patronized as a child. A few years ago, I returned to the new and improved Hilltop Branch Library in Columbus for a program during Black History Month to promote my latest novel, *Starlight Passage*. Yes, my books were on the shelves, and my fans were there to thank me for writing the kinds of stories they loved. What a wonderful turn of events.

In the upcoming chapters you will meet many courageous, talented, self-confident women who have taken charge of their futures and are selling their dreams. You will be offered tips on showcasing your talent and ideas on how to develop and benefit from your assets. I've included lots of practical information on ways to make yourself memorable, but most of all, you will be given tips on adopting attitudes that will help make your journey as satisfying, successful, and exciting as mine.

By defining and incorporating positive attitudinal characteristics into the day-to-day rhythm of your life, you are able to create a personal promotional campaign that brings results. My plan, designed to help women step out with attitude, is based on what I call the Three D's of Life: Desire, Discipline, and Drive.

The strength and motivation that fuel my journey come from the loving support of family, friends, professional colleagues, sisters, teachers, church members, and others in the community who validate my mission. Self-knowledge is the key to maximizing potential, so first we must truly understand what it is we most *desire* from life. If we are not crystal clear about what we want, how can we possibly articulate our dreams to others? In the following chapters, I will provide an assessment process that will help you define, acknowledge, and express what has been on your mind so you can finally transform mental wandering into actualization. Internalization of a long-held desire creates a persistent hunger that will not be satisfied until it is permitted to spring forth with a life force of its own.

By leading *disciplined* lives women learn how to confront fears, freeing themselves to pursue change. Women of color need a strong sense of self, tempered by humility, appreciation, and flexibility in order to stay the course—and to achieve extraordinary success. A disciplined mind, an organized approach, and a realistic attitude are prerequisites for keeping commitments to ourselves.

Working toward increased visibility is, and should be, an evolutionary process that keeps you growing and learning. We are all *driven* by different reasons to spotlight ourselves, but no matter what propels us to step out, it is vital that we have a solid understanding of what is fueling our quest.

If you have been standing in the shadows, enviously watching others take their places in the spotlight, believe me, you can, too—without feeling guilty. The journey to personal and professional fulfillment can be difficult, with challenges and obstacles at every turn, but women with drive and persistence can make the trip a joyful experience with a bounty of rewards along the way.

PART 1

Desire

You are what you think about most.

LES BROWN, MOTIVATIONAL SPEAKER

Mary Jane Gone Bye-Bye

Maria D. Dowd

Executive producer, African American Women on Tour

As little girls—with feet strapped into black, patent-leather Mary Janes, with our lacy socks and Vaseline-shiny brown legs—we were encouraged to sit still and not scuff up those black shiny shoes and ashen up our little brown legs. We were taught to sit quietly, "ladylike" while our brothers—with muddy brown sneakers, untied laces, and play-worn pant knees—kicked up their heels and slid feet first into home plate. Mama simply shook her head and promised to replace the boys' iron-on patches. Too often, the double standard rang loud and clear: girls sit still and be quiet, boys live life to the fullest.

As women-children, we watched and studied with quiet reserve the ways of fast, pride-filled women, and the ways of the God-fearing, church-goin' sisters, wondering which would determine our fate: to be a rebel or to live with restraint. Should we trade in the proverbial Mary Janes and lacy socks for seamed stockings, garters, and high heels so we, too, could kick up our heels? While the men could do their "thang" on Saturday nights and *maybe* make it to church on Sunday mornings, women filled the pews, sitting still and quiet like good Christian women were supposed to do. The double standard continued to ring loud and clear.

As we crossed into womanhood, we accepted the familial and political correctness of basking in our husband's accomplishments and our children's achievements, remaining quiet about what was happening on our own personal and professional fronts. After all, "pride-filled" women were sinful women and self-promotion was a male-only thing. Being good mothers, we sat still, afraid to scuff up our own shiny Mary Janes while mentally fitting our daughters' feet with Reeboks. The double standard continued to ring loud and clear.

In the workplace, those Mary Janes began to feel tighter and those lacy socks began to scratch as we downplayed our talents, skills, accomplishments, and dreams. As our feet began to ache, we yearned for answers, and we started to learn lessons from our past: the double standards and mixed messages we had been given so long ago were obviously the cause of our hurtin' feet.

We began to seek out safe empowering places to learn and share—like African American Women on Tour. We began to seek out enlightening literature like *Steppin' Out with Attitude: Sister, Sell Your Dream!* and soon, we realized that we didn't *have to* sit quietly. We could kick off our Mary Janes and run around in our lacy-socked feet if we so chose.

Now, we can be still and quiet when we *choose* to be because we understand the value of meditation and visualization. We have come to realize that society's drummer ain't always on *our* beat. So we have to find our own drummers, fill ourselves with confidence and wisdom, and acquire the skills we need in order to know that it is okay to step out—with *attitude*.

True liberation comes with Steppin' out barefoot, experiencing the magnificent feeling of wiggling our T.O.E.S.— our Tenacity, our Oneness, our Enthusiasm, and our Saleswomanship. Mary Jane has gone bye-bye.

1
What's on Your Mind?

Attitude Focus: Confronting Change
How can a woman coming from a world that tells her to
go to school
get a job
get married
Buy a house with a family room and a white picket fence
have 2.5 children
send them to college
Retire and live happily ever after
Dare to give all that up
So she can fly?

ELMA L. JACKSON GREEN

COME TO GRIPS WITH THE NEED TO ACT

The alarm clock rings. You smash the button to shut off the demanding buzz that interrupted your dream and pull the blanket up under your chin, reluctant to get up and face another day. The sound of rain pounding against the windows reinforces your desire to turn over, go back to sleep, and forget about going into the office today. But you can't possibly take a sick day now. There's a stack of work on your desk. Your boss warned everyone not to be late for the eight A.M. staff meeting today, and a coworker is depending on you to pick her up on your way into town.

With a groan you sit up, throw your legs over the side of the bed, and wonder how much longer you can keep going at this pace. You've been on the job for a long time. The pay is good and you enjoy your coworkers, but you are keenly aware that something is missing. It's been a frustrating roller-coaster ride—juggling office politics while waiting for the promotion you know you deserve. Now it seems as if the routine aspects of the job have stifled your creativity. You're ready to give up on trying to get management to take your ideas and suggestions seriously. You've simply settled into the rut of marking time, glad to have a steady paycheck coming into your bank account twice a month.

The dream that was so rudely interrupted by the shrilling alarm still hangs in the back of your mind as you bathe and dress. Making your way to the kitchen, you refuse to allow yourself to dwell on the possibility of stepping out to do your own thing, let alone contemplate the changes that you would have to make in your life if you acted on what has been on your mind for months: quit your job and strike out on your own. Such a move would be complicated and risky, yet all day long you keep thinking about it because you know it is definitely time for something to give.

ATTITUDE ADJUSTMENT TIP #1

Give in to the vision.

At a recent networking mixer for the membership of the National Coalition of 100 Black Women, I moved from table to table introducing myself, explaining the mission of the organization to potential new members. I sat and chatted with one young lady for nearly twenty minutes. She was in banking, loved books, and had read several of mine. She was articulate, charming, an ideal candidate for our organization. As I stood to leave, I handed her my business card and asked for hers. The card she handed me was a personal one without any mention of the bank where she worked, and it was the most attractive business card I had ever seen! It captured my interest because I was looking for someone to design new stationery for me. I commented on the unusual color and logo and asked her who had done it. "I did," she answered, adding, "I fool around with graphic design on the side." She actually lowered her eyes and her voice as she said this! I was shocked! I said, rather sternly, "You need to put that on your personal business cards. I could use your help. Do you realize that I almost left here without knowing of your talent? Why didn't you tell me earlier?" She shrugged, seemingly embarrassed. I shook my head and told her, "I'll be calling you real soon."

Many sisters are marking time until they get the money, the support, the courage, or the nod of approval from "someone" before they permit themselves to seriously consider making major changes in their lives.

The prospect of change is connected to a complex set of emotions: Hope. Anticipation. Promise. Fear. Intellectually you know that starting over with a new set of circumstances may seem to be the best answer to your dilemma, but in your heart you feel threatened and downright scared.

Taking risks involving one's career and future earning power is difficult, and especially so for African-Americans because, historically, change has been closely connected to traumatic events. Forced separations of families during slavery and the constant threat of eviction from areas where blacks were not welcome was part of everyday life. Equating stability with safety make us instinctively shun the idea of going off into an unknown direction without a safety net to catch us. But as the days, weeks, and even years slip past, you may come to realize that you have no choice but to take charge of your future. You have to embrace your dream.

The author Gwyn McGee recounts how, when she was a child growing up in Gary, Indiana, her "head was packed with the things that enthralled me. Ballet, mermaids, musicals, rhythmic songs, and stories took me to fanciful places. There was nothing I didn't think was possible." This enthusiasm, or "naïveté," as she puts it, launched her life journey from college dropout to conversion to the Black Muslim faith to burger flipper to news director of a radio station, and eventually to her current career as a noted romance author. "No matter how hard the road, I never lost the childlike belief that miracles could always happen," she admits. "This has been the life raft that has gotten me to the other side when nothing else was available. It is also the foundation of my writing career."

Early in her career, when faced with overwhelming criticism of one of her novels and the vocal concern of her publisher, Gwyn's creative confidence was shaken to the core. She decided to change her style, and write what she thought her critics wanted instead of what was in her heart. The results? "I felt inside as if I were writing with a tiny piece of chalk on a huge blackboard," she says. "Finally I could not eke out one more word. My creative drive vanished and I was paralyzed with fright." When her spirits were at their lowest, a colleague in the publishing industry called to inform her of the rapid sales of the book the critics had panned. Gwyn did some checking to confirm this report, and quickly realized that the print run of the book she had been told would not sell had actually sold out! "My creative self had been vindicated," Gwyn says. "I made a pact with myself that day. I promised always to trust my creative source, to know that it is infinite and beyond rational thought. It dwells outside the parameters of the status quo. This source has never failed me, and it's available to all of us, no matter what our dreams may be."

In the crowded and competitive world of publishing, how does Gwyn raise her visibility to create a memorable impression? She adopted the pen name Eboni Snoe, dresses only in black and white when she meet her fans, and wears glamorous hats and gloves!

* * *

When criticism comes unexpectedly, you have no choice but to deal with it, utilizing the skills, talent, and intuition that allow you to keep going. It is hard to focus on the positive aspects of negative feedback because of the pain you are feeling. Unpleasant experiences wipe out our ability to envision the benefits that a new set of circumstances might bring.

Changes in the workplace can mean you will have to get to know and understand a new management team—but perhaps your new boss will notice and respect your talent a little more than your previous supervisor. Addressing a new audience means learning a new set of rules, devising a new plan for survival—but it might also force you to make some much-needed changes that could create favorable conditions for that promotion you've been praying for or that contract you've been after.

Starting your own business or striking out on your own with a creative venture requires drastic adjustments in many areas of your life. Now you will be in charge. You will finally be able to implement all those ideas that no one would listen to, but you will also be responsible for all those things you didn't have to worry about earlier. Shifts in static situations often initiate feelings of anxiousness and inadequacy. But remember, change is a natural part of life, and moving through it with a positive approach will permit you to take advantage of the new opportunities that appear on the horizon. It's all in the attitude you decide to adopt.

IDENTIFYING YOUR LIFE MISSION

> Too many people pass away with their songs unsung, their gifts unwrapped, their talents unused, and their treasures left buried.
>
> *Vickie Daniel, vocalist and record company owner*

Vickie Daniel worked as a registered psychiatric nurse in the Indianapolis area for many years while she was simultaneously engaged in her part-time profession as a jazz vocalist and actress. Performing in local clubs, at national conferences, and holding down a demanding stage role playing Madame C. J. Walker at the Walker Theatre in Indianapolis brought her a great deal of satisfaction, publicity, and recognition for her talent. She was thrilled to be able to use her gift of song to entertain and inform, but singing in clubs at night and getting up to go to work the next day was leaving her exhausted, frustrated, and under a great deal of pressure

Vicki says she struggled constantly with feelings of not being "good enough" and lacked the courage to quit her day job to pursue a musical career full time. Paralyzed by her own idea of perfection, Vickie kept her dream on the back burner, until a conversation with a sister changed her life.

"I remember a sistah telling me that I would probably end up as nothing more than an old woman in a nursing home being rolled into the day room to sing for the other residents," Vickie recalls. "I jokingly said that if I did live in a nursing home, I would have blue hair and everyone would call me Sarah Vaughan!"

This joking comeback was delivered in a lighthearted manner, but in reality Vickie was angry. The sister's words haunted her. The image of herself in a wheelchair, singing for old ladies, reminded Vickie that time was quickly ticking by. She began to think of the missed dreams and life unlived that would be her legacy if she continued on her current path. She turned to prayer and asked God to assist her in "perfecting" the gifts He had placed in trust with her.

After twelve years as a registered nurse, Vickie quit her job and launched Benu Museek, a recording company that specializes in soothing sounds for the spirit, soul, and body. She was already well known in music circles, so her idea to combine her medical training with her musical talent was brilliant. Her goal, to assist in the total healing process through music, helps people find their divine purpose in life. This venture has widened her audience, allowing Vickie to serve others while pursuing her dream of being a full-time musician. Unexpected dividends have been bestowed upon this courageous, soft-spoken sister: She recently married the "brother" who sings with her. In her promotional materials, Vickie say that she and her husband are "a life and a love . . . doing music that heals and mends forgotten gifts and unrealized dreams."

Vickie Daniel's Mission Statement

TO CREATE HEALING SOUNDS FOR THOSE WHOSE LIVES NEED SPIRITUAL LIFTING. TO PROVIDE HEALING SOUNDS TO PROMOTE SELF-ACTUALIZATION OF GOD-GIVEN GIFTS, TALENTS, AND BURIED TREASURES.

She truly has the best of both worlds!

ATTITUDE ADJUSTMENT TIP #2

Focus on purpose.

There are several ways to begin this process, starting with simply interviewing *yourself*. Over a period of days, weeks, or even months, channel energy into defining what you believe you have been put on this earth to do. Don't rush the process. Pay attention to what you do well, what brings you pleasure, and how you can contribute to improving circumstances within an environment that is important to you. Your community, church, school, place of employment, favorite charitable organization, or cultural or ethnic group may be waiting for you to make a commitment.

Focusing on purpose creates a sense of empowerment. By investing time in serious research about who you are, where your talents lie, and what you have to offer the world, you will then be able to draft and articulate a mission statement to serve as a road map for the unfolding of your life. After gaining a better understanding of where your true interests lie, you will begin to share your talent with others. Then, support will surface as those who are in a position to help you follow the path you were destined to travel, gravitate into your world.

If you decide to drastically change your current situation, be brave, be patient, be honest. Don't allow fear of losing what has become familiar to prevent you from developing your potential or fulfilling what you consider your destiny. Acting on your vision can be a truly exhilarating experience, but only if you first come to grips with what has been on your mind— day and night, month after month, year after year.

Action Steps

Answer these questions:

1. What do you truly want and how much do you want it?

_____

2. Do you believe you can convince others of the value of your idea/skill/talent? _____

_____

3. Why? List three reasons._____

_____

_____

4. Do you believe you have what it takes to go the distance to promote your service/product? _____

_____

5. Why do you believe this? _____

_____

Some women immediately know the answers to these questions because they have been thinking, dreaming, and planning for a long time, allowing their visions of the future to crystallize and became real. Such women have high expectations of themselves and are focused on making a difference.

However, you may be uncertain about the changes you want to make. You may have a vague sense of wanting: more control over your life, more emotional support on your job, or more financial stability. You may have difficulty articulating what you want to do and how you plan to achieve it, and perhaps there is a lingering emptiness you have lived with so long that it has almost become natural, comfortable. You can't remember when you did not feel it. If this is the case, it's time to take stock, analyze your assets, and chart a new course of action.

ATTITUDE ADJUSTMENT TIP #3

Isolate what you think about most.

By clearing your mind of fragmented dreams and unresolved issues, you can zero in on what is most important to you. Whatever you spend most of your time thinking about may be closely associated with what you are currently doing, and the transition from dreaming to acting might not be as difficult as you first thought. For many sisters, the skills developed in the world of work, or a passionately pursued hobby, often provide the kind of experiences that can facilitate change.

On the other hand, you may find that your dreams are focused on a field or industry that is very much outside of your current experience. You may have had little or no exposure to a subject that intrigues you, but the attraction is so strong you cannot ignore it. You feel overwhelmed by everything you *don't* know and practicality overrules the yearnings of your heart. Don't be alarmed. Yes, the risk factor seems high, but passion often outweighs preparation. You can study. You can adopt new paradigms and learn. You can master new skills. Think of yourself as a curious explorer about to embark on a wonderful adventure.

Exercise

Using the four-word groupings below, choose the one that most closely fits your behavior in either a work setting or a social environment.

1. *Self-assured, decisive, risk taker, competitive.*
   These are qualities of a take-charge person.

2. *Expansive, empathetic, positive, gracious.*
   These are qualities of a persuasive person.

3. *Calm, sincere, stable, prepared.*
   These are qualities of a reliable person.

4. *Organized, inquisitive, questioning, guarded.*
   These are qualities of an analytical person.

All of us probably have some qualities of each group, but knowing your dominant behavioral traits can help you focus on your life's mission. Think back to a time when you did something really well. Recall the feelings and emotions that surfaced. Draw on those memories, allowing yourself to relive the sense of achievement, satisfaction, and hope that succeeding brought.

When I was young, I discovered that the feelings triggered by successfully completing an assignment were nice. The emotions I felt when accomplishing a goal, being recognized for doing well, or of finishing a task to my own and others' satisfaction instilled a sense of control and empowerment that I quickly embraced. Determined to keep these feelings alive, I refused to focus on my limitations.

What good does it do continually to tell yourself, "I don't have the experience, the education, or the money to accomplish what I dream about?" You have to start somewhere, so take small steps and begin working through obstacles while focusing on what you *know* you do well.

TAKE AIM

If the obstacle standing between you and your life mission is the fear of hurting, offending, or disappointing someone close to you, you will probably be reluctant to take any action. I know what you are worried about. What will my friends and family say and think of me if I quit my job and go into debt to start my business? Will I be alienated from my coworkers if I go after the new management position at work? Should I do it quietly, or openly lobby for the position? Will my club members be jealous of me if I get on TV and snag media attention when I promote the annual fund-raiser? What if my plans don't work out? How can I possibly face anyone?

ATTITUDE ADJUSTMENT TIP #4

Don't be naïve.

During many of the workshops and focus groups that I have conducted over the years, I routinely hear my sisters say that they have been holding back from showcasing some skill or talent because of a fear of alienating themselves from a parent, coworker, sibling, club member, or friend who either doesn't understand or doesn't have confidence in what they want to do. This realization can be extremely painful, leaving sisters in a quandary about what to do. Should they abandon their project or dreams to escape feelings of guilt? Or should they go forward and risk a breakdown of the relationship, further isolating themselves?

Face the facts. Everyone is not going to be pleased with your decision to enhance your visibility at the office, in the community, or in the competitive marketplace.

Be honest—with yourself and those you worry about offending. Enhancing your visibility is something you *have* to do to reach the goals you've set for yourself. You are not being self-centered or selfish.

Ideally, those who are closest to you are on your side, encouraging you to go after your dreams as they applaud your decision to step out and speak up. Unfortunately, however, this is not always the case. Those who are not pleased about your proposed actions may criticize your dream—to your face or, more often, behind your back. This is a reality, but you don't have to allow it to sabotage your mission or undermine your confidence. Rise above it by keeping your eyes focused on a much larger picture—the goals you have set for yourself.

Karen E. Quinones Miller, who grew up in a low-income family in Harlem, dropped out of school in the eighth grade, as did all of her brothers and sisters. While her mother was not pleased with the fact that Karen had given up on her education, she encouraged her daughter to read the daily newspaper and write letters to the editor if she felt strongly about something.

Karen eventually got her GED, became a single mother, then started working as a secretary in the circulation department of the Philadelphia *Daily News*, a paper that Karen felt had never provided sufficient news coverage for people of color.

"One day while I was talking to another secretary about my inability to afford dance lessons for my daughter," Karen says, "a vice-president of the company walked past and broke into our conversation. He said, 'Karen, you should not feel bad that you can't give your daughter everything you'd like to give her. Be happy that you can put food on the table and clothes on her back.' Five minutes later I heard this same VP discussing, with my boss, his plan to purchase a twenty-foot yacht."

This conversation hit Karen like a bolt of lightning, forcing her to acknowledge the great gap between herself and those for whom she worked. "I realized how far out of the loop I was," Karen says. "I wasn't even in the same arena, and I didn't like it. I was dissatisfied with my life and I knew that if I didn't do something soon, things would never change. I had been too concerned about survival to think enough about my future."

When the *Daily News'* coverage of a march for *Roe vs. Wade* took precedence over a big march in support of affirmative action, Karen stepped out with attitude and wrote a letter of protest, using this situation as an example of the paper's lack of coverage of news of importance to African-Americans. "I had no fear about taking this letter to my boss, who invited me to his office to discuss my observations with him. He told me that he had heard similar complaints before, but the problem was they didn't have enough minorities writing for the paper. When I asked what he intended to do about that, he smiled and sarcastically replied that there was nothing he could do because the paper was under a hiring freeze. Then, he looked at his watch and said he had enjoyed talking to me!"

This blatant dismissal shocked Karen, who promptly informed her boss that he had wasted her time because nothing had been accomplished. "He got angry then and said if I didn't think the paper was doing a good job, maybe I should get a job writing and stop sitting around complaining."

Karen was boiling mad when she left his office, but as she walked to her desk, she decided to accept his challenge. "I went downstairs, thought about it some more, and gave my two weeks' notice. I had decided to quit my job to go to school to study journalism."

Her gutsy decision was met with a great deal of resistance from family and friends. "I soon realized that my plan was a threat to the people who were close to me," Karen relates. "I threatened their comfort level. Everyone said I was being selfish, that I would deprive my daughter of time with her mother if I attempted to be a single parent, go to school, and hold down a part-time job. I lost a dear friend during this time because he just didn't believe I would ever be able to balance everything I was trying to do. Sadly, most of my close relationships deteriorated because I had decided to improve myself."

Karen moved past the pain of losing close friendships, got

financial aid, and enrolled at Temple University. Against the wishes of her professors, she took her infant daughter, Camille, to classes with her. "It was tough, but I was determined to change the system to fit what I needed. Soon the professors and classmates supported me and fell in love with Camille."

What did Karen do next? A year after graduating with a 3.58 grade-point average, she got a job as a staff writer with *The Philadelphia Inquirer*, the *Daily News'* biggest competitor. In 1992, while working there, she wrote a feature story that was picked up by a wire service and eventually appeared with her byline in the *Daily News*—the paper she had left in order to fulfill her dream. This made Karen very happy. According to Karen E. Quinones Miller, "Success is definitely the sweetest revenge."

ATTITUDE ADJUSTMENT TIP #5

Adopt an attitude of gratitude.

When life's problems, complications, and setbacks threaten to engulf us, we feel as if we are swimming in the dark. It is easy to forget all the things we should be grateful for when dealing with misfortune or loss. The fact that you are reading this book means that circumstances in your life have come together to give you hope and a vision for the future. Your health, your intelligence, and the people and experiences that have carried you this far, as well as the mistakes and stumbles you've endured, create the tapestry that is you. Whether good or bad, happy or sad, all of our experiences provide lessons in living that shape and prepare us for the future. Here are a few survival tips:

Step 1. Communicate, in a positive manner, with those who express concern or bewilderment about your desire and need to showcase your talent. Tell them about your long-range plans and why you believe you will achieve them. Don't put yourself down or belittle any aspect of your mission. Use language and terms with which they can relate. If they are truly interested in your future, they will stick by you as you step out to deliver your message and attract the attention you feel you deserve. You may discover that the person you thought was least supportive simply did not know what had been on your mind for a very long time, or how important it was to you.

Step 2. Reach out and bring the skeptics into your dream. Allow them to participate in some aspect of your plan as you step out and toot your own horn. If your sister is artistic, ask her to help design your promotional material. If a coworker is good at writing proposals, ask for her opinion of the one you have drafted. If an uncle plays the piano, invite him to play a musical interlude during the program you are chairing. Those who appear standoffish and aloof to your dream may be standing on the sidelines watching, hoping to be included, recognized, and allowed to experience your journey with you.

Step 3. Move past those who truly do not wish you well. Ask yourself this question: Will what I plan to do favorably impact the lives of others? If the answer is yes, move forward and get busy. Don't give your time or energy to those who clearly are not on your side.

I am an educator by profession, trained to serve the needs of those who hunger for knowledge and want to improve themselves. I am sure that is why my first works of fiction were historically based. I felt, and continue to feel, obligated to share the historical information I uncover about my race and my culture with readers. As a child I found great pleasure in reading. The library and all of its books were a treasury of knowledge and wonderful experiences. As I grew to adulthood, I became more and more intrigued by language, books of an historical nature, and the memorable characters in the stories that I read. In college, I majored in foreign language and eventually found deep satisfaction in teaching both young people and adults how to master a language. Later in life, when I realized that I could no longer ignore that voice that had been nagging me for years, I knew I was destined to write fictional stories based on factual history of unusual aspects of black life and culture, focusing on women. I wanted to share the intriguing facts about black Americans I had uncovered in my research. It took five years to complete my first book and it was rejected thirty-two times. I refused to give up on my dream, and the greatest professional risk I ever took was leaving full-time employment as a teacher to self-publish my novel *Emily, the Yellow Rose*. I was given plenty of advice by friends, colleagues, and professionals in the industry on why I should not do it. I did not let their reservations deter me from taking action. I listened, weighed their advice against my desire, and went ahead with my plan. I have to admit that at times, my decision brought anxiety and disappointment as well as physical and financial exhaustion, but I also experienced a great deal of joy and satisfaction knowing that I was fulfilling my mission to serve my race by telling stories that I felt were important. Determined not to live out my life regretting never having tried, I fulfilled my desire to become a published author, and it was the decision that completely changed my life. Because I stepped out, ignoring the nonbelievers, I defined my course and knew there would be no turning back.

Two Things You Can Do Now

1. *Draft your mission statement.* Refer to Vickie Daniel's mission statement on page 11 as an example. To begin the process, trace the source of what matters most. Answer these questions:

- What excites me and creates a sense of anticipation?

- What makes me smile?

- What motivates me to get involved in a project, learn more about a subject, or take a stand on a particular issue?

- What five things do I value highly?

- Where do I hold deep-seated beliefs?

- Am I following in the footsteps of a family member or carving out a niche of my own?

- How can I become better acquainted with the people and/or circumstances that have influenced me and shaped my desires, career path, or hobby?

- What obstacles keep me from engaging in my passion?

- How can these roadblocks be eliminated or diminished?

- What do I want to be remembered for accomplishing?

- How do I prioritize the use of my time?

Reduce the information to three or four sentences that clearly reflect where you are headed and why. This is an evolutionary process that takes time, but going through it can help you zero in on what really matters and where your life mission lies.

2. *Write your bio.* This should be a focused, descriptive piece that tells people who you are and what you are about. It is not the same as a résumé or curriculum vitae. This biographical sketch can be used for introductions, as an effective marketing tool to showcase your talent, and as a valuable documentation of your achievements. Include a photo if you like, and remember to update it regularly, creating an ongoing record of your progress on your mission statement.

For an example of an attractive, effective biographical piece, see p. 140.

2

It Ain't Necessarily So

Attitude Focus: Beating the Odds
I pledge Allegiance
To the Unity of womanhood
For the values we have
The uplifting of each other
Through God's love and mercy
Let's fill our cups
Get out of our ruts
Stand real tough
For liberty and justice for all.

JACQUELINE OLURIN

After careful thought, you have decided it is time to go after that promotion, make your fund-raising event the most successful ever, turn your hobby into a money-making venture, or sell that screenplay you stashed in the bottom drawer of your desk two years ago. So, where do you start? What's the first step toward increasing the odds that you will get the attention of those you must impress, influence, or persuade? The answer? Do your homework.

GATHERING AMMUNITION

Credibility is your best vehicle for enhancing visibility. Whether you are targeting upper management at your place of employment, a producer at a television station, or the congregation at your church, you must know what you are talking about in order to get your audience to listen to you with interest and excitement. An in-depth knowledge of the subject at hand, coupled with an established credibility in your field, greatly increases the odds of receiving an enthusiastic reception.

For an example, let's say you have a military background and are contemplating writing a book profiling African-American women combat veterans. You open the newspaper and see that a female veteran of the Persian Gulf War is presenting a lecture on her life in military service. You are interested in meeting this sister because she has "been there, done that" and must know what she is talking about. If the same program were to feature a white male college professor who had never seen active duty discussing statistics on the subject, you might think twice before taking the time to attend. Your enthusiasm and level of interest are definitely connected to the life experiences of the messenger.

Hopefully, you have already established a good reputation in your field and may be considered an expert. Formal recognition and endorsements that carry weight provide credentials that immediately put your target audience at ease.

However, if you have not yet accumulated the experience needed to be considered credible, get busy. Focus on expanding your base of knowledge by becoming actively engaged in your area of interest. Get to know people who can guide you toward the experiences you need. Interacting with industry-related professionals will allow you to gain exposure while creating valuable relationships.

Beating the odds means being prepared, informed, and

aware of the constant changes that affect your target audience. Staying in the game requires credentials—the ammunition necessary to defend your position and sell your dream.

ATTITUDE ADJUSTMENT TIP #1

Don't believe the hype.

The statistical data that you gather while doing niche research can be enlightening as well as frightening. Don't allow what you discover to dampen the fire in your heart, because usually there are exceptions to every stated fact.

A 1991 study by Gale Research tells us that 50 percent of businesses owned by black women fail within four years. This little nugget of information could make you second-guess your decision to hang out your shingle or to support a sister who is thinking of becoming an entrepreneur.

Over and over again writers are told that less than 5 percent of those who seek publication ever reach that pinnacle of accomplishment. Such discouraging odds could make you shut off your computer and stuff your unfinished manuscript into a closet.

In a recent issue of *Black Enterprise* magazine the president of a sales, marketing, and public relations firm involved with launching new fashion designers said that no designer should even attempt to launch a line of clothing with less than a $5 million investment. Say what?

Well, don't believe the hype, sisters. There *are* exceptions to all of this madness. Despite the industry hype about the need for heavy capital to get started, Toni Whittaker was able to establish her clothing store in a trendy location where she currently sells a ready-to-wear line in the $500-to-$3,500 price range. How did this sister do it? Certainly not by investing $5 million.

Born in Camden, South Carolina, Toni Whittaker knew by the age of six that she wanted to be a fashion designer. Her dream never wavered, and she went on to receive a bachelor's degree in fashion design from Syracuse University. "Because I came from a small town, I had to catch up when I entered Syracuse," Toni says. "I had not had as much exposure to art and design as the white students and I was amazed at how much I had to learn. My plan was to get a degree, then teach fashion design while working toward starting my own business. My exposure to different kinds of people was truly the best experience I had at Syracuse University. It was a broadening experience. Moving into different environments is very important. I tell my sisters, never say no to anything. Learn by seeing and doing. I became a student of people, and at Syracuse, I learned how to think. I learned how to defend my creations by never setting out to please the instructor. I believe I am a good teacher today because I can look at a student's work and even if I don't like it, I appreciate it if they can defend why they did it."

After receiving her degree, she went on to get a bachelor of science degree in textile technology from North Carolina State, and studied for her master's at Colorado State, concentrating on the business side of the fashion industry. She was determined to open her own design shop.

Of financing her venture Toni says, "What I *didn't* have did not stop me. Some people can't start at the bottom. I can, and I did. My first shop space was in a loft that cost a hundred dollars a month, and all I had was a new Bernina sewing machine. But that's all I needed if I was going to do custom work. By going to family members for a thirteen-thousand-dollar loan, I was able to lease the space, purchase fabric, and hire a staff. I made fifty garments."

Toni opened her store, stepping out with a limited amount of initial stock, but she soon parlayed those fifty pieces of clothing into a thriving fashion business.

"I did a fashion show to get my first client and I worked in a fabric store for minimum wage to get exposure and find potential clients. When a client would give me a deposit, I would buy the fabric, and when she paid the balance I could pay my rent. Now my store is at street level, and I get business from word of mouth."

Custom design means working very closely with clients, often having to understand their personalities and habits. "In my designs, I try to follow my heart," says Toni. "In my business, I give people what they want, but I will not prostitute my creations. I recommend, but I don't preach. My clients must trust me and appreciate what I offer. If a person wants a Toni Whittaker, then they don't want a dress *made* by Toni Whittaker—they want a *Toni Whittaker*."

When asked to define a Toni Whittaker design, Toni replies, "Definition? Wildly pretty clothes. Very feminine. You have to walk, sit, and get in the car like a lady if you wear my designs. I don't do a lot of trendy things. I do trendy accessories—funky, with attitude and display, but my garments are classics. My first ready-to-wear show will be in New York in 1998. The fee to show was two thousand dollars, the samples were costly, but I got my name into circulation. I am totally independent. I use my own money, so I don't have to go to someone to help me finance my line. I own my own company and nobody owns me. It all depends on what you want. I want to be known as a black-owned female company one hundred percent so I can give jobs to my nieces and nephews. I was given a small house that needed work, so I put on a new roof and remodeled it myself. Now, I own my own home—it is small but it's mine. I will live rent-free the rest of my life."

Toni's Tips for Enhancing Visibility

- If you have a gut feeling about a dream, act on it.

- Be prepared to be alone—a lot.

- Be aware that there are people waiting for you to fail.

- Support your sisters. Show up!

For Toni, taking the attitude of dismissing the hype meant focusing on creating something from what was available. She never wasted time lamenting over what was beyond her reach.

CHECK THINGS OUT FOR YOURSELF

The head learns new things, but the heart forever
practices old experiences.
Henry Ward Beecher

Armed with information, you have a very good chance of
getting what you want. Remember, statistics are simply aver-
ages. You are special. Make up your mind to be the exception,
the one to shatter those myths that keep so many sisters from
even trying. I operate on the fifty-fifty rule. No matter what
the statistics say, I focus on the fact that once I put forth an
idea about a project or make an attempt to access someone
with my message, I will either be accepted or rejected. Case
closed. Those odds are really not so bad.

If you are lucky enough to snag the attention of your target audience, a relationship quickly develops as information
is exchanged. If you can fill a need, provide a valid service, or
positively impact the lives of others, both you and your message will suddenly rise in value.

Julia Shaw now owns her own literary marketing and
events management firm, but for years she worked as a
cashier for the New York Transit Authority. "I was miserable,"
Julia says. "Day after day I was counting as much as $150,000
of somebody else's money while my own life was simply on
hold. I knew I could not do this for the rest of my life."

After a long day at work, Julia found joy in spending time
with her children. A book lover, she was always on the look-
out for books written by black authors, featuring black children. "During these times [early eighties] it was very difficult
to find such books," she remembers. "At first I thought there
were *none* around, then I met a children's writer, John
Steptoe, who opened my eyes to a hidden treasure trove of
stories written for children like mine. He told me about other
authors and gave me titles to look for in the public and school
libraries, as well as local bookstores. I did my homework and
began to check things out for myself. I was amazed at what I
found—or did *not* find—especially in the public school system."

This awakening led Julia to seek employment with a book distributor, and she began selling books to the New York City Board of Education. "My original mission had been to communicate the existence of black books to my children. By taking this job, I was able to widen my mission to exposing the public school system to more multicultural material." Soon Julia was promoted to sales manager and began supervising other sales reps. A significant part of her job was to come up with promotional campaigns during Black History Month and to call on bookstores and help publicize authors and their titles. "I learned a lot about promotion," Julia says. "I learned to be results-oriented and responsible. It was excellent training. I began to think about going out on my own."

Ten years ago, Julia opened the doors of Shaw Literary Group (SLG), a multiservice agency that targets the African-American marketplace. "SLG provides services in events management for authors, conference organization, product marketing, and design of promotional campaigns. My goal is to help clients gain visibility through strategic market placement. We penetrate a three-hundred-billion-dollars-per-year consumer base," she says.

According to Julia, the most difficult aspect of developing a strategic placement plan is to identify the client's true market. "I have to find different ways to tap into the appropriate markets in order for my client to meet her objectives. The African-American market is 'markets within markets.' Some people don't understand this. Just because a product or service comes from a black person, it is not going to appeal to every African-American. We have to become very specific, starting with small outlets, then expanding to larger audiences. I try to assess my client's personality, then put her in the best venue that allows her to shine. If the enormity of the trade show atmosphere makes an author uncomfortable, I will try to showcase her in a more intimate setting with a targeted audience, like a performance or a reading. "

One of SLG's first productions was the Literary Showcase at the famous jazz club Birdland in Manhattan. It was an immediate hit because of its unusual mix of nightclub atmos-

phere and literary theme. Shaw made another innovative
move at the 1991 Kwaanza Expo in New York. "I brought in
high-profile authors and placed them at various vendors'
booths throughout the expo instead of clumping them
together in one section. This effectively placed my clients
where the numbers were, and people shopping at the expo
got in line to meet high profile authors. Making contact with
large numbers of people with a common interest pays off,"
says Julia, who knows that maximum exposure is what it's all
about.

Julia's company has worked with such organizations as
African American Women on Tour, Black Expo USA, Books
Across Ghana, International African Arts Festival, and the
Madam C. J. Walker Foundation. She told me some of her
organizational secrets.

Julia's Tips for Producing a Successful Event

- Make sure you can access adequate resources—both
  human and financial.

- Create a plan that includes detailed logistics.

- Be flexible, make changes as needed to keep things going.

- Be a willing team player.

- Delegate responsibility when appropriate, but be knowledgeable about all aspects of the project by checking
  things out for yourself.

ATTITUDE ADJUSTMENT TIP #2

Decide to beat the odds!

I do believe that black women face more obstacles than
others, but it doesn't mean that our chances of succeeding are
any less than those of our sisters who are white, Asian, or
Latino. Unfortunately, too many of us have become brain-

washed into believing that whatever is written, announced on TV, or told to us by so-called experts is the absolute truth.

Don't let anyone convince you that the road will be so steep, the odds stacked so high against you, and the path so convoluted that it's better not to try.

Think about all the articles you've read with discouraging statistics related to a single woman's chance of finding a mate, especially if she is African-American, divorced, and has children. The relationship experts will make you downright depressed. According to them, large numbers of black women wind up alone because they outnumber black men, and too many once-eligible brothers are either in jail, unemployed, or gay. Don't buy into that tired myth. As a divorced thirty-nine-year-old mother of two, I beat the odds and found Mr. Right. We've been married now for eleven years. So, sisters, there are plenty of serious candidates walking around looking good and looking for Miss Right. With the right attitude, an open mind, and an adventurous approach, you too can beat any odds.

When I began writing, in the early 1980s, I was often told that blacks did not read many books and there was no market for African-American romantic novels. I *never* believed that to be true, because I knew the marketing data had never been properly gathered. Now, ten years later, several major publishers are marketing entire lines of ethnic romance books for black, Hispanic, and Asian women, releasing several titles a month. If I had let those so-called statistics sway my decision to become a novelist, I never would have dared put pen to paper to write my first book.

TIMING IS EVERYTHING

In March of 1987, Adrienne M. Shabazz took her nine children and fled a fifteen-year marriage in which she had suffered verbal, physical, and mental abuse. Without sufficient education or job skills to adequately support her family, she swallowed her pride and went on welfare. However, this was not the kind of life she had envisioned for herself and her children, so she decided to go to back to school.

Within two years, Adrienne acquired an associate's degree in mental health/mental retardation. She says, "I chose this field because I wanted a degree that would enable me to counsel substance abusers and alcoholics. Since I witnessed the problems that many in my community were having with substance abuse, I felt that not only would I be able to provide for my family, but I would provide a needed service to my people as well."

Raising nine children and going to school kept Adrienne very busy, but the time came when she realized that along with her new degree, she needed work experience. "The best way to get it, as far as I was concerned, was to volunteer," she says. "I knew that volunteer experience counted as much as paid work experience, and the good thing was that I found myself in a position to choose the agency that would provide the exposure I needed."

Determined to stay involved in her community, she filled volunteer positions with a variety of agencies over a period of two and a half years. Adrienne spoke up on behalf of abused children, taught parenting classes to high school students, expanded emergency shelters for homeless youth, and gave instruction on independent living. These selfless activities on behalf of those less fortunate than she brought Adrienne immense visibility, creating her reputation as a sister who was deeply committed to helping women and children turn their lives around.

Three years later, she earned a bachelor of science degree, and is currently working in a salaried position as a case manager with the city of Fort Worth, Texas, developing programs for drug awareness and prevention. In 1995, her daughter Tiwoni won the 1995 *Ladies Home Journal* contest "My Special Mom" with a story she submitted about Adrienne, providing her with more visibility than she ever dreamed of having!

How was Adrienne Shabazz able to beat the odds? Why did she become a mentor and a role model when so many of her sisters were content to remain stuck in the demeaning cycle of abuse and public assistance? It was Adrienne's unconditional love for her children that infused her with the discipline and tenacity necessary to survive and thrive. Her decision to create a decent lifestyle for her family and herself motivated her to become an example of what it means to be a responsible, caring parent. To keep going forward when things got rough, Adrienne's attitude toward serving others inspired her to touch the life of one more abused, neglected, and hopeless woman who, in turn, renewed Adrienne's faith in herself. Adrienne's next dream? She wants to tour the country meeting and encouraging other women to *believe and achieve*.

ATTITUDE ADJUSTMENT TIP #3

Seek opportunities to influence.

The position you have your eye on at your company may never before have been filled by a woman, let alone a woman of color. The project you are now in charge of may never have had the company's support. The startup capital needed to launch your restaurant may seem impossible to find, and the children's book you have sent to agents and publishers may have been rejected dozens of times. None of this matters. Not if you believe that what you plan to do will have a favorable impact on your company, the community, the marketplace, and the consumer you are trying to reach. Trust me, your message will eventually hit home, but how it is received can depend heavily on two things: preparation and timing.

With careful preparation you can impact your audience, but you must take the time to carefully construct the showcase for your talent.

When you deliver a message that is intended to make a difference is as important as *what* you say. What issues are of utmost importance to your boss or your company at this time? Are you the one to offer a solution? What problems in your community need to be tackled *now*? Can your service address those issues? What type of product is your audience searching for? Can you provide what they want? If you are prepared to give people what they need or desire and your timing is right, you will receive a positive response. Spotlighting what you do best becomes a reciprocal process, and soon you will be pleasantly surprised at how much you receive from those you set out to influence.

The time of day, season of the year, or placement on the agenda can impact the receptivity of your message. Try, as much as possible, to influence these variables. I always advise that if you can choose to be first or last on the agenda, be first. Audiences pay more attention to the first speaker on a program because they have no other speaker against whom to measure the current performance. People listen with expectation, and if you give them what they came to hear, you will be long remembered. Your boss will pay attention to your sales pitch for your project if you catch him early because his mind will not be cluttered with all that has happened throughout his busy day.

And don't forget the weather! If you live in an area where weather conditions can affect your audience's mobility, be it rain, sleet, or extreme heat, be aware that people often make decisions on the basis of the local weather report. Don't get caught standing at the podium facing an empty room because Mother Nature was working against you.

During the summer of 1996, I was scheduled for a book signing at the same time and on the same night that the Olympic runner Michael Johnson was going for the gold. I am sure neither my publisher nor the bookstore owner had even thought about this when the date for my signing was originally set. The turnout was low that night, and I, along with the few faithful fans who did show up, talked of how much we hated missing the historic event. Eventually, the bookstore owner set his small TV on top of the counter and we watched the race. Needless to say, timing that night definitely worked against me. After that experience, I began asking more questions and taking a closer look at what else might be going on before committing to an appearance that may already be doomed.

Proper timing can create immediate interest, inspiring your audience to embrace you, but there are times when the window of opportunity is short-lived. So you must have your antennae up and be aware of what is going on that might impact your plans.

Don't go to your supervisor with an innovative marketing idea after she has returned from headquarters, where there was a planned meeting to launch a new product. You should be well enough in the loop to grasp opportunities to impact decisions long before they are made. If you aren't getting the vital information that you need, find out why, then make yourself better known in the circles where information is shared so your input can be better timed.

If the grand opening of your soul-food restaurant comes two weeks after a local competitor's well-publicized debut, be prepared to be disappointed. The media blitz given the restaurant across town will most likely not be repeated for you. You're old news. The reporters and editors who covered your competition have moved on to something else.

ATTITUDE ADJUSTMENT TIP #4

Forget the tried and true.

Five years ago, after experiencing the frustration of trying to find quality child care for her family, Janice Robinson made up her mind to open her own day-care center. This decision inspired her to go back to school and complete her degree in early childhood education. Next, she took a position in child-care administration with the Philadelphia public school system. Because of her commitment to children and her work as an early-childhood specialist and parent educator, in 1995 Janice launched her own magazine, *Successful Black Parenting*.

This innovative sister is the publisher and president of the first national parenting publication targeted toward African-American families. "I knew I had to establish strategic alliances with established magazine publishers that reached my target audience," says Janice. "I needed support from people like John Johnson of *Ebony* and *Jet,* and Clarence Smith of *Essence,* but they refused to meet with me." After her repeated calls, Clarence Smith did break down and agree to give Janice and her two partners exactly five minutes of his time.

"Our goal was to create a joint venture with *Essence,*" she says. "My partners, Charisse and Marta, and I knew what we were going to say, but we could not decide on what to wear. We knew we wanted to be different—innovative. After much discussion, we decided not to wear business suits, and had three T-shirts made with the cover of our magazine on the back. Each shirt had one word from the NIKE slogan 'Just Do It' spelled out on the front."

The plan was for each woman to wear a shirt and together they would spell out their plea for Smith to "Just Do It!"—take them on in a joint venture. However, the plan began to break apart when Charisse had to drop out of the meeting because of an emergency. But Janice and Marta decided to go ahead with only two words, "Do It!" on their shirts, figuring Smith would still get the message. Walking down the streets of New York on their way to the meeting, the two sisters drew a lot of laughs and attention with what now was being interpreted as a sexual proposition!

Janice says with a laugh, "We met with Clarence Smith. He was very impressed with our presentation, but he was a little slow. He didn't get the message until the very end of the meeting. The partnership did not happen as we had hoped, but the publisher of *Essence* never forgot us!"

After launching her publication, Janice won many awards for entrepreneurial excellence, appeared on CNN and CNBC, and was profiled in *USA Today.* Not surprisingly, *Essence* was one of the first publications to cover the achievements of this savvy sister in its magazine.

INNOVATIVE ACTION STEPS

Come up with a new angle to make your product or service stand out. Showcasing your talent or product in a unique environment might generate a whole new attitude about what you have to offer. For example, if the grand opening of your type of business has traditionally been held on location, go off-site to a museum, university, or cultural center.

I had a very memorable experience in 1997 when I was a workshop presenter at the Annual Conference of the Black Caucus of the American Library Association held in Winston-Salem, North Carolina. When I arrived I discovered that in addition to using the local convention center for conference sessions, many events were to be held off-site at local art galleries, branch libraries, and various locations on the campus of Winston-Salem State University. This approach provided conference attendees, a great opportunity to get out, see the city, and make new friends. On my return from an awards ceremony that had been held at an art gallery, I passed an African-American bookstore and decided to drop in to introduce myself. The owners of Special Occasions, Ed and Miriam McCarter, were a delightful couple—happy to meet me and eager to talk about books. As we chatted, many of their customers, whom I soon discovered were fans of mine, came up and introduced themselves to me. Soon an impromptu book signing followed, and I had a lively afternoon visiting with my newfound friends. Needless to say, my visibility in Winston-Salem was raised that day simply because I had an opportunity to get out and explore new territory.

A method of spreading the word that has worked for me is to solicit assistance by adopting the "each one reach one" method. I prepare postage-paid postcards or flyers promoting my newest release and distribute them, asking each person to simply mail it along to a colleague or friend who would be interested in my books. Word of mouth is the best thing going in any target community.

Create a unique, high-profile happening like a fund-raising raffle or a silent auction that will bring local celebrities to your event or business. This will give your customers an opportunity to mix and mingle with high-profile people and contribute to a worthy cause while expanding the customer base of your venture. Go after publicity in alternative, smaller media outlets such as cable TV programs, neighborhood newspapers, and fraternal and social organizations' newsletters, and use personal networks more aggressively.

What You Can Do Now

Step 1. Review the mission statement you created earlier. Are your goals realistically tied to the base of knowledge you have accumulated? Are you close to being considered an expert?

Step 2. Assess your readiness to deliver your message by playing the devil's advocate. Prepare a list of questions that most likely will be thrown at you. Write down the answers and rehearse them. Your knowledge of the subject and your credibility *will* be put to the test.

Step 3. Seek stories of like-minded people who have managed to beat the odds. How did they achieve what they set out to accomplish? Study their strategies, compare your obstacles to theirs. Adopt any habits or advice they give that is appropriate to your particular situation.

Step 4. Using folders, computer files, a calendar, or notebooks, prepare a guidebook of strategies you can use to monitor your progress on a regular basis.

In the early 1980s I found myself divorced, raising two preteen daughters, and holding down two jobs to make ends meet—not a high point in my life, and not a time when I felt particularly creative. However, at a social function I happened to attend, I met a well-known filmmaker who had been coproducer of *The Buddy Holly Story*. He took an immediate interest in me and we wound up chatting in a corner of the room. I was overwhelmed by him and by all of the movie people at the affair. In a timid voice I cautiously talked about myself, telling him I was a teacher, but I really wanted to write novels—when the time was right. I told him of my desire to write a book about African-Americans who got wealthy during the 1920 oil boom in Texas. I wanted to craft books based in black history that would be entertaining and informative, allowing others to feel proud about the positive black heroes and heroines I planned to create.

The producer listened to me, paying close attention, as if he truly cared, then said in a very authoritative manner, "What are you waiting for? Call yourself a writer, dammit. How else are you ever going to become one?"

Terrified, I took his advice and stopped putting off my dream. I joined a writers' group, began researching my story, and surveyed the owners of black bookstores and their customers. Sixteen years and five novels later, I have a network of black booksellers who support my books, those same people who were encouraging from the beginning. And I am also still in touch with the film producer. I visit him whenever I go to Los Angeles. He has become a mentor, my harshest critic, my shoulder to cry on, and a soul-mate with whom I celebrate. He helped me beat the odds and received the first autographed copy of my oilfield story, which turned out to be *Black Gold*.

3

I Can Do That!

Attitude Focus: Value Your Assets
For if a man think himself to be something, when he is
nothing, he deceiveth himself. But let every man prove his own
work, and then shall he have rejoicing in himself alone, and
not in another.

GALATIANS 6:4

*T*he guest speaker at a professional women's organization asked everyone in the room to stand up. She told the group that she was going to ask a series of questions, and if we could answer "yes" to any of them, sit down. I was curious about the game, because I knew the topic for the meeting was "Getting Organized."

The first question was "Did you leave your house without making your bed?" About one third of the women sat down—not surprising, since it was ten o'clock on a Saturday morning. I never leave my beds unmade, so I remained standing. Next question, "Do you have stacks of unopened mail sitting at home?" There was laughter, and more ladies sat down. "Are your waste baskets overflowing?" A few more admitted to the disorganization in their lives, and took their seats. "Is the top of your desk buried under paper?" Quite a few attendees sank down into their chairs. The questions continued in this vein, all of them focused on the mountain of tasks women often let pile up as they go about their busy lives.

When the last question was asked, I looked behind me and was shocked to find that I was standing alone. My colleagues roared with laughter, amazed that I turned out to be the most organized person in the group. For some reason I felt embarrassed to accept the prize—a book on how to get organized.

I am certain that one of my most valuable assets is my ability to plan and organize. I like the feeling of knowing that things will run much more smoothly if I am properly prepared. My background in education taught me that preparation is key to successful classroom management, and as a staff person in the world of nonprofits, I had to devise effective ways to organize and train thousands of individuals for hundreds of tasks. I learned very soon that the only way to pull off such assignments was to start early, make lots of lists, pay attention to details, and keep the overall objective uppermost in my mind.

When I decided to write *Wild Embers*, my novel about a nurse who falls in love with a Tuskegee airman during World War II, I knew that the writing would only be as good as the research and planning that went into the book. Uncovering the story of the black experience during World War II was more difficult than I had expected, and with no military background of my own, I soon became overwhelmed and frustrated, wondering whether I was in over my head. But I persevered, traveling to Ohio, Alabama, and Washington, D.C., to find the stories to shape the book. This was a monumental task, but I pulled it off because I focused on a narrow period of time, and organized the historical framework in a chronological manner that made it easier to integrate the stories into the fictional aspects of the book. By remaining methodical in my approach, I began to understand what it takes for me to do my best work. Advance planning keeps me grounded and not easily rattled. I know that I can reach my objectives as long as I maintain a firm grasp on as many variables as possible, have a plan, follow it, and refuse to allow distractions or clutter to creep in and settle down.

Go back and review the behavioral characteristics that you identified on page 14 in Chapter 1. Are you pragmatic, organized, and detail-oriented? Are you social, creative, and idealistic? A combination of both? Take the time to think seriously about what you have going for yourself. How can the specific traits that are uniquely yours qualify as assets—assets that can help you strengthen and showcase your skills?

ATTITUDE ADJUSTMENT TIP #1

Speak honestly about your assets.

"My greatest asset is my ability to influence people," says Debra A. Miller, the 1997 president of Public Relations Society of America (PRSA). This sister, the first person of color to lead the 17,500-member organization in its forty-seven-year history, speaks with confidence and commitment when she says, "I know I can communicate in a variety of situations, to a very broad audience. I know who I am, what I need to accomplish, and what I want to leave with people. I have learned how to be a walking sound bite."

Debra remembers when she was not so confident. "In 1977 I attended my first national PRSA conference in New Orleans. When I quietly slipped into the assembly room and sat in the back, I realized that of the approximately two hundred people in attendance, I was the only black person—besides the wait staff—in the room. Even more discouraging, there were no more than fifteen or twenty other women at the meeting. I felt as if I didn't belong, as if someone was going to put me out at any moment. But that didn't happen and I didn't leave. The longer I sat there, the more I began to imagine myself sitting up there on the dais, looking out. I never told anyone about my vision, but holding on to it kept me working toward the day when I would lead that organization."

Debra's commitment to PRSA continued as she went about her business, gathering twenty years of experience in marketing, advertising, research, and management for a variety of organizations. In 1994, she won the spot of national secretary for PRSA and also launched her own PR firm, D. Miller and Associates, Inc., to give advice, provide analysis, and troubleshoot PR campaigns for companies and organizations that want to communicate more effectively with audiences of color.

In 1995, Debra actively campaigned for the position of national treasurer of PRSA, but failed to receive the nomination, though she was obviously the most qualified candidate. Winning that spot would have put her in direct line for the presidency, so it was not going to come her way very easily. However, this gutsy sister decided to take on her challenger in a publicized debate, something unheard of within this organization. By actively running on a platform that stressed her commitment to controlling expenses, Debra D. Miller came out the winner.

When she accepted the presidency of PRSA in 1997, Debra made history. "I marketed myself aggressively. I set out to make solid alliances with a broad constituency. This helped immensely in making my term of office a valuable, rewarding experience. I feel that women have to do more of this. They need to be better connected and less skeptical. Often we are not sure about where we need to be. We can't be everywhere. It is important to distinguish ourselves in areas where we feel comfortable—where we will get the most bang for our bucks, so to speak. We must use our resources to move on. Change makes one take chances. I chose to devote myself to PRSA to gain a strong network, and since there is a small number of minorities in the profession, it worked to my advantage. I got noticed, I learned, and I got professional development."

Today, she manages D. Miller and Associates by using free-lance professionals on a contractual basis, while working full time as the assistant dean of the School of Journalism at

Florida International University. "I realized early on that I did not want to manage employees, though I knew that most small firms failed because only one person was involved in the day-to-day aspects of the business. I knew I needed someone to go out and get the business while others stayed in the office and did the work, but I didn't want somebody else's rent dependent on me. I decided to work alone. I accomplished this by referring clients to other firms to get the job done. I say that I specialize in 'beyond the press release,'" she says, laughing, confidently admitting that she does not advertise, nor even have business cards. All of her work comes from referrals resulting from the kind of reputation she has built.

"A good reputation is simply one that tells customers that your company's products and services will meet their needs. It is the collective outcome of building trust and gaining credibility."

When asked for words of wisdom to share with her sisters, Debra replies, "Ain't no hill for a stepper. You either stand for something or you'll fall for anything. If life is a journey, then life's greatest tragedy is not enjoying the trip."

There will always be someone who will try to poot on your toot!

> Maria D. Dowd, executive director, African
> American Women on Tour

SEIZE THE DAY

Growth comes with experience. If you focus too long on your shortcomings, you will block access to paths that could allow you to move closer to your goals.

Shortly after graduating from high school, Aubrey Vaughan began researching the Detroit area for opportunities to work as a professional model. It didn't take long for her to discover that the best-paying and most prestigious jobs in her community were connected to the automobile industry, so she set her sights on becoming an auto show spokesperson. Aubrey was savvy enough to know that more than a pretty face, a shapely body, and a desirable height and weight would be required, so she enrolled in a series of narration and commercial acting classes to perfect her elocution skills. She dreamed of the day when she would cheerfully deliver her sales pitch from the top of a revolving turntable in the center of a showroom.

Aubrey put her heart into her classes, eventually gaining enough confidence to begin auditioning for various talent agencies. "I noted early on that the decision makers were the auto executives," Aubrey says. "My goal was to convince them and the agents that I was competent and capable." However, as word of her ambition circulated among her friends, she began to pick up on negative vibes. "A few 'friends' seemed downright determined to plant nasty seeds of doubt in my mind," she recalls. "Even the mother of a little boy I used to baby-sit said it was ridiculous for a woman of my complexion [brown] with no apparently striking physical traits to believe that she would actually be paid to model. An agent told me I had an interesting look, but I was too ethnic to find lucrative work in the traditional Midwest market. Those words unnerved me, but I wasn't ready to give up."

Aubrey persevered through a series of rejections until a popular working actor noticed her and suggested she audition for Pontiac. This determined sister grabbed the opportunity and managed to survive the first round of cuts, but was not selected as a model. The executives at Pontiac told her not to worry, she had been placed high on the list for selection the following year. Disappointed yet optimistic, this sister dug in for the long haul and continued preparing for a spot in the national auto show circuit.

When the date for the following year's auditions came around, Aubrey was six months' pregnant, and showing every bit of it. Undaunted, she decided to take an assertive approach, explaining to her agent how her outgoing personality and training in narration made her an asset and the best possible choice for Pontiac Motors, even in her advanced state of pregnancy. The agent was wary, but she relented and sent Aubrey out for the audition to compete with fifteen beautiful *Bay*

Watch body-types for one of six coveted modeling spots.

What happened? Aubrey Vaughan got the job! Here's why.

"I used my obvious with-child state as a major selling point," Aubrey recalls. "I explained to the advertising executives how, as a soon-to-be-mom, I was a real person with whom consumers could relate. I was delighted when the GM executives agreed. I was more than just a pretty face with a girlish figure and tight perfect abs! I became a symbol of the modern working woman, the busy sister who needs reliable transportation! My dream had finally come true. I went on to model successfully for eight years—doing auto show narration, print assignments, and national commercials. Earning success wasn't easy, but I've never once regretted seizing the day!"

Follow your instincts if you must consider adjusting your plans. Don't relinquish a dream just because things are not going along exactly the way you had hoped. Think about the long-term effects of the decisions you make. If Aubrey Vaughan had let pregnancy derail her dream of being a model, she might have lost out on a very significant opportunity to enhance her visibility in an industry that remains extremely competitive and difficult to enter.

ATTITUDE ADJUSTMENT TIP #2

Be honest when facing your shortcomings.

As You See It

Your definition of reality comes from your perception of the events you witness and the behaviors in which you engage. Your reality will be colored by the emotions, problems, setbacks, and successes that you experience—but remember, reality has two sides: how it looks to you and how it comes across to others.

ATTITUDE ADJUSTMENT TIP #3

Adopt a positive demeanor.

As you begin to formulate your plan to step out and bring attention to yourself, consider how you can integrate the ten positive qualities listed below into your daily interactions with people at work and in the community. Doing this can ensure that your attitude is working for you and you come across as you hope, increasing your chances of being remembered in a positive way.

Ten Positive Qualities

Amiability

Compassion

Cooperativeness

Courtesy

Diligence

Discretion

Efficiency

Fair-mindedness

Frankness

Generosity

These qualities definitely shape your reputation—the most valuable asset anyone can possess. When you are selling yourself, you are selling your reputation, so guard it carefully and never let your standards slip.

Dr. Martha J. Wong is a second-generation Chinese-American who made history when she was the first Asian-American to be elected to serve on the Houston City Council. This pioneer in both the political and educational arenas served as the first Asian-American school principal in the state of Texas.

Martha says, "My most important assets are my friendly personality and positive outlook, second only to my cultural heritage, which certainly helps boost my visibility. As an Asian female, even as an elected official, I often feel that people don't see me, or they see me in a very distant way. When I am in a crowd there are usually very few Asians, so I am very outgoing. It is easy for me to take the initiative, shake hands, and introduce myself to strangers. When asked to speak, I do speak out."

Councilwoman Wong recently taught a fourth-grade class how to register to vote as part of President Clinton's Teach America program. "Doing this allowed children to get close to me and learn about what I do. It let them see that holding political office is possible for all kinds of people, including Asian women, and hopefully I can inspire more children to serve their communities."

In the Asian household, according to Martha, the male is king. In her family, however, things were different. Martha's father encouraged his children to talk and debate issues at the dinner table, and doing this helped Martha learn how to express and defend her position on issues. "This was very unusual for a Chinese family," she says. "Chinese girls are taught to be quiet, listen, and do the work. Because my father permitted me to disagree with him, I have never been afraid to disagree with people of power. I have always felt confident pressing a point, speaking up, or debating. My training as a classroom teacher also helped me learn how to gain control of a group and hold its attention. I know how to make words important enough to get people to listen."

This very busy sister has experienced firsthand some of the cultural issues related to self-promotion. "The Asian culture says that we are to be very modest, that we are not to tell people how wonderful we are. That is ingrained in me, and though I am a successful politician, sometimes it is still hard for me to do. It is easier for me to accept praise if I include my staff. People appreciate this very much, but when I have to defend myself, I do. When male members of the city council try to take credit for things my office has done, I have no difficulty correcting them—in a gracious manner. I often have to remind them that *I* am the chairperson of a particular committee or that *my* staff did the research for a bill when it is obvious they didn't do their homework."

Martha Wong gives her sisters some helpful tips that a former boss gave her.

Martha Wong's Helpful Tips

- You don't have to tell everybody everything. Don't give away your trade secrets or feel pressured to divulge information you'd rather keep to yourself. Unfortunately, women tend to do this.

- You must find work that allows your personal and professional lives to blend and complement each other. If you have to live separate lives, it will be very difficult.

Councilwoman Wong has achieved a good balance. Her training as an educator helps her to be a good public official and advocate. "I can impact lives and make a difference by speaking out and taking a stand," she says. "I support activities that say, 'This is what I believe in.' Time is precious and choices need to be made."

EXPRESS YOURSELF

> The global economy does not trade in Black English.
> *Earl Graves, publisher, Black Enterprise*

I have to agree with the editor and publisher of *Black Enterprise* magazine. We live in a world where standard English is the universal language of global communication and there is no reason for our children to be taught that street slang, jargon, substandard English, or so-called Black English has a place in the world of work or play. The debate over the placement of Ebonics in our public school curriculum has caused quite a stir, but whether or not Ebonics can be considered a true language is not the issue, as far as I'm concerned. It may have valid roots in African languages, but black Americans have been out of Africa for a very long time. How much longer do proponents of Ebonics think it will it take for blacks to assimilate? What matters now is that African-Americans acquire the skills—one of which is clearly spoken standard English—needed to make it in the larger world, beyond the comfortable enclaves where Ebonics may indeed be spoken and respected.

I have worked as a teacher of English as a second language for many years, instructing adults and children from around the world. I know from experience that teachers do not need to speak Chinese to teach a child from China how to read and speak standard English. So why the need to learn Ebonics? Why are black children considered so strange and unique that legions of educators must learn a new language in order to reach them? Don't believe the hype. The most important thing we sisters can do is help our children learn to speak English well, with confidence and clarity. That's what really counts.

Speaking well may be the single most important asset you can have if you want to stand out. It does not matter if you are in a business setting talking with your boss, in an intimate conversation with a trusted confidante, or in a public forum speaking to hundreds of people. You cannot overestimate the value of using proper, standard English. Having good communication skills means speaking clearly and concisely, communicating your message in the simplest of terms, and using words to empower your message without complicating the message itself.

When you open your mouth, you are opening yourself up to immediate scrutiny. What you say and the way you say it, along with your physical image (which we will tackle in a later chapter), creates a lasting first impression. Don't take chances. If you don't express yourself in solid, fluent language, everything else will be forgotten, overshadowed by that shortcoming.

If you feel your verbal skills need some attention, here are a few suggestions.

Action Steps

1. Take a course at a community college on public speaking.
2. Make arrangements with an instructor at a local high school or university to help you improve your verbal expression. You must be willing to take constructive criticism.
3. Join a professional speakers organization like Toastmasters. There are chapters in most major cities.
4. Seek opportunities to speak before local organizations and groups. This is a chance to enhance visibility *and* get in some practice.
5. Watch TV and listen carefully to reporters, announcers, and professional speakers.
6. Attend forums to watch speakers in action.
7. Pay attention to what good speakers say and analyze their facial expressions.
8. Pay attention to the body language used by people when speaking.
9. Take notes. What makes a presenter good or not so good?
10. Record your voice and your message. How do you sound? If improvement is needed, work on enunciation, content, clarity, and vocabulary.

HIGHER LEARNING

Having a college degree is not a prerequisite to success, but it can certainly qualify as an asset. Statistics show that the more formal education a woman has, the greater her earning power. Having financial stability increases the probability that you will be able to engage in the type of work you desire. Also, if you are in good financial shape, you'll be able to afford more sophisticated promotional activities to get your name and face recognized. Financial stability allows you to travel more frequently and easily. You can attend conferences where you can be seen and heard, or hire professionals who can help you get noticed. Having the money to dress and live in the manner consistent with your professional and personal objectives will help you move closer to your definition of success.

Feelings of inadequacy and low self-esteem are closely connected to financial failure. If you do not feel good about yourself, you surely can't convince others of your marketability. Financial and emotional stability create a heightened sense of self-assurance that can bring confidence and optimism to the forefront.

ATTITUDE ADJUSTMENT TIP #4

You are never too old to learn.

"I used to be one of those sad sisters, lamenting over what could have been," says the author and publisher Linda Waters. "As I stood in my hair salon day after day cutting and curling the hair of professional men and women, I listened to them unburden themselves about the woes of their important jobs and fabulous careers."

Linda began to feel that she had missed out on a crucial part of life by not finishing college. She dreamed of changing her situation, of writing articles on topics other than hair care, and of doing anything other than having her hands in suds, dandruff, and water all day. The daydreams persisted, until one day she abruptly closed her salon, enrolled her daughter in kindergarten, and headed to college as a thirty-something freshman.

"I prayed that God would give me the strength to walk out of the hair business and never look back," Linda said. "It was truly the work of God that I was able to walk away from a paying job and put myself in a student environment without any money or the possibility of earning real money for at least three years. I just knew I had to put a foot out and take a step in the direction I wished to go."

Linda enrolled in a scriptwriting class, but had to drop it owing to a family crisis. She soon found another writing class that was held in the instructor's home. There, she began to learn the mechanics of how to create and chart a story. This experience led Linda to pursue a degree in English and eventually to go back to the scriptwriting class she had dropped.

"I just had to finish it," she said. "I stuck with it and completed my first movie script, which I hope to sell one day. I am very proud of myself for going back to retake the class I had dropped. There is significant satisfaction that comes from sticking with something to the end."

Though Linda has not yet sold her movie script, she has completed her degree, published three novels, accepted a position teaching English at a local high school, and has become a locally syndicated newspaper columnist. She even went one step further to showcase her talent by founding a newspaper devoted to women's issues where she welcomes editorials on a variety of subjects. It is appropriately titled *It's None of My Business . . . But*. Now, this hairdresser-turned-educator–publishing tycoon is one of the most visible sisters in Houston.

YOUR CIRCLE OF FRIENDS

My friend Linda Waters is also very savvy when it comes to computers. I am only interested in knowing how to process the words I need to finish the book I am writing. I'm fine not knowing everything, so when I needed some slick promotional materials—fast—I called Linda. She jumped at the opportunity to help me out and quickly scanned in my photos, entered the text, and delivered professional-quality brochures and posters to me within days. All she asked in return was for me to read and comment on the first draft of her novel. Bartering among friends is a great way to solve problems and get a very good deal.

If you are lucky enough to have supportive, trustworthy friends and acquaintances, consider them definite assets. Don't be shy about asking for help. If your sorority sister's first cousin is the editor at the newspaper, tell her what's going on and let her hook you up. The little old ladies in your grandmother's sewing circle may have deeper roots in the community and better access to people in power than you can begin to imagine. People love to feel needed, so include other sisters and let their talent shine in the spotlight you create. Don't be too proud to admit when you need help.

ATTITUDE ADJUSTMENT TIP #5

Accept the fact that others have a right to their opinions.

Allowing yourself to be more open to suggestions from others can bring unexpected dividends. Too often we shut off the voice of opposition, unable to believe that anyone could possibly understand our particular situation. Ignoring constructive criticism and candid feedback is foolish. Yes, negative comments can hurt and anger you, but they *will* come your way. Be wise enough to accept such observations when they are valid, make adjustments, and move on.

Three talented sisters in the Dallas area are celebrating the first anniversary of their author escort service, TNT Driving. The marketing director, Dianna, told me the business was born when she impulsively told the author and *Essence* magazine senior editor Susan Taylor that the next time she came to Dallas, she wanted the author to use her driving service. Susan enthusiastically agreed to use her company—not knowing it didn't yet exist! But this high-profile author's commitment launched the business, and now, TNT Driving Service is one of only a few escort services specializing in providing African-American female drivers for African-American authors. Dianna admitted that the first year definitely had its rough spots and the group of women made many mistakes. But like a true trailblazer, she said, "Yes, I got told about myself in plain English every time things went wrong. It was tough, but I adopted the motto 'Grow and go!' We took the advice that was valid, pushed on to the next level, and we're still in the game."

I urge my sisters to follow this advice and be grateful for any feedback you can get. An attitude of gratitude will take you to new levels!

What You Can Do Now

Step 1. Using your personal records (Rolodex, phone book, membership lists, etc.), analyze your support network. Call people and tell them what you're doing. Discover what connections and talents exist among your friends. Barter and exchange appropriate services.

Step 2. Access published resources for finding like-minded women. Lists of organizations that serve targeted communities and steps on how to approach them are included in "Recommended Reading and Resources," page 277.

Step 3. Keep your name and your needs circulating among the professionals in your field. Someone will surface who can help you out.

4

Replay That Tape

Attitude Focus: Visualizing the Future
True.
I have been asleep and
Silent without motion
Or cause.
I have met blank days and
Seen myself in future's
Mirror.
Absorbing all that was me
When I was myself asleep,
I have awakened
In a season that requires
That I be exactly who
I am.

CHERYL FARRIS

*T*he lights slowly dim until the room is completely black. The
muted whispers of those around me taper off into silence and

the creaking sounds that were coming from the chairs stop as everyone settles down. Even the cranky baby in the back of the auditorium suddenly stops crying and the restless little boy who had been running up and down the aisle returns to his seat and flops down.

Soon a stirring melody bursts from the finely tuned sound system, sweeping over the audience in an emotional wave. The darkened screen at the front of the theater comes to life as an incredibly blue sky fills the huge expanse of canvas. Next, the camera pans down to a shiny 1922 Buick roadster barreling down a dusty country road toward a big white farmhouse in the distance.

I slip down in my seat until my neck is resting on its edge and press my hands to my knees to stop them from shaking. I stare at the images before me, holding my breath in anticipation because the scenes are quite familiar.

The movie continues. Behind the wheel of the car sits a handsome, debonair man with a determined set to his jaw. He has light brown skin, wavy dark hair, and a face illuminated by a boyish innocence that competes with his sexy, self-assured attitude. The man brushes specks of dust from his lapels, then pulls a wad of cash from the breast pocket of his velvet-collared jacket and carelessly tosses the money onto the empty seat beside him.

Gunning the engine, he rounds a bend in the road, roars to a stop at the edge of the farm, then quickly grabs the money in a clenched fist and gets out. He strides impatiently to the front of the car. Fanning the bills, the gambler props one foot on the chrome bumper and squints across the land toward a beautiful woman sitting proudly on a horse at the foot of a tall oil derrick.

The sun bounces off the woman's reddish-brown hair, which has been pulled back from her face with a red bandanna. She shifts her position atop her striking chestnut mare to look at the man but deliberately refuses to acknowledge his presence.

He sets out on foot toward her.

The screen credits for *Black Gold* begin to roll.

The Widow, Leela Wilder . . . . *Vanessa Williams*
The Gambler, Carey Logan . . . . *Mario Van Peebles*
The Wildcatter, Victor Beaufort . . . . *Samuel L. Jackson*

Screenplay based on the novel by Anita Richmond Bunkley

This is where my fantasy usually ends, though at times I must admit that I allow myself to go so far as to conjure up images of sitting in the audience at the Academy Awards ceremony with the stars, applauding as one of them accepts an Oscar. Or I might decide to bring the after-Oscars party into focus, visualizing myself sipping champagne and making small talk with celebrities at the oh-so-chic affair after the awards. Dreaming? Maybe. Crazy? I don't think so. Possible? Definitely!

CREATING MENTAL SCENARIOS

Our ability to control our thoughts is the only true power we have. All women, and especially African-American women, must realize the enormous potential of this God-given force and put it to better use. Neither unemployment, downsizing, poverty, nor rejection can wipe out your ability to control what goes on in your mind. It's the one domain that totally and absolutely belongs to you. It's what kept our enslaved ancestors alive—believing that a better day would come.

Conjuring up scenarios such as the one described above occupies an important place in my life, inspiring me to write a better sentence, work harder to make a deadline, and concentrate on fulfilling my potential as a creative individual.

I set aside a portion of each day to engage in such visualization exercises and never feel guilty about the time I devote to my foray into dreamland. This is the fuel that nourishes the creative spirit, allowing it to survive those rocky periods when everything seems to be fuzzy.

ATTITUDE ADJUSTMENT TIP #1

Meditate or you will stagnate. If you stagnate you are dead.

If you have a dream, a goal, a purpose in life, nourish it by visualizing yourself at the ultimate high point—the pinnacle of your success—and you will feel as if you are already there.

Creative visualization is not child's play, though children routinely create fantasy worlds to act out what catches their fancy. It is interesting that adults are quick to humor and encourage this behavior. They laugh as the kids interact in their make-believe worlds and talk with imaginary playmates. Mothers and fathers watch and coo in admiration. Isn't she cute? Will you look at that? My, my, what an active imagination she has! But when a mature woman starts daydreaming or talking to others about accomplishing something that friends and family consider absolutely impossible, her ideas are often met with skeptical approval, ridicule, cautious support, or stern words of unsolicited advice.

Fear of disapproval has caused many of my sisters to shun creative dreaming. This fear acts like a paralysis, locking their brains in a permanent state of complacency, preventing them from seeing, feeling, smelling, and touching the vision that lies at the back of their minds.

The ability to mentally shape the future is at the heart of stepping out to sell a dream. If you can't bring forth a clear picture of where you want to go and how you plan to get there, you can't possibly survive the journey.

African-American women must learn to explore and strengthen their relationship with the higher spiritual source—the source that connects all of us to the universality of the world. According to the results of a study done by the Institute for Social Research at the University of Michigan, African-Americans are generally more religious and participate in higher levels of spiritual activity in their daily lives than whites. These results were published in the *Journal for the Scientific Study of Religion* (as cited in David Briggs's article in the *Houston Chronicle*, Mar. 9, 1997). It is well documented that the black church has traditionally been pivotal in effecting social and economic change in the lives of African-Americans, and it is estimated that 39 percent of blacks read religious material every day. We spend more time in spiritual contemplation than whites, putting prayer and devotion high on our list of priorities.

It is this personal connection with a higher source of power and our historical involvement with action-based faith that has allowed us to survive as a race. Participating in creative visualization exercises in order to achieve a goal is simply another way of expressing our faith in ourselves.

Spending time each morning in spiritual devotion helps me get centered before starting my day. Reading scripture and inspirational passages and listening to motivational tapes fire me up with excitement, preparing me for the long stretch of creative effort I face.

I encourage all of my sisters to set aside time to get in touch with the life-giving power that guides us on our journeys, because we surely are not walking these paths alone. In our own unique ways, we must strengthen the spiritual connection that links us to our futures, showers us with blessings, and gives us the strength to pursue the paths we choose. Adopting a more spiritual attitude helps us energize, focus, and reinforce our belief that the decisions we make about our life's work are based on solid ground and are the ones we were meant to make.

Our thoughts and how we focus mental energy is what sets humans apart from lower species and is the source of all inspiration. Inventors, artists, scientists, educators, and religious and political leaders would never have accomplished anything if first they hadn't seen themselves doing it and envisioned the results of their efforts. Only you can create your future. No one else is going to do it for you. So what are you waiting for?

ATTITUDE ADJUSTMENT TIP #2

Allow yourself some quiet time every day.

Mental wandering is one thing, but focused visualization is quite another.

As an author, one of the most common questions I am asked when I speak to a group of readers or writers is where I get the inspiration for the characters and plots in my novels. The answer is simple. Everyday life. Ideas for stories and characters come at me like an avalanche because I keep my antennae up, my eyes open, and my ears finely tuned to what is going on. Incidents, unusual people, and tales of tragedy as well as triumph are in the news every day, fueling my imagination.

In order to become more receptive to visual stimuli you must know what you want, sense that it is near, and commit to having it soon! Here are several activities to help develop your imagination:

- Concentrate on the images that attract you in magazines, books, and newspapers.

- Observe people during social activities and while you are traveling.

- Listen to the unique expressions people use to convey certain feelings.

- Use a small tape recorder to capture incidents, quotes, jokes, or other scenes from life.

- Embrace images of success and memorize the feelings that come with them.

When you make that great speech, impress your boss, accept that promotion, pull off a successful event, or snag that account you've been after, you validate your perceived ability to master a task. By successfully incorporating resources at your disposal with the skills that you possess, you can get results.

No matter what anyone says, what you consider attainable is neither preposterous, unreachable, nor foolish. Look around. Others have done exactly what you propose. Movies do get made from books. Poor people do become millionaires. Teachers do touch children's lives. Academy Awards do get won. Small businesses do thrive. Inventions do get patented. By whom and why? By people with a solid sense of self who understand what they have been called to do. They dare to take risks, relying more on themselves than others as they step out on faith with no more than a dream and a desire to sell it to the world. Why? Because they absolutely have no other choice.

I first met the author Terry McMillan in 1989 at a book signing in Houston, Texas. She was promoting her second book, *Disappearing Acts,* and was still trying to get the word out about her talent. The tiny African-American bookstore where she was appearing was crowded.

I was anxious to meet the woman who in *Disappearing Acts* had written so brashly and boldly about a sister's struggle to hold on to the man in her life. This book was among the first from a major publishing house to focus on the lives of middle-class African-American women. Terry had claimed her place in the writing world, one I wanted to be a part of too.

I was sitting very close to Terry and even had a chance to chat with her for a few minutes between autographs. When she learned that I was a writer, she made a gracious offer I'll never forget. She invited me to sign my self-published book, *Emily, the Yellow Rose*, right along with her! Of course I declined, but I gave her an autographed copy, letting her know that my goal was to be published by a major house soon. She smiled, gave me a thumbs-up, and kept on signing her books.

I, like Terry, have been a single parent, writing and struggling to raise a family alone. Her story, told with humor and sincerity, touched me and many other sisters as the type of novel that we wanted to read. Terry told the audience her personal story, relating that at the time she got her publishing contract she had been broke and desperate, but filled with faith. I, and many of the women in the room, could certainly identify with that.

Someone in the audience asked whether Terry would like to see her book turned into a movie. She laughed and nodded, a gleam of certainty in her eyes, and I could tell she had already visualized this! Her positive attitude and determination buoyed me. That night I left the bookstore with a personally autographed copy of her book. She wrote:

TO ANITA—TO A FELLOW WRITER!! GOOD LUCK WITH YOUR WORK— LOOKING FORWARD! WARMLY, TERRY MCMILLAN, 12/2/89

I was inspired and more determined than ever to take my books to my target audience.

Six years later, when I sat in the theater watching *Waiting to Exhale*, I felt proud, excited, and spiritually connected. Terry had done it! Finally, an African-American woman's story had made it to the big screen and the characters were well developed, positive, smart, attractive black women—not the worn-out mammy/maid stereotypes we sisters have been forced to endure for so long. Terry never gave up on her dream. I am convinced that someday it will happen for my books, too.

ATTITUDE ADJUSTMENT TIP #3

Feed your faith.

The telephone rings. It's the call you've been waiting for. The editor of a major publishing house wants to buy your book. I visualized this scene over and over, even rehearsing what I would say, absolutely believing it would happen to me. It did. In 1992, when my agent informed me that Penguin USA, one of the nation's largest and most-respected publishing houses, wanted to publish *Black Gold* and was offering me a two-book contract, I felt as if I was standing smack in the middle of the dream sequence I had lived with for years. It happened exactly as I had envisioned. Later when friends asked me if I had been surprised about the contract, I had to answer no. I had *expected* this to come. The only question was when.

Before I became a published author I used to go into B. Dalton, Crown, Waldenbooks, and various African-American bookstores and imagine that my books were already there for sale. I would walk around and study book covers, analyze the in-store displays, and investigate how the books were placed on the shelves. In airports and drugstores I would look at the racks and envision my novels alongside those of other authors whom I had read and admired. In 1995, I stepped off a plane in Chicago and went directly to a nearby airport newsstand to see if my first paperback release, *Black Gold*, was on the shelf. I was so excited to find it racked high on a wall, shining like a star among all the other titles. I stood silently for a long time just looking at it. A woman reached past me, took down a copy, and went to the cashier to pay for it. I smiled as I watched her tuck it into her carry-on bag. I had envisioned that scenario so many times, and now it was real!

ATTITUDE ADJUSTMENT TIP #4

Adopt an open attitude toward things that are new.

I firmly believe that everything happens for a reason. No matter how difficult or stressful a situation may seem, how you deal with the problem is largely determined by your attitude. When my two daughters were small and I would fix Kool-aid for them and their playmates, one child would invariably tell me, "It's too sour," while another would say, "It's not sweet enough." I always found it very interesting that the same message could be conveyed in two very different attitudes. How does life taste to you?

Allow yourself to be more adventurous and experimental. Taking the positive view of a difficult situation helps you stay focused and in control. Anger, jealousy, and resentment are emotional triggers that drain energy, interfering with your ability to tap into your creative resources and begin working on the problem. People who bitch and groan and have nothing good to say about anything or anybody can't possibly expect to succeed. The precious energy that should be focused on finding creative solutions is squandered on dreary complaints.

Too many of my sisters seem to be extremely "nearsighted," but nothing is really wrong with their eyes. They may have 20/20 vision, yet they tend to focus on the lack of opportunities within their immediate environment, allowing their potential to be defined by the limited experiences they have had and the less-than-supportive influences around them. I encourage these sisters to seek people and situations that will fill their days with a variety of positive life experiences. They must dream harder and longer and with more imagination. Here are some steps to help my sisters do just that:

Action Steps

Step 1. Create a private space where you can surround yourself with materials such as posters, photos, maps, artwork, and other visuals related to your field that will fire you up.

Step 2. Resolve to spend time in this space on a regular basis, fueling your imagination.

Step 3. Go where you want to be. Visit high-rise buildings, theaters, auditoriums, museums, banks, universities, bookstores. Walk the halls. Ride the elevators. Observe the decor. Experience the sights, smells, and sounds of the environment where you expect to achieve maximum success.

Step 4. Spend time with professionals in your field or industry. Talk to people who can influence your journey in a positive way. Act like a sponge and absorb the knowledge that your peers and mentors possess.

Step 5. Tap into sources of information to fuel your visualization exercises. Books, magazines, tapes, and videos can transport you directly into your new reality.

Institutions like public libraries and government and consumer-oriented bureaus that deal with public information have free material that can help you enhance your ability to visualize in a creative manner.

Exercise

As you sit alone in your quiet place, letting your mind drift, a series of vivid, exciting images will come to you. See yourself at the peak of your success. You are claiming it, owning, it, rejoicing in it, and sharing it.

Step 1. In a notebook or computer file, state your objective by finishing these sentences:

a. I see myself _____

b. I am here because_____

c. With me is/are _____

d. I expect _____

Step 2. Make a chronological list of all the activities you must undertake to transform this goal into reality. The objective and the actions steps create the bridge that will take you from mental wandering to actuality.

An example

Below is an example of the results of one sister's completion of the exercise described above.

Objective (Step 1): My next sales pitch will snag a major account for my company, Cellular Phone, Inc. This will prove that I have the negotiation skills required to become a part of the firm's premier sales team.

Action steps (Step 2). This is the sister's list of the activities she must undertake to make her dream a reality.

1. Gather background information, statistics, history on the company I plan to target. Analyze my competition.

2. Identify and make contact with the "gatekeeper" (the person who can facilitate entry) at the office of my targeted contact.
3. Finalize my sales proposal by a targeted date.
4. Do a needs assessment on the target audience. (Vital! You must SERVE the needs of those you expect to persuade.)
5. Determine who in my network can help with preparations/ introductions.
6. Call and speak with the contact appropriate to what I have to offer.
7. Position the focus of my proposal as necessary to the success of the company. Demonstrate via statistics, history, projections, and references why my company should be awarded the contract.
8. Ask for an appointment. If rejected, thank the contact for considering me and inquire about a possible follow-up at a later date. Immediately target another company.
9. If accepted, set the date of my presentation.
10. If possible, meet the person/s to whom I will pitch my proposal and visit the room/setting where the pitch will be made.
11. Troubleshoot the presentation by playing devil's advocate. Ask hard questions. Pay attention to details.
12. Rehearse my presentation.
13. Plan my wardrobe so my image is appropriate to the audience.
14. Rehearse my presentation.
15. Solicit feedback from my mentor/trusted adviser.
16. Incorporate valid suggestions into my presentation.
17. Think positive thoughts.
18. Approach the task with an attitude of enthusiasm.
19. Make my best presentation.
20. Expect the positive outcome that I have visualized for this meeting.

Consider this process like a videotape, one that you can replay over and over, applying these two steps to whatever project or objective you are working on. Planning is key to ensuring that the process unfolds in an effective manner. By routinely engaging in the visualization process, you will keep your creative energy high and a positive attitude in place.

Success is inspiration taken to a level of imagination that shapes it into something real.

The first writers' conference I ever attended was in 1982, held at the University of Houston. The experience was a true reality check. There were only two other black writers in attendance. None of the workshops addressed marketing to the African-American audience that I planned to reach with my stories. The scenario was extremely discouraging. As I sat listening to the editors, agents, and published authors, fear set in and paralyzed me. When the time came for my scheduled meeting with a top New York agent, I almost canceled. But I took a deep breath, said a prayer, and went into the room.

We discussed my work in progress. She asked to see few chapters. I was excited. She was very encouraging. But a few weeks later she rejected me, confirming my suspicion that my target audience—the African-American woman—had not been identified as the formidable market I knew it would be. I also knew that I had a long way to go before my work would be good enough to be published. I made up my mind to study, study, study. Nine years later, I signed a contract with that very same agent, and she negotiated my hardcover deal for two works of African-American women's fiction, *Black Gold* and *Wild Embers*. I continue to treasure Denise Marcil's commitment to my career.

Examples abound of sisters who developed a vision, kept it alive, and saw it come true for them. Margarite grew up in an emotionally abusive environment. A bright girl, though bored in high school, she wound up graduating with lower-than-average grades. When she left home to make her way in the world, she worked at a minimum-wage job in a fast-food restaurant and shared a small apartment with three other girls. They partied every night and gave little thought to the future, let alone building careers.

Soon Margarite became frustrated and grew tired of the nonstop nightclubbing that consumed them. She realized there had to be a better life for her than earning four-fifty an hour and wearing a uniform she hated, but she had no idea what to do because she had never been encouraged to focus on anything or set any goals for herself. She had simply grown up with little direction or support.

The longer Margarite worked at her low-paying, unin-spired job, the more depressed she became. Soon she began calling in sick and missing work; eventually she was fired. This turn of events depressed her even more, and without a good reference she was not motivated to get serious about her job hunt. After bumming off her roommates for a few months, they began making noise about putting her out if she didn't get a job and pay her share of the rent.

One morning Margarite read a help-wanted ad placed by a nearby dry cleaner's. They wanted someone to do minor repairs on clothing. Margarite perked up. She knew how to sew and had made many of her own clothes while in high school. The pay was no better than at the fast-food place, but she rationalized that this type of work would be easier than standing on her feet flipping hamburgers all day, so she went to the dry cleaner's and applied. Because she had no refer-ences, the manager hired her on a thirty-day-trial basis.

The work was not so bad. Margarite quickly discovered that she enjoyed seeing the finished product when a zipper had been replaced, or a rip in a seam was repaired so neatly that no one could tell the garment had been damaged. Handling pretty dresses and working on well-tailored suits was exciting. She had never come in contact with expensive clothing before and she began looking at people in an entirely different light.

Margarite began reading *Vogue* and *Harper's Bazaar* and tore photos of beautiful dresses out of magazines to put them on the walls of her room. She started watching the fashion shows instead of MTV. She got up enough nerve to venture into the pricey stores in the malls to examine high-quality suits and dresses to see how they were put together, and soon began visualizing herself working as a buyer for one of the upscale retail stores. Gradually, Margarite started to improve her own appearance. When her roommates took notice, she brushed them off, unable to share her vision with them, fearing they would laugh at her ambition or try to discourage her from going after a dream that seemed impossible.

One day, Mrs. Williams, a very stylish woman who was a regular customer at the dry cleaner's where Margarite worked, brought in a white silk blouse that had a large tear in one of the cuffs. The manager told the customer that the blouse was ruined. Mrs. Williams handed it to the manager and told him to discard it. He tossed it into a rag bin nearby.

From her sewing machine behind the counter, Margarite had watched this exchange with interest. That evening, before leaving work, she salvaged the blouse from the rag bin and took it home. After examining how the blouse was constructed, she came up with a creative solution. She replaced both of the cuffs on the blouse with wide bands of white satin ribbon.

A few days later when Mrs. Williams came in, Margarite showed her what she had done. The woman was extremely grateful and impressed with the young lady's creativity and the quality of her workmanship. The two women began to talk and Margarite took a chance—sharing her dream of working at an upscale women's clothing store.

It turned out that Mrs. Williams worked in the sales department of a major downtown retailer. Margarite had suspected as much from the quality of her clothes. Mrs. Williams took a liking to Margarite and when there was an opening in the alterations department at the retail store where Mrs. Williams worked, she let Marguerite know and said she'd give her a reference. Margarite got the job—and eventually moved up to become a buyer for one of the most prestigious retail chains in the nation. Just as she had visualized!

Because Margarite had a vision and acted on it, she was able to find her niche as well as the happiness that came from doing what she loved.

A dream builder seeks creative solutions to obstacles and

does not settle for circumstances as they are. Strengthen your resolve to serve the needs of others, and suddenly a vast reservoir of possibilities will be at your disposal. What you *can* do, you *must* do, and bringing your sisters along on your imaginative journeys will help you live a life of courageous inspiration. Shun mediocrity like the plague. Whatever has deep meaning for you can be translated into a clear mental picture. Remain dedicated to keeping that image in focus, in front of you, and fresh. Bring it forth on a regular basis and replay that tape again and again and again!

5

Fly Away Home

Attitude Focus: Giving Back
Any definition of a successful life must include serving others.
PRESIDENT GEORGE BUSH

*I*n 1989, in the course of coordinating a feature called "Essence on the Mall" for *Essence* magazine's cover model search, Maria Dowd realized that her sisters were hungry for anything that centered on *them* and the issues that affected their futures. "It was amazing how black women responded," Maria remembers. "They were ecstatic about such an event. It made me realize that a 'feel-good' conference, or a 'traveling reunion for sisters' that was chock full of uplifting messages, informative and insightful seminars, celebrity guests, Afrocentric goods, and networking galore, was exactly what they wanted."

In 1991, trusting her instincts that it was the right time to move forward on her concept, Maria stepped out into the marketplace and launched her first African American Women on Tour conference in San Diego, California. With little money, lots of courage, the help of sister-friends in San Diego, and the support of Susan Taylor, the editor-in-chief of *Essence* magazine, the two-and-a-half-day gathering was an immediate success.

"Very soon," Maria says, "the drum began to beat about the little conference that could."

Two years later, Maria took another giant step, expanding the conference to Oakland and Los Angeles. Unfortunately, things did not go smoothly. The conference experienced a major setback when a high-profile celebrity who was scheduled to appear in Los Angeles canceled. Maria admits that it took two years to recover financially from this unexpected episode, but public interest in her venture remained high.

Undaunted, Maria—who says the entrepreneurial spirit runs strong in her family—plunged ahead, expanding the conference farther, reaching out to sisters in Washington, D.C., and again in Oakland, and adding New Orleans. But once again, financial tragedy struck when the numbers didn't pan out in New Orleans, and she was forced to cancel the entire conference in the final hours.

Did Maria give up? Not on your life! She shrewdly negotiated for additional time to pay the bills she had amassed in New Orleans. She contacted the hotels, contractors, and suppliers, telling them, "You have to trust me. I *will* pay you. I just need time." Luckily, they trusted her and she made good on her promise.

Today, African American Women on Tour is the most successful, visible, and valuable empowerment conference for black women in the country, drawing thousands of talented, focused sisters together in six major cities every year.

A divorced mother of two, Maria found her niche and is currently experiencing the joy of independence that she was able to obtain by stepping out to make real what she had only envisioned. She says that the women who attend her conferences often arrive at the hotels expressing the following attitude: "I'm going to get the max *out* of this and I'm going to be the max *in* this. I am here because I want to be, and I owe this to myself."

Releasing your dream to the world creates energy, which

in turn generates momentum. Once this force is let loose, a shift in mental attitude occurs that inspires others to flock to you with offers of help. Accept these offers in the spirit of gratitude, and be prepared to reciprocate in some way, someday.

The difference between holding back or stepping out is often tied to issues of support, and feelings of isolation are common among highly successful people. Some high achievers were loners in their youth, others may have been considered "outsiders" during high school and college years. Maybe they did march to the beat of a different drummer or carve their paths out of the wilderness, but through it all, many revealed that even though going after their dreams separated them from their peers, they were willing to live with this sense of isolation in order to fulfill their perceived destinies. However, now that they have made it, they are eager to give back by extending a helping hand.

VOLUNTEERISM: AN AMERICAN EXPERIENCE

The pioneer, can-do spirit that inspired men and women to carve a nation out of a wilderness left a legacy of sharing and support that is synonymous with America. This sense of obligation, to neighbors and strangers, remains deeply imbedded in the American psyche and is a curious phenomenon in the eyes of many underdeveloped countries throughout the world.

Early settlers who were separated by great distances often depended on the kindness of strangers to survive. When towns were established, everyone helped construct buildings, pooling resources to create a city.

Today, in many parts of the country, disadvantaged segments of the population still depend on charitable organizations and the kindness of strangers to maintain minimum standards of living. Millions are tied to the generosity of thousands of people who routinely reach out and give back to those in need. For empathetic individuals, heads of corporations, and members of charitable institutions, volunteering is a part of everyday life, as important as getting up in the morning and going to work.

Companies large and small routinely consider their communities' needs when developing their business strategies. Local entrepreneurs are keenly aware of the responsibility they have to serve the communities where they do business. Successful CEOs and committed entrepreneurs often sit on boards and serve on committees of nonprofit organizations. They do not do this solely to enhance their visibility, though that is certainly an important by-product of such involvement; they do this to help find solutions to community problems and increase standards of living for the residents of those communities.

ATTITUDE ADJUSTMENT TIP #1

Practice putting yourself in another person's place.

When you see hopeless homeless sisters, try to put yourself in their place. What do they need that you can provide? How can you fit service into your life? Sure, we have to be careful about opening ourselves up to strangers. That's a fact of life in these times, but take the time to consider what you have to give. Think about causes you can support. The joy received from helping others build better lives is immeasurable and will be returned tenfold.

THE IMPORTANCE OF ROLE MODELS

Because many black women in positions of power had few role models or mentors to advise them, they are cautious about approaching other successful sisters to ask for advice. But the truth is, most successful people *want* to reach out to help a colleague, and they keep their eyes open for suitable candidates to assist.

ATTITUDE ADJUSTMENT TIP #2

Don't be afraid of competition.

The security that comes with achievement prepares successful women to share. They don't worry that their ideas and tips for making it in their professions will be stolen or adopted by others. Circulating valuable information brings savvy sisters a sense of accomplishment, identifying them among their peers as people who truly care. They actively seek opportunities to help others avoid the pitfalls they have experienced.

During her ten years in the hair-care industry, Geri Rowe has traveled the globe, sharing her techniques and expertise in the beauty industry with international audiences around the world. From New Zealand to the Caribbean to Canada and Mexico, this international educator captures the attention of fashionable women of all races and ethnic backgrounds as she demonstrates new products and influences styling trends.

"My entrepreneurial spirit goes back to my high school days, when I sold popcorn to raise money to sponsor myself as homecoming queen," says Geri, who understood at an early age that she had to be responsible for enhancing her own visibility. "My dad was a self-employed payroll clerk and auditor. Working for him after school allowed me to identify with the satisfaction and sense of reward he felt at achieving his goals through his work."

With a degree in business, Geri started a career in corporate America, managing a temporary employment agency. There, she recruited and hired staff, managed sales reps, and set corporate sales quotas. She stayed with the company for eleven years, but she was not happy and never recaptured that sense of satisfaction that she felt when working for her dad. "After the birth of my son," Geri relates, "I realized that if I was going to be a positive role model, I needed to feel positive about my work. I wanted to be able to demonstrate to my son that he had options—that he did not have to work for someone else."

Geri, who had always enjoyed hairstyling, art, and fashion, began thinking, researching, and planning to open her own beauty salon. She enrolled in cosmetology courses at the community college, passed her exams, and became a state-certified cosmetologist. She focused on making her mark in the health and beauty industry. A major influence was the story of Madame C. J. Walker, who pioneered the black hair-care industry in 1905 and made a fortune serving her sisters. She became America's first black female millionaire.

Within a year after passing her exams, Geri Rowe opened the doors of The Hair Shoppe. "Once I was in business for myself, I began networking at church, supermarkets, toll booths, happy hours, and many social functions. I even recruited telemarketers to call potential customers and sell my products and promote the services of my salon," Geri says. "The business took off, breaking even in six months."

Now, Geri employs a variety of hairstylists with different backgrounds. "The diversity of my employees has allowed me to learn many techniques. As the lead stylist in my own salon, I feel it is important to attend every educational event that has value, regardless of where it is. It is a challenge to meet the demands of parenthood, run a salon, and travel so frequently, but when I think about all the women, past and present, who have been role models for me, I simply become inspired to achieve even more."

SERVICE COUNTS

Many Fortune 500 companies have community involvement programs to encourage employees to serve or enhance unmet needs in the community. A large number of corporations have formal policies granting employees paid leave for service and education-related activities. Others allow staff to fulfill their obligations on company time.

A 1995 research report from the Center for Corporate Community Relations, conducted through Boston College (*A*

Center Research Report, Chestnut Hill, MA 02167-3835, phone 617 552-4545), found that 53 percent of 190 companies surveyed included community relations in their strategic plans. Eighty-five percent encouraged managers to get involved in the community. Over 90 percent said that such programs improve the company's public image while positively impacting employees' morale.

For five years I worked as the director of volunteers for the American Red Cross, the premier volunteer-based organization in the world. Recruiting, training, and supervising thousands of volunteers in the greater Houston area gave me an opportunity to meet generous, unselfish people, many from local corporations, who willingly gave their time, talent, and money to help those in need.

When Hurricane Alicia hit the Gulf Coast area in 1982, the appeal went out for thousands of volunteers and I found myself interviewing CEOs, lawyers, CPAs, doctors, and teachers, as well as truck drivers, students, and mothers. I found myself training a huge number of people from a vast variety of backgrounds and educational levels in how to ease the suffering of those who had experienced devastating loss.

My major task was to match volunteers with specific tasks that needed to be done, and to get them into the affected area as quickly as possible. The interview process was vital to creating a corps of people who could immediately go in and help the community recover from the disaster. On the basis of whatever information I could quickly gather during an initial interview, I began to set up training sessions. It was hectic and time-consuming work, and many people complained about the time and effort that went into the screening process. However, I refused to change my approach. I knew that it was necessary to place the right person in the right position in order to give him or her the most satisfying and effective volunteer experience—and get the job done.

If a person's skills and interests have been properly matched to the job they are expected to do, they feel that their time and talent are valued. It was my job was to make sure this happened.

The people I trained and placed in the program during this disaster didn't volunteer in order to showcase themselves, but you can bet that's exactly what happened in many cases. As they stepped in to do their part, they were automatically provided an opportunity to share skills, expertise, and experience. During the long hours of work involved in helping disaster victims, many volunteers' actions were noted and remembered, and their talents were sought out for other positions long after the crisis had passed. Once certificates of appreciation had been bestowed, many companies' managers contacted me to express thanks, adding that their employees' volunteer service would become a part of their performance record.

What You Can Do Now

Step 1. Study your company's annual report to see how and where your company has been involved in the community.

Step 2. Check with the appropriate department to learn how you can participate in the programs they support.

Step 3. Investigate the requirements to participate in your company's loaned executive program. This type of exchange presents an opportunity to enter a new environment and donate and showcase your talent, while expanding your network.

Step 4. Take the initiative to organize a group of your coworkers to tackle a community project such as repairing houses for the elderly, cleaning a local park, or participating in a marathon/walk to raise funds for a worthwhile cause. You will be amazed at the variety of volunteer opportunities that exist where your talent and time can make a difference in a community and in someone's life.

Step 5. Make your expectations known. When corporations commit to a community project, the CEOs are not bashful about setting objectives for public awareness and visibility. You should be equally candid. If your forte is event planning and you really want to be in charge of coordinating the program or arranging for appearances of celebrity participants, speak up! Don't get stuck in a backroom folding napkins or making lemonade, which could easily sour your volunteer experience.

Research the Program

Before making a commitment to an organization or a cause, it's a good idea to do a little research.

Ten Questions to Ask Before Volunteering

1. What is the mission statement of the organization?
2. Do the objectives of the organization fit with your values and interests?
3. Does the organization have reputable backing and support?
4. What obstacles exist to achieving its objectives?
5. What is its track record in accomplishing stated objectives?
6. Is a volunteer training, supervision, and recognition program in place?
7. Is there sufficient manpower to accomplish the objectives?
8. Are both short- and long-term activities available for the scope of service?
9. Is the geographic area of service realistic and convenient for you?
10. Is there opportunity to move up the volunteer ranks as your experience and expertise increase?

BE A BUDDY: MENTORING

Mentoring is one of the most popular kinds of volunteer activities. Generally it's a flexible activity that provides an immediate sense of reward. By giving instruction or advice in an area where you have a high level of comfort, you strengthen your own sense of assurance and build your self-confidence.

The Houston Chapter of the Coalition of 100 Black Women has a Role Model Program that attracts female college students from across the state who are looking for mentors. Members are encouraged to mentor students who are interested in careers in education, business, law, social services, medicine, and communications. The girls live with their mentor for three days. During this time, the mentor takes the student to work with her, providing an insider's view of a field or profession that the girl might otherwise never get to experience. The young women also participate in group activities and cultural outings and discussions of their various experiences. This program has been very successful and the limited spots are coveted. Several of the original students are now professional women who have become mentors themselves.

Mentoring is an intimate experience that creates an opportunity to establish instant rapport with the recipient of your services and provides you with immediate gratification.

In a mentoring program one can easily find corporate CEOs, busy entrepreneurs, socialites, and homemakers alongside teachers, students, and unemployed people—all willing to give their time to help young people move ahead with their lives. Mentoring affords us the opportunity to make friends and gain valuable insight and knowledge about the young people of today.

The emotional and spiritual rewards that come from helping youths recognize and utilize their full potential cannot be measured. If done with sincerity and enthusiasm, coaching the young sisters and brothers of our communities will definitely impact the future of our nation. Exposure to your wisdom, experience, and talent could be the deciding factor in turning a young person's life around. By offering an out-stretched hand, you can positively impact your community in a variety of critical ways.

Learning and Growth from Mentoring

If you are receptive and alert, volunteer involvement can mean gaining new skills and enhancing leadership qualities, as well as exposing your talent to a new audience. These are benefits that you receive simply by reaching out. Your organizational contacts can provide written commendations that you can use as references and your volunteer record can be a valuable documentation of your generous spirit. Both can be important resources to improve your chances for promotions, raises, or new responsibilities. Characteristics such as dependability, organization, punctuality, flexibility, and the ability to interact with a wide variety of people can be considered as positive attributes to add to your personnel file. It's a win-win situation when you decide to give back, so donate your time where you believe you can do the most good, and the pay-off will astound you.

> Too often we fail as human beings to recognize the contributions of our living jewels until after they're gone.
>
> *Carolyn Campbell, television news reporter*

As a young girl, Carolyn Campbell had bright eyes and big dreams about getting into the crazy business of covering the news. Her vision was realized through the help of a man who stepped forward and became her mentor.

"When I got out of college," says Carolyn, who is a general assignment television news reporter for Station KHOU-TV in Houston, a CBS affiliate, "the opportunities to grow and learn from my mistakes were few." She got lucky when Varee Shields, the editor of the African-American newspaper the *Forward Times*, hired her as a free-lance reporter. "It was one of my first 'real jobs' in journalism," she relates. "Mr. Shields actually *paid* me for my stories, which at the time were mediocre at best. He patiently critiqued my writing, discussed story ideas, and helped me understand there was always a story behind the story. When I started working at KHOU-TV, I called him often, just to bounce ideas and perspectives off of him. He was always available to listen and offer an encouraging word. For a young 'wannabe' journalist I couldn't have had a more nurturing and talented mentor. He was my cheerleader, inspiring me to stretch myself and work harder, so I could fly higher."

And fly higher she did. Carolyn has worked as a stringer for Black Entertainment Television and National Black Network News, and in 1984 she won the Broadcast Media Award for Outstanding Coverage of Mental Health Issues. This busy sister continues the legacy of her mentor by working with interns at her television station. "It takes more to help our students," she says of the young African-Americans with whom she interacts. "They don't arrive with a sense of entitlement. They feel overwhelmed by the television studio and are in awe of the on-air talent. I try to help them develop a sense of belonging and the confidence to fully participate in the intern experience." She has some advice to pass on.

Carolyn's Tips for Effective Mentoring

1. Find the time. Busy people don't always have control of their time.
2. Make a commitment to being a good mentor, not just playing a role.
3. Have patience. Mentoring requires a nurturing personality.
4. Stick with it until a bond has developed.
5. Don't give up if things don't click right away.
6. Give the relationship time to gel.
7. Stay in touch with those you have helped. Let them feel you truly cared.

The entire community benefits when sisters take responsibility for helping others make something of their lives.

ATTITUDE ADJUSTMENT TIP #3

Don't expect reciprocity for your service or donation.

The sense of satisfaction generated by giving back and helping others must be the reason you get involved. You should not anticipate pay, perks, gifts, or even thanks as you set out to serve. As your volunteer experiences grow, so will your visibility. Companies often highlight their volunteers' activities in trade publications and the local press. Involvement at the local level of an organization may lead to unexpected opportunities to network and share your talent on a national scale. You never know who is watching, so do your best and stay enthusiastic. Soon, your name might be on everyone's list and you'll be sought out to serve in places you never imagined.

Action Steps

1. Commit to providing someone with a service that only you can offer.
2. Target an appropriate organization/institution by contacting your local volunteer clearinghouse or calling a national organization that may have branches in your area.
3. Approach your commitment seriously by following through on promises and being punctual and dependable.
4. Learn all you can about the organization, not just where you fit in.

ATTITUDE ADJUSTMENT TIP #4

Share your service experience.

Serve your brothers and sisters in the same way you would expect to be assisted. If appropriate, bring your own children or young people in your community along with you on your volunteer assignment and show them the ropes.

When I was working with the Red Cross, I was a single mother with two preteen daughters, and many of my assignments involved weekend and evening hours, so my girls were often right there by my side. While recruiting instructors for the summer learn-to-swim classes, I was pleased that both my girls, who are excellent swimmers, expressed interest. They signed up to work as aides for the volunteer swimming instructors at the public pools around the city.

The experience meant rising before dawn every day during summer vacation to catch a ride with a volunteer who would take them all over the city of Houston—into neighborhoods they knew nothing about. This exposure allowed them to make new friends and see how children lived in circumstances very different from theirs. Soon, I overheard them expressing concern for others, pride in themselves, and a heightened sense of how fortunate they were to be able to help other children who wanted to learn to swim. Later when they began seeking employment and applying to colleges, references were needed. Those Red Cross instructors were eager to vouch for my daughters' dependability, responsibility, and personal character. They had already established reputations as trustworthy girls who were good candidates for college life and for employment.

Exposing our youth to the joy of serving will heighten their sense of self-worth and foster attitudes of gratitude that soon become contagious.

ATTITUDE ADJUSTMENT TIP #5

Stop saying you're too busy.

Busy people get things done—at least they should, otherwise, what are they doing with their time? When your church, community, sorority, professional association, job, family, and friends all want a piece of you, it's easy to feel overwhelmed. As you rush through your hectic days, interacting with so many people, every minute is precious. You start your day determined to fulfill everything on your agenda, and when someone asks if you can squeeze in one more thing, you say, "I can't. I'm just too busy." Or perhaps your standard line is "My plate is already full." If you are constantly telling people that you are operating on overload and can't possibly take on one more project, maybe it's time to take a closer look at what is going on.

Perhaps all of this is true—but could it be that you have simply fallen into the dreary habit of proclaiming overload in order to make an excuse not to serve? Or could this be a ploy to make others believe that you are in such high demand that everything must be going well? If so, forget it. Such put-offs are tiresome expressions that eventually become unbelievable.

One of the busiest sisters on the planet must be the legendary jazz singer and actress Nancy Wilson. With over sixty recordings to her credit during a career that has spanned forty-five years, she is indeed a living icon in her industry. She's also my homegirl. We attended the same high school in Columbus, Ohio, though at different times, and I remember when she began her singing career in the local clubs around town. Nancy was brave enough to go out on her own and create a fabulous, enduring career when few mainstream clubs were open to black female entertainers. Everyone in Columbus was and still is extremely proud of her.

I finally got to meet Nancy Wilson up close and personal three years ago at a reception preceding a huge gala fundraiser for the Urban League. She had interrupted her busy schedule to help raise funds for a worthwhile cause. Because of a delayed flight, she arrived late, for which she apologized profusely; then she warmly greeted the anxious crowd. As I watched her, I knew she was a sincere sister who was genuinely involved in the organization that would benefit from her appearance. I wanted to do more than just shake her hand, I wanted to *know* Nancy Wilson. When I finally got close to her, I told her I was from Columbus. She laughed and gave me a warm hug. I asked her if she liked to read to pass the time while she was on the road enduring a grueling schedule. Her eyes lit up and she affirmed my instinct that education and books are very important to her. She can rattle off titles like a librarian and it is clear that she is very supportive of her sister writers. I told her I was an author and asked whether I could leave copies of my novels at the front desk of her hotel. She was delighted and grateful for my offer. That evening when I got home I personally autographed *Black Gold* and *Wild Embers* to Nancy Wilson, drafted a letter introducing myself, and put everything in a large envelope that was delivered to her hotel first thing the next morning. About two weeks later, in the middle of the night, my phone rang. It was Nancy. She was in Las Vegas and had just finished her singing engagement, and was back in her room. She wanted to thank me and tell me how much she enjoyed my books and that they had made her time on the road more enjoyable. She asked what she could do to help my career. I asked her whether she would give me a quote to print on the jacket of my next book and told her I'd stay in touch. She came through, graciously providing a supportive message to use in promotion of *Wild Embers*, my World War II saga that has scenes in our hometown. When I asked her to share words of wisdom for this book, about keeping perspective, she readily agreed to write the foreword to Part 3. We have talked on the phone many times since then, and I always send her books and notices to let her know when I am in her audience. As diverse and demanding as her stellar career has been, Nancy Wilson always finds time to volunteer her services to worthy causes. I know she's a sister who cares. She knows I'm a sister who shares.

How and Where to Get Involved

There are many fraternal, social, and community-based organizations whose mission statements are centered around helping black women. Seek them out. Donate some time to helping these organizations serve the less fortunate. There are mutual benefits to serving that can help both you and the organization of your choice. Public and private schools are desperate for adult involvement with their students. If you can, make a regular contribution as a tutor or try to give a few hours whenever you can. Career days and special fairs are great times to go into the school to talk about your profession, read stories, demonstrate a craft, or introduce the students to a rewarding hobby that brings you pleasure.

Hospitals, geriatric centers, literacy organizations, and a host of organizations targeted to children and young adults will also welcome you with open arms.

One way to find out how to get involved is to contact the Points of Light Foundation. It is an independent nonprofit organization dedicated to engaging more people in effective community volunteer service by working with local volunteer centers, corporate volunteer councils, the media, and local businesses. For information on a chapter in your area, call 202–223-9186.

Part I Worksheet

Assessment Questions

1. What do I think about most? _____
_____

2. What do I truly want to become, to accomplish, or to change? _____
_____

3. What really matters in my life? _____
_____

4. What is my greatest strength/talent? _____
_____

5. What makes me feel special? _____
_____

6. What is very difficult for me? _____
_____

7. Who can help me reach my goals? _____
_____

8. Who or what will most likely hinder my progress? _____

_____

9. What do I have to share? _____

_____

Action Steps

1. Set aside time each day to engage in visualization exercises.

2. Write down exactly what you dream about *most*. _____

   _____

3. Write down the obstacles facing you and divide them into
   two categories:

   a. Those that you can eliminate quickly. _____

   _____

   b. Those that will take longer than six months to resolve.

   _____

4. List the names of people who can help you. _____

   _____

5. Make a one-year plan by stating your goals in clear, specific language.

   Example: I will appear on a minimum of two radio programs each month this year. I will do this by sending press
   kits and making follow-up phone calls to the producers of
   the radio programs found in my media directory (available at the library) that have programs suitable for my
   message. The *short-range* goals might be perfecting the
   text of your message, having professional photos taken, or
   creating press materials. Later in the book I'll give you the
   steps to do this, from the right kind of paper to the proper
   format to the kinds of photos to how to write a press

release.

Write down what can you do today, this week, this month, then by the end of the year to move a step closer to each of the goals you have written down._____

_____

_____

6. Make a three-year plan.

Example: My objectives.

- This year I will join and become active in the local chapter of the Houston Business Women's Association.

- I will offer to present a workshop for them on *Steppin' Out with Attitude* for the fall meeting.

- I will circulate my promotional materials at the next meeting.

- I will express my desire to become a board member, with the goal of doing so in 1999.

- Next year I will respond to the call for speakers and submit an outline of my workshop to be presented at the regional conference.

- Within three years I will give a keynote speech, then run for a spot on the regional board of directors.

    Becoming an active participant in my local association is the first step to networking with the people who are in a position to help me move into a larger spotlight. I will make a timetable on a large wall calendar, charting anticipated progress toward these objectives. As I meet each one, I will revise and expand my plan to include the next five years.

7. Make a five-year plan.

Example: Within five years I will expand my retail space or move my office to a location that will provide better access to my clientele. Such a long-term plan will require steps related to industry forecasting, market analysis, demographics, growth projections, and local building codes.

If you need assistance to accomplish this objective, and most likely you will, turn to your local Small Business Administration office or the library of a business school connected to a university in your area. In either place you will find plans, statistics, and studies to help you make the important decisions that facilitate your reaching your objectives.

PART 2

Discipline

The reward is not so great without the struggle.

WILMA RUDOLPH, OLYMPIC GOLD MEDALIST

The Will to Find a Way

Kathryn Leary

CEO, The Leary Group, Inc.

When I decided to go to Japan to create opportunities for minority and small-business owners to enter the Japanese market, I knew that the general perception of Japan among African-Americans was not favorable. One of my goals was to help debunk these various myths. My experience shows that what most small-enterprise owners crave more than anything else is a sense of comfort that there are systematic procedures to help them establish themselves in their target market. They want direction. It's like learning to draw: Do you start with the eyes or the nose or the chin?

Like most other people doing business, I've stumbled a few times along the way. But the formula for success is no mystery. It's a matter of being methodical, persistent, curious, and receptive. You need to learn about the people you are trying to sell to. You must understand marketing. The basic concepts and principles apply in Japan as they do anywhere else. Build and maintain a strong, diversified network. Each element in a network can be a resource, provide leads and answers to questions, open new doors, and illuminate possibilities. Establish your credibility, for this is the ultimate purpose of networking.

Achieving success isn't accomplished through magic. It takes discipline. You have to work at maintaining your contacts. You have to keep people informed. You have to make your presence known. And most important, you have to be patient.

6

Stick with It!

Attitude Focus: Living with Commitment
Success requires a willingness to give up a great deal of your personal life.

MIGNON WYATT, OWNER, LE CHATEAU DELAWARE
BED AND BREAKFAST

*I*n the summer of 1997, I was invited by Donna Lucas of X-Pression bookstore in Indianapolis to participate in a literary café as part of the Indiana Black Expo. Of course I jumped at the invitation, fully aware of the huge numbers of people drawn to this grand showcase of black talent every year—one of the largest expositions in the nation.

Convinced that this was an opportunity not to be missed, I looked forward to being onstage with such successful authors as E. Lynn Harris, Tina Ansa, Dawn Turner Trice, and Kimberly Lawson Robey. An added bonus was the appearance of the actress-comedienne Kim Coles, who was promoting her new book, *I'm Single, But It Will Cost You*. The comedian Sinbad even showed up to share a few laughs with the audience!

While in Indianapolis, Donna Lucas had arranged for me and several other participating authors to stay in a bed and breakfast called Le Chateau Delaware, a grand Italian-style mansion in the historic district of the city. What a treat! We were all very impressed with the spacious rooms, the rich decor, the winding staircases, and most of all, the hospitality of the owner, Mignon Wyatt, a petite, soft-spoken African-American woman who had created a warm, inviting atmosphere for her literary guests to enjoy.

In this extraordinarily beautiful setting, Mignon and I had time to chat while I was eating breakfast before my early-morning departure. She told me how she had fulfilled her dream of owning such a historic house. "I simply went after what I wanted," she says. "When I saw this house, I knew immediately that it was *the* house for my bed and breakfast. I went up to the front door, rang the bell, and told the owner that I wanted to buy it. My timing and my instincts proved correct. The owner confessed that he was ready to get out from under maintaining the place, and was interested in my proposal. The house did need a great deal of attention, so I made him an offer that I felt was fair, and, as I had visualized, he accepted! Very soon after, I was in business."

Mignon feels that entrepreneurial women must first germinate an idea until they visualize *how* it can become reality. "I had worked at many different jobs in the past," she says. "Sometimes it was for other people—when I worked for the airlines—and often for myself as I bought and sold real estate. I knew I wanted to be in control of my future. I visualized myself running my own hotel-type establishment, so I began to search for the perfect setting. Driving around town, I kept my eyes open and my ears tuned to pick up on any leads. When I saw it, immediately I knew that the Chateau Delaware was exactly the type of place I had in mind.

"Next, it was necessary to do research to determine if there truly was a need for my type of business. I checked with other bed-and-breakfast owners in the city and talked frankly with them. They were very helpful, and I saw that the field was pretty open—there was room for me. And though I quickly became known as the "black bed and breakfast," I never set out to serve only people of color. I have clients of all races, even many who come from Europe to stay with me, but in Indianapolis, I still seem to be known as the black-owned establishment. My research proved that there was an customer base coming through the city that was large enough to produce a satisfactory income, but it does take a lot of work to keep my name in circulation and to bring in sufficient clientele to keep things running smoothly."

Mignon admits that the hospitality business is tough. "You must have the discipline to stick with it, day after day, and follow through, even when things do not go as planned." In her business there are peak and off-peak times, so she must be creative in attracting other types of events in order to keep her income stable. She showcases artists, hosts meetings and receptions, and makes her establishment available for affairs held by social and charitable groups.

"The biggest drawback is that I really do have to be on-site most of the time. Even with help, I am the one responsible. It is like having a guest in my home. I act as hostess and oversee the day-to-day activities myself. It ties me down and is extremely hard work, but this is what I wanted."

> Approach every challenge with your best effort. When you succeed, you know why. If you do not succeed, there is no need to look back.
> *Sally Shipman, executive director,*
> *Coalition for the Homeless*

Do you wonder what keeps some women pushing forward after setbacks and disappointments, while others simply throw up their hands and give up?

Do you marvel at the way successful, high-profile people find the hours in their busy days to accomplish all that they do, while you fall into bed exhausted and dissatisfied, angry with yourself for not having done more?

There are women who can plow through a series of discouraging obstacles, only to emerge smarter and more energized, eager for another challenge, while others are left by the wayside, broken and bitter. What sets the first group apart? I believe that organization, effective time management, focused energy, and a realistic attitude are the prerequisites for maintaining the kind of commitment needed to keep high-achieving sisters going forward day in and day out with no thought whatsoever to giving up on their dreams.

If you have decided to step out into the marketplace with your talent, service, or product, you will need a strong sense of self, along with a big dose of humility, and a flexible attitude to stay the course. Many people start off on their journey all fired up, but in time, enthusiasm fizzles and they stray off the path, in much the same way that New Year's Eve resolutions dissolve and fade away before Valentine's Day.

COMPLACENCY ERODES THE FOUNDATION OF SUCCESS

On an isolated backroad in the Texas hill country, a small red car moves slowly along a rutted, winding road. At a break in the sagging rail fence that runs parallel to the road, the car comes to a stop and a woman wearing a white straw hat gets out.

Patricia Smith Prather, urban archaeologist, author, historian, and preservationist, strides purposefully across the road and enters an overgrown cemetery that is dotted with weathered tombstones. She seems to be in a hurry, but it is really excitement that makes her dart so quickly from one headstone to the next. Letting out a yelp of surprise and discovery, she drops to her knees, opens a notebook and eagerly begins to copy the inscription from a slab of marble sticking out of the ground.

No, Pat has not discovered the grave of a long-lost relative or a famous person. The body that lies in the ground is a Texas Trailblazer—a man or a woman of African descent who played a major role in Texas history but whose accomplishments had never been documented in history books or archival material.

Fifteen years ago, when Patricia Smith Prather set out on

her mission to document the lives of prominent early African-American Texans, many educators, social historians, archivists, and experts in the field of genealogical research warned her not to even try. They told her that there was little or no documented history available and she would be wasting her time.

But Pat was not willing to give up so easily, nor was she going to remain complacent about the lack of information available on people of color who helped shaped the history of her native state. Traveling backroads, visiting rural libraries and courthouses, she spent hours sifting through forgotten papers, books, and souvenir materials that had been stored in churches, warehouses, and abandoned businesses for over a century. She knocked on doors, interviewing descendants of slaves who had been the ancestors of unheralded leaders, whenever she was lucky enough to locate them.

Today, Patricia is the highly visible executive director of the Texas Trailblazer Preservation Association in Houston, as well as a published author, a much sought after lecturer, a tour guide, and the winner of numerous awards for her ground-breaking research. Media coverage has made her a local celebrity and an oft-quoted expert on issues related to blacks in Texas. The research, writing, and eventual publication of her book *Texas Trailblazer Series* was accomplished over a span of five years.

"There are few shortcuts to success," says Pat when asked about her ability to stick with her commitment. "Take one step at a time. Set reasonable time frames to accomplish your goals, but work on them every day. I live by the lyrics of James Weldon Johnson's "Lift Every Voice and Sing": 'Facing the rising sun of a new day begun . . . Let us march on til victory is won.' If we face each day as a new beginning, we will reach our goals."

DISCOVERING YOU

A decision to discover who you are means making a commitment to better understand your potential. This is not easily accomplished, and it will take time, assistance from those who care, and an open mind to allow you to examine unexplored aspects of yourself. Change takes courage. Altering your behavior and attitudes means altering the attitudes that others have toward you, as well as the way they will interact with you in the future. Get ready to have your commitment repeatedly tested, but never allow the attitudes of others to pull you off-track.

As you move along the never-ending journey of achieving goals, there will be joyful times, boring times, and moments of great disappointment. Triumph will be countered by setback, and the worst things that *can* happen *will* happen to you, making you falter, question your mission, but hopefully, regroup and simply take a different path.

ATTITUDE ADJUSTMENT TIP #1

Find a way.

The biggest obstacle I ever faced was doubting myself.
Raquel A. Gonzales, wife, mother, educator

Born forty-seven years ago in Mexico City, Raquel Gonzales admits that she felt restless while growing up, wanting more for herself and her community. Determined to change things when she was a teenager, she and her two sisters began teaching religion classes in their father's garage. Soon they had sixty-plus children crowded together in the stuffy garage, and that was when Raquel says she first acquired a sense of purpose. "I knew God had something special for me to do in this life."

After moving to Texas and graduating from high school came two years of college, marriage, and a decision to become a stay-at-home mom, raising four children. But when the time came to reenter the world of work after seventeen years of being a full-time homemaker, Raquel was wary of the stiff competition she knew she would face from younger, more educated candidates.

"When I went to my first job interview at a nearby elementary school after being out of the workforce for so long, I felt that selling myself was very important," she remembers.

Her husband helped her write a résumé highlighting the valuable experience she had gained from her volunteer work in the school, the church, and the community. She wore a three-piece suit, carried her husband's old briefcase, and rehearsed answers to questions she felt would be asked. The interview was a success and Raquel was given a position as a teacher's assistant.

Once employed, she grabbed this opportunity and made the most of it by getting involved with committees, accepting assignments that other teachers shunned, and making herself visible to administrators at the district level. Often, she volunteered to make presentations to the staff. This drive to stand out brought Raquel a scholarship to finish her interrupted degree at Houston Baptist University, and initiated a stunning career in the field of education.

With her new degree, Raquel began work as a certified second-grade bilingual teacher. It soon became obvious, however, that she and her Spanish-speaking students were often excluded from schoolwide activities and were looked down upon by her coworkers. Immediately, Raquel set out to change things! By repeatedly inviting coworkers into her classroom and pressing district administrators to pay attention to the progress of her pupils, Raquel eventually caught the eye of the district superintendent. Soon she was granted permission to attend workshops and conferences, and the negative attitudes of her coworkers toward bilingual students started to ease.

Raquel says, "The Hispanic culture does not view women as independent and expects us to be the foundation for a family. This can lead to feeling guilty if one tries to achieve a profession. I had to believe in myself and not be afraid to take risks. I had to work hard, discipline myself, and set goals, always with the sense that God's plan was being fulfilled."

In 1995, Raquel won a full scholarship to obtain a master's degree in educational supervision from St. Thomas

University in Houston, Texas, and six months before gradua-
tion, was offered the position of Bilingual/ESL Coordinator
for the Fort Bend Independent School District. She had traveled a long way, from teaching Bible lessons in a garage in
Mexico City to the administrative offices of a major educational system!

The process of growing and experiencing new challenges
will force you to discover how far you can push yourself and
how much heat you can take. You'll be surprised by what you
learn. When your spirits sag and your soul actually hurts
from constant worry, it can become difficult to remain optimistic. You want to appear confident and self-assured without coming off as overbearing or intimidating, and while
some sisters are able to manage this delicate balance, others
have a long way to go.

If a sister's self-esteem has been eroded over a long period
of time and her personal self-image has become distorted,
can it ever be repaired? Are the scars that come from
repeated rejection and disappointment permanent, or can
they eventually be erased? It is true that many women, of all
races, have been victimized, both emotionally and physically,
and will carry deep scars all their lives. Yet there are just as
many who have suffered greatly and nevertheless manage to
heal and move on. They never see themselves as losers, only
as challenged once again.

Unfortunately, there are sisters who suffer simply from a
victim mentality and it makes them quick to blame anything
and everyone but themselves for their unhappiness and
defeat. They've convinced themselves that their cultural heritage or skin color is a barrier that will forever keep them
classified as second-class citizens.

No one can deny that racism and sexism are alive and
thriving in this country, and the battle for civil rights still
rages. Stories in the news prove that prejudice and racial
hatred have deep roots in our land, giving men and women of
color reason to lash out at those who want to perpetuate ugly
stereotypes and preconceived notions that have plagued all of
us too long.

Yes, large numbers of women—African-Americans, His-panics, Asians, and white women, too—suffer oppression and are treated unjustly, but we cannot be intimidated into letting such tragic situations turn us away from pursuing our dreams. We are the ones who must take responsibility for the future, taking risks to put ourselves on the front line over and over again. I suggest that we stop for a moment and ask, "How much do I want to change my life and who will benefit from what I plan to do?"

African-American women, especially, must be willing to prioritize and organize in order to reach the goals they set for themselves, their families, and their communities. Trust and cooperation are vital to making progress. Undermining one another when we need to pull together will have devastating repercussions on the future.

We have had fine, strong examples to lead us on our jour-neys. Haven't we witnessed the steady commitment and unflagging patience of our parents, grandparents, and neigh-bors as they organized voter registration drives, civil rights protest marches, boycotts, block parties, family reunions, and community activities that eventually brought positive results? Haven't we reaped the benefits of their efforts which, more often than not, were carried out under much more danger-ous, volatile circumstances than we now face?

As a child, I watched my parents and neighbors take on the mayor of our city as they pressured him to install a traffic light on a busy street that the children of my neighborhood had to cross in order to get to school. My mother spent hours in the hallways of city hall, not backing down when she was excluded from meetings or her phone calls went unanswered. For months she gathered signatures, made endless visits to city council meetings, ignoring the hurtful things that were said to her and her neighbors. They refused to give up on their mission.

Eventually the mayor gave in and the light was installed. As a young girl, I was very impressed to see my mother's pic-ture in the local white newspaper, smiling, standing on the corner watching as children safely crossed the street. Now, more than forty years later, the stoplight at the corner of Central and Cable in Columbus, Ohio, is still operating. Every time I pass it I am reminded again of the many lives it has saved and accidents it has prevented—as well as the courage and commitment it took for my mother to step out with a real attitude and get the job done.

KEEPING WATCH

Often, the results of a public appeal or a tactic to create change are not evident right away. We start to panic when there is no immediate feedback. We begin to worry that no one has heard our message or even cares about what we have to say. I urge my sisters not to let such uneasy lulls fool them or lure them into a state of despair. Experience has taught me that this is the time to adopt great patience, become content to wait, and carry on with your original plan. During this quiet time, much more is going on than you can possibly imagine—things over which you do not have control.

Relax. If you are presenting your case to the proper audience and your mission has been clearly defined, trust me, something will come of your effort. Concentrate on spending downtime preparing for what comes next, be it good news or bad, so that you can take your quest to the next level with confidence and unwavering strength.

Sisters, we must be consistent in our efforts and optimistic in our attitudes if we expect others to help us. Getting too caught up in the moment can cloud your vision, and who knows what kind of impact a conversation, a meeting, or a letter written today will have months or years from now?

GETTING YOUR ACT TOGETHER

"Organization" is another word for planning. It's impossible to maneuver the bumpy road to heightened visibility without taking time to get yourself, your working environment, and your tools in order. You don't need to be a perfectionist, but you do need to have a sense of balance and the ability to work efficiently on your project. It's time to get down to business.

According to a report from Day Runner, Inc., a leading maker of personal organizers, 73 percent of Americans say that they are *very* or *insanely* busy. Many sisters complain routinely that there are not enough hours in the day. They stress themselves out over all the unfinished business that remains undone when they fall into bed, too tired to do what would probably help solve most of their problems: Take a few minutes to plan.

ATTITUDE ADJUSTMENT TIP #2

Make each moment count.

While surfing the Internet one day, LaNita Filer-Jones decided to read the on-line message boards on organization. She had become increasingly dissatisfied with her part-time job with a major shipping company, and now she came across an announcement from DayMaster, Inc., a company that manufactures Christ-centered organizational tools such as relationship/personality planners and organizers—a new concept in time management that intrigued her. LaNita promptly contacted the company and arranged a meeting with the president to discuss her interest in networking, as well as her desire to enter the field of public relations.

"I immediately knew God had placed me right where I belonged. He directed this path—my path—to DayMaster," LaNita reveals. She signed on with the fledgling company as an independent consultant, holding on to her day job as she learned how to sell and promote DayMaster products. Within eight months, LaNita had done so well she was offered a full-time position as public relations and sales manager for the company.

Now this highly organized sister travels the country conducting training sessions, speaking to audiences on the topic of time management, and spreading the word about the importance of planning.

"I want to help people find balance in all areas of their lives—family, personal relationships, career, and spiritual," she says. "Effective time management can help you build better relationships, establish priorities, get control of your schedule, and remain Christ-centered."

If you are stressed out and trying to get control, LaNita advocates prioritizing your to-do's by implementing these five D's:

1. Dump—everything that is in your mind onto a piece of paper.
2. Delay—everything that does not need to be done in the next few days.
3. Delegate—everything that does not require your personal attention.
4. Delete—everything that is not essential to your life purpose.
5. Do—everything else in a manageable way.

A lot of energy goes into imagining, creating, and getting results from your personal promotional plan. The reward for your efforts will be greatly accelerated if you can remain in control of your time. Do what works best for you. If you tend to run late and are usually pressed for time in the morning, make it a habit to get up thirty minutes earlier. The clock in my office is always ten minutes fast. When I get engrossed in my writing and time flies by, I can't tell you how many times those extra ten minutes have saved me from missing an important phone call or an outside appointment.

TEN TIME MANAGEMENT TIPS

1. *Plan.* Spend a few minutes at the end of each day anticipating what you have to face tomorrow. This can help you find that elusive twenty-fifth hour that you have been longing for.
2. *Make a to-do list.* Jot down, in order of importance, the tasks that need your attention.

3. *Invest in the calendar,* personal organizer, computer program, or notebook that works for you. Above all, keep it simple. A complicated system only increases your level of frustration.

4. *Don't procrastinate.* It's a subversive habit that can easily become comfortable. Tackle whatever you've been putting off the longest, first.

5. *Avoid clutter.* Stop moving paper around—at home or the office. Once you pick it up, act on it or throw it away.

6. *Pay for help.* Stop trying to do everything yourself. If you can afford to pay for support, that's great. If not, consider bartering or trading to get the help you need.

7. *Guard your time.* Don't allow unwanted interruptions to undermine your plan. Control time-wasting habits like TV, unnecessary shopping, or visiting on the phone that easily get out of hand.

8. *Don't become a workaholic.* Strive for balance in commitments. Activities that are simply fun or bring you pleasure can renew energy, allowing you to accomplish more.

9. *Say no, and mean it.* Don't feel guilty about turning people down.

10. *Protect your health.* Arrange your activities in blocks of time that allow you to take frequent breaks. Long stretches at a computer can cause physical injury and mental fatigue.

ON THE HOME FRONT

Many sisters are carving office space out of their private domains to set up shop and launch a business, develop creative projects, or simply expand on official work space. For a variety of reasons, more people are opting to establish home-based work spaces that are functional and convenient, over which they have control. To make sure the space you create will meet your expectations and to get the job done in a professional manner, do some advance planning. Here are a few things to consider.

- Seek peace. Locate your office in the quietest part of your home, even if it is in the basement. By avoiding high-traffic areas, you become less accessible to the rest of the family, increasing your odds of being left alone.

- Get what you need. Use a comfortable chair, a desk/table that adequately serves your purpose, and decent lighting in your space. It's okay to improvise on bookcases, filing cabinets, and other storage equipment, but when it comes to where you sit and read, don't compromise on physical comfort.

- Invest in the equipment and software that will keep you competitive. Today, having a computer, a fax machine, and a telephone answering service or second phone line are expected. Just be sure your space has enough electrical outlets to serve all of your equipment.

- Treat your office with respect. Just because your office is in your home is no reason to allow functions other than work-related activities to take place there.

- Schedule time in your office and stick to it, using a timer if needed.

- Explore possible tax deductions for maintaining a home office.

ATTITUDE ADJUSTMENT TIP #3

Adopt an attitude of positive persistence.

It is easy to attribute the negative things that happen to us to other people's ignorance, racism, or jealousy. But this is really a cop-out—a defense tactic that never garners positive results. By actively managing your disappointment, anger, and frustration, instead of simply lashing out, you can learn to become more positive, remaining focused and persistent.

To stick with your commitment, make a decision to be the

best, not just good enough. Some sisters are always *getting
ready* to do something, convinced they are not quite prepared
to take on the challenge or succeed at a task. They start each
sentence with "I'm fixin' to . . ." or "After my kids get
older . . ." or "If I had the money . . . ," procrastinating to the
point that no one takes them seriously, and they lose credibility, which fuels unattractive stereotypes.

Action Steps

1. Do an honest self-assessment. Living with commitment
   can be lonely. Are you willing to discipline yourself and
   avoid distractions that eat into your time?
2. Be reliable and on time. If you have problems in this area,
   use a calendar to track how often you are late for a meeting or miss returning a phone call. See if there are patterns that need to be changed.
3. Stick by your convictions. Speak up for a sister if you support her view or opinion, even if yours is the only voice in
   the room.

ATTITUDE ADJUSTMENT TIP #4

Think highly of yourself and what you have to offer.

Using self-deprecating language reinforces others' beliefs
that you probably don't have what it takes to succeed. For
example, if you make a presentation at work, and a colleague
tells you how great it was, don't mumble some halfhearted
reply like "Thanks, but I doubt it will impress my supervisor.
He's never going to promote me." Don't slip into the habit of
putting yourself down, and *never* affirm, even jokingly, some
less than positive comment that someone else makes about
you. It is vital to condition yourself to speak publicly in gracious, positive terms, even about people and situations that
hurt. Vent your anger in a safe place with someone who can

serve as a buffer between you and the audience you seek. Look for the uplifting aspect of a painful situation and concentrate on the good that can come from a disappointing experience instead of whining about the setback it appears to be.

What You Can Do Now

- Believe that *you*—your service, talent, product—have value. When you open your mouth to talk about your dream, people will trust you to deliver.

- Do your part, in any possible way, to help counter the negative images too often perpetuated by the media about your race and culture.

- Keep commitments.

- Stop worrying about being liked.

- Concentrate on being respected.

Learning to live with commitment requires daily renewal of vows made to stay on target. Each of us is uniquely capable of traveling the paths we set for ourselves. Understanding what is needed to persevere in the face of certain rejection and hardship comes with each step we take, each mile we cover, and each smile we put on another sister's face.

7

Accentuate the Positive

Attitude Focus: The Winning Spirit
People fall down. Winners get up.
BONNIE ST. JOHN DEANE, OLYMPIC SKI MEDALIST

At sixteen, Bonnie St. John Deane was a young African-American girl with one leg and very big dreams. Within five years, this amputee became an Olympic ski medalist, a Harvard honors graduate, and a Rhodes scholar. Featured on *NBC Nightly News* as one of the five most inspiring women in the nation, her winning spirit and focused determination were felt all the way to the White House, where she eventually worked as Director of Human Capital Issues in President Clinton's administration. On Wall Street she spent time as a financial analyst, and she has sat in the boardrooms of major corporations across the country. Bonnie now works full time in her own business as an inspirational speaker, sharing her journey with those who want to achieve peak performance.

Entering the Winner's Circle

Bonnie entered the 1984 Olympics determined to win. Skiing on one leg, she knew her competition was stiff, but also knew that she was mentally and physically prepared for the challenge. When the time came for her long-awaited downhill race, she shoved off, totally focused on winning. But disaster struck near the end of the run when she hit an icy patch and fell, interrupting the course she had set for her future. Disappointed and stunned, Bonnie knew she had suffered a severe setback, but this courageous young woman didn't just lie in the snow feeling sorry for herself; she got up, refocused, and finished the race.

When the event was over and the performances of the athletes had been rated, Bonnie was shocked to learn that her overall time was good enough to win her the bronze medal. Later, when thinking about the performance of the gold medal winner, Bonnie remembered that her competitor had also fallen down, but she realized that the victor's quick recovery was what had paid off and pushed her to first place.

Bonnie says, "I learned an important lesson from that experience. Falling down does not signal the end of the race. It's how fast you get up that matters."

Survival Tips from Bonnie St. John Deane

- Step forward. Ask for more responsibility.

- Stop cheating yourself. Reach out to women who can help you.

- Listen, challenge, inspire.

- Get involved. Become a member of the club.

- Make it your job to become visible without becoming a "glory hound."

- Target, interview, invite. Turn visibility into access by involving those who can help you get noticed.

- Write an article or do a study using people in your industry/events on your calendar.

- Offer to draft your own recommendations, facilitating their timely submission.

- Make rain. Do whatever you do best to attract the attention you deserve.

- Find out who controls the clouds you will need to produce the rain you want to make.

"I had achieved most of the honors I've won by 1986," says Bonnie. "Yet between 1987 and 1993 I was in the media no more than two or three times. Now that I have begun making motivational and inspirational speaking engagements, I am on TV, radio, and featured in magazines on a regular basis. What changed? It is not what I had accomplished, but it was what I learned. I learned how to use the system and I learned the importance of taking time to help the media do their job. Publicity does not go to the *deserving*, it goes to those who are *in* the system, working it."

THE WORDS OF A CHAMPION

Though reluctant to admit it, I am old enough to remember when the heavyweight boxing champion Cassius Clay shocked the world by changing his name to Muhammed Ali and refusing to be drafted to fight in the Vietnam War. He stood by his convictions and his word. He went to jail.

As a champion, he had no problem declaring, with great bravado and absolutely no shame, that he was "the greatest" boxer ever to enter the ring. The world watched in awe as he proved his bold pronouncements to be true.

Certainly, such unabashed bragging and immodest behavior prompted disapproving comments among fans and exclamations of horror among sports professionals. How could anyone be so brash and rude? But in the end, we all had to give the brother credit. He *was* "the greatest."

As a nation, we allowed Muhammed Ali to brag, forgave his irritating behavior, and applauded his achievements. His loud declarations of superiority and rapid-fire poetry taunted and teased, initially shocking us, then just as quickly filled us with pride. We began to admire his cocky, self-assured attitude. Stunned into silence, we waited anxiously to see what he would do next. Why? Because we were convinced that this man was a rare exception, someone unafraid of boasting about his prowess as a boxer and quite prepared to live up to the challengers he faced.

ATTITUDE ADJUSTMENT TIP #1

Put praise into perspective.

The truth is that the majority of Americans would never dare make such open claims of greatness, even if given permission to do so. According to Pamela J. Benoit, in her book *Telling the Success Story*, most Americans are quite humble. Instead of bragging, the author says, we are more likely to modestly downplay our achievements by attributing our success to hard work, overcoming obstacles, luck, and sharing responsibility with cooperative associates. When publicly honored, we tend to shy away from behavior that might be considered vain or self-centered in favor of explanations that insulate us against any type of criticism.

As difficult as it may be, I believe accepting accolades for outstanding performance should be an enjoyable, rewarding experience. Moments of praise are well deserved if you put in long hours of focused activity that require discipline and personal sacrifice. When the hard work pays off, you should step into the limelight and soak up the glory, letting everyone know how much you appreciate the honor of being recognized for staying the course. Right? Well, maybe.

In truth, it is not easy for most of us to be the focus of a great deal of attention. Why? Because good manners still prevail. We have been conditioned to adopt a position of modesty, and we fear offending those who are less successful, or who are envious of our good luck and accomplishments.

In a recent interview (the *Houston Chronicle*, Jan. 16, 1997), the Academy Award–winning actress Meryl Streep said that her grandmother used to tell her, "Fools' names and fools' faces always appear in public places." This actress says she had to work hard to overcome shyness and get used to the public recognition created by her stardom.

If you find it difficult to accept compliments, praise, or formal recognition, here are a few tips that can help:

Action Steps

1. Become accountable for your future. Review, mentally or on paper, the steps taken and the obstacles overcome to reach this point in your life.
2. Envision yourself in the spotlight and focus on the emotions that follow. What are they? Fear? Pride? Embarrassment? Joy? Relief? Examine the origin of your feelings.
3. Write down what made you uncomfortable at a time when you were praised.

   a. Was it the person bestowing the recognition?

   b. The setting where the words of praise were delivered?

   c. The responsibility that came with being called a winner?

   d. The fear of not being able to live up to new standards?

   e. An uneasiness at being singled out, separating you from your peers?

   f. Feelings that you aren't worthy and don't deserve the honor?

Face these issues with honesty and work on eliminating unfounded fears.

4. Shut off negative self-talk. It undermines feelings of worthiness.
5. Relax. Take deep breaths. Tension generates unwarranted fear and increases feelings of insecurity.
6. Decide to have a good time and enjoy an upcoming recognition event.
7. Rehearse your acceptance speech.
8. Remember to give credit to your success entourage—those who support you in your work/efforts to achieve goals.
9. Don't lose control of the moment by rambling. It's your time to shine, so make yourself even more memorable by delivering a dynamite, focused message.
10. When a recognition event is over, evaluate the moment. Are you satisfied with the way you acted? If not, why not?

All of us share a universal desire to feel accepted, included, valued, and loved. Knowing how to graciously accept praise is key to nurturing the positive attitudes you will need to keep your promotional plan moving forward. You want to be number one and you want to capture the prize, yet you do not want to alienate people or fall prey to jealous back-stabbing. Shaping a satisfying career can create extremely delicate and competitive situations where only one person *will* emerge the winner. You want to be that person.

In accepting praise and honors, one of the major reasons we are so careful about what we say and how we say it is to avoid offending those with whom we work and live. It is vital to remain confident that you deserve the attention you get, even when confronted by those who may think otherwise.

TIME TO LET GO

Making a decision to spotlight yourself brings a responsibility to accept the difficult choices that follow. This can mean reevaluating relationships that have stagnated, removing people from your life who may be doing you more harm than good, or changing your thinking about a certain issue. It also means shifting people around as new players enter and leave your support network. When faced with letting go of a relationship that may be comfortable, but not particularly healthy, you may experience feelings of guilt, sadness, or disillusionment.

There will always be negative people who come in and out of your life. Some will be obvious in their displeasure with what you are doing, others will be quite subtle in their lack of support and in the way they disguise their envy or fear of your potential success. Motivated by ignorance, jealousy, greed, or insecurity, these people cannot help you sell your dream or fulfill your mission. They are the ones who grumble, complain, and attack anyone who emerges as a threat, goes against them, or does not share their opinions. As you strive to become a better person, they strive to go "one better."

The motivational speaker Les Brown calls these influences "toxic people," and I agree with him. They pollute dreams and poison the atmosphere, tainting positive persistence with negative doubt. Casting aside such nonproductive people and ridding yourself of their insidious influence is vital to your survival. Don't feel guilty about letting them go.

The oft-referred-to African-American syndrome of "crabs in a bucket" is unfortunate, but true: Infighting and back-stabbing do exist within our race, as well as others, so keep your antennae tuned for the creative ways your so-called friends can undercut your enthusiasm. Jealous of anything new and different, especially the fresh, success-oriented image you will soon begin to project, they engage in subtle unsupportive behavior that you must vigilantly detect and ignore.

Every creative sister whose work is subject to review and comment by professional critics understands that there *will* be times when someone does not like or understand your effort. The prospect of negative opinion is not something artists look forward to, but it comes with the territory. Savvy sisters quickly learn to separate professional opinion from personal attack, and are secure enough in their talent to ignore deliberately uncomplimentary messages.

ATTITUDE ADJUSTMENT TIP #2

Don't create excuses to lose.

If you are committed to your mission and hungry for success, you already see yourself winning. You know it will take an incredible amount of energy and highly creative methods to achieve the lofty goals you have set, but you also know that faith and commitment can take you wherever you see yourself going. True winners do not construct roadblocks that make the journey any harder than it has to be.

TOP TEN EXCUSES NOT TO STEP OUT

1. I don't have the money.
2. I don't have the time.
3. I can't risk my job security.
4. I don't have a degree.
5. A black woman will never be supported in this.
6. My husband/family doesn't want me to do this.
7. I don't have anyone to watch my kids.
8. I'm getting along fine the way things are now.
9. I can't speak in front of an audience.
10. I am not comfortable meeting new people.

I have heard these excuses from many women who asked for advice on how to move forward with their dreams. Certainly, these can be genuine stumbling blocks, but every one of them can be overcome. Your desire to change must be strong and you must be surrounded by people who *can* and *will* positively influence your commitment to change.

YOUR SUCCESS ENTOURAGE

Success shouldn't be based on how much better or worse you are living than your sisters, but on how good you feel about what you have accomplished.
Tiwoni Shabazz-Lynch, president, African American Writers Society

In a recent edition of *Sisterspeak,* the official newsletter of African American Women on Tour, the clinical psychologist Dr. E. Carol Webster refers to the people in your life who **do** understand your mission and want to help you thrive and survive as your "success entourage." I love that term because it implies that supporters in large numbers are surrounding you, encouraging and nurturing your growth and achievements.

Dr. Webster, who specializes in helping individuals attain and cope with high levels of success, is the author of several books on success management. She says, "It's a difficult climb to the top, so women should set their sights high and become determined self-promoters. Don't hold back. Tell people what's great about you and why they should do business with you. Successful people know the value of self-exaltation, of expecting great things of themselves. They make sure that others know about their accomplishments. Forget what people told you as a child: "'Children should be seen and not heard.' You are a grown-up now!"

Striving to enrich the positive, supportive relationships that exist in your life leaves little time for preoccupation with the gloomy naysayers who would steer you off-course. Adding people of quality to your inner circle leads to a positively charged atmosphere where confidence is high. None of us can survive this journey alone, so be grateful for the lessons in life that your success entourage has to offer. Say thank you, often, and mean it.

ATTITUDE ADJUSTMENT TIP #3

Stay in control of your feelings.

"Trust me to do my thing," says Sibyl Avery Jackson, a communications professional who, after thirteen years of successful work in the field of public relations, found herself dealing with a boss who thought he knew more than she did.

"His knowledge of my job responsibilities could be written on a piece of confetti," says this Spelman College graduate, a sister who has written speeches for politicians and coached corporate executives.

In her position as external affairs manager for a major wireless company, Sibyl's duties included public relations, corporate giving, and community, government, and media relations—but on the organizational chart she became a direct report to the newly hired vice president of sales and marketing.

"Imagine my shock when, after briefing my new boss on my job responsibilities and showing him newspaper clippings and videos of news placements I had made, he told me that from now on all requests from the media had to be submitted in writing for his review before the company would release a statement to the press!"

Sibyl stayed calm, explaining how hard she had worked to cultivate relationships with local, and even international, technology reporters, stressing the importance of media accessibility. The new policy, in her opinion, could damage the company's positioning. "It all fell on deaf ears," she says. "He was in control and things were going to be done his way."

Furious, Sibyl returned to her office, but did not lose her cool in front of her coworkers or discuss the situation with them. "The devil must have been a dust bunny on the lamp shade in my boss's office because I immediately got a call from one of my favorite reporters who was on a tight deadline for an article in which he was profiling the two local cellular companies. He wanted to highlight some of my company's products. I knew we had the best wireless technology and were providing superior customer service, but I could say nothing about this without my boss's approval."

Visions of the credibility loss she would suffer passed before her eyes, but she gently explained the company's new policy. "It was one of the most embarrassing moments of my career," she says. "The reporter pleaded with me to make an exception, and for a moment, I considered honoring his request." With her boss in the field, she rationalized that she could have easily ignored his directive, granted the interview, and saved the company the embarrassment of not being included in the profile.

"But just as I entertained that thought, a light bulb went off in my head," she says. "This was the perfect opportunity to show my boss what a mistake he was making by not trusting me to 'do my thing.'"

The next morning when she got to her office, there was a message on her voice-mail from the company president. He wanted to see Sibyl in his office right away. He had seen the article in the evening paper and was not a happy camper. "I confidently took the elevator to the next floor and entered the president's office. I was surprised to see my new boss sitting opposite the president's desk, fumbling his hands like a nervous schoolboy in the principal's office. Holding up the newspaper, the president asked me to explain why our company had appeared so evasive in the article when our competitor had strutted its stuff like a proud peacock. I thought he would explode when I told him about our new media policy. He looked at me, turned to my boss, then said we would talk later."

An hour passed before Sibyl's new boss stuck his head in her door and without explanation told her to disregard the policy he had earlier instituted. From that day on, until she resigned two years later to start her own PR firm, Sibyl Avery Jackson was left alone to "do her thing."

DISTANCE YOURSELF FROM NEGATIVE INFLUENCES

Reduce the temptation to engage in emotionally destructive conversations and behavior by steering clear of those who may carry your message to the wrong ears. Draw into yourself, pulling strength from your own determination to decompress the destructive and hurtful situation you are facing.

Action Steps

1. Eliminate the habit of expressing skepticism when your ideas or plans are challenged.
2. If someone hurts you, never focus on revenge.
3. Seek out positive, like-minded people with whom you can discuss your disappointments.
4. If emerging from an abusive, unsupportive environment, get professional help to learn how to focus on loving yourself.
5. Set aside a specific time to do something that simply makes you feel better.

I have been very fortunate to have had many positive black men in my family upon whom to model the male characters in my books. My father, brother, uncles, and husbands (yes, there were two) are all caring, intelligent, responsible black men. I receive quite a few fan letters from readers who applaud the positive images of black men and women that I create in my books, and they encourage me to keep doing just that. They are tired of the ghettoized stereotypes they see in books and films about African-American people. My fans tell me that their sons and daughters experience a sense of great pride when they read my stories. It makes me feel good to know that my commitment to positive images has an impact on the way we see and feel about ourselves.

FILL YOUR OWN CUP FIRST

An old saying goes: "Fill your own cup first, and nourish others from the overflow." Okay, it's time to get tough—to focus on what *you* want. If you have resolved to pay more attention to your professional, spiritual, and emotional needs, you want to maintain that upbeat, positive attitude. Poised for success, you're ready to fly, but for some reason, a nebulous barrier keeps popping up. You worry that you may never make it to that higher level you are so determined to reach.

ATTITUDE ADJUSTMENT TIP #4

Make a decision to act on your own behalf.

Step back and think things over. Perhaps you have zeroed in on your mission so keenly that you are now paralyzed, unable to move to the next stage. Overwhelmed by the tasks that have consumed you to this point, you have not taken the time to lift your head and prepare for what lies on the horizon. If you feel you are in such a place and can't seem to get through a rough spot, try reaching out to someone whose life can benefit from your presence. Thinking of others while focusing on yourself goes a long way in helping you step back and gain perspective in order to change the circumstances that are blocking your progress.

In 1994, Karen White-Owens's life changed drastically when her mother was diagnosed with lung cancer. At the time Karen was working in a demanding job as a senior managed-care information analyst, and her plans were for a secure future with the company. However, when tragedy struck, Karen immediately took a family/medical leave of absence in order to care for her mother and share her final days.

After withdrawing from the world of work, Karen felt lost. "I have never been idle," says Karen. "Most of my adult life I have worked two, even three jobs. But for the first time in my life, without a job to go to every day, I had no routine, nothing to do but watch my only parent slowly waste away."

To fill the hours, Karen began writing a book, something her busy career had always prevented her from doing. Each day Karen's story and characters grew, and her goal became to finish the book before her mother died. Karen focused all of her energy on her mission, but sadly, her mother's condition deteriorated quickly and she passed away within weeks of her diagnosis, never reading Karen's story.

"During the most difficult period in my life I managed to complete seven chapters of my romance novel," Karen said, amazed that she had been able to use this unexpected setback to move forward on a closely held but long-delayed dream. She finished the book and it is currently under consideration by two publishing houses. "As a tribute to my mother I plan to publish under her name because without her I would never have had the courage to try something so different from the life I was living. When I think of that time in my life—and I do think of it often— I realize that my mother and I took that final journey together and I was able to find a new outlet to express my creative side. New doors have opened for me and I have discovered a wealth of strength I never knew I had."

WATCH THE CLOCK

I have a few rules that I've adopted to help me stay on target with deadlines and commitments. My family and close friends know what they are and don't consider me selfish for guarding my time so carefully. I never watch television in the morning, I rarely do lunch, and I have been known to turn off the phone for days at a time. Voice-mail is a godsend, allowing me to call back and communicate with people when I can concentrate just on them. These simple acts do wonders for protecting my writing time, and I never feel guilty about explaining them to an insistent sister who threatens to get me off-track.

Don't beat yourself up because you must take a hard line about guarding your time. Set limits and boundaries and stick by them. Refusing to engage in lengthy conversations with people who have little to say, have a score to settle, or express a less than optimistic attitude will prevent you from taking care of business. Don't hesitate to take any action necessary to screen your calls and prevent interruptive influences of a negative nature that might lure you from your work.

If asked to participate in an event or give support to an activity that is emotionally charged or very controversial, proceed with caution. Is your heart really in it? Some people love a good fight and want lots of company while they engage in verbal and emotional warfare. They thrive on finding fault, criticizing, and expressing their opinions of people, situations, programs, or projects that don't meet with their approval. It is not a good idea to jump on every bandwagon that passes, no matter how convincing the cause may seem. Don't feel bad about telling an insistent sister that you need time to consider her request before plunging into a situation that could possibly have disastrous ramifications or make you question your values.

You are the most important player in your promotional campaign, so take the necessary steps to care for yourself emotionally and spiritually. Whatever helps you stay focused and centered—whether meditation, exercise, reading, or spiritual discussion—work toward remaining calm and positive, even when it seems as if everything around you is flying apart.

8

The Long Campaign

Attitude Focus: Talk the Talk
Those who target an ethnic audience with a special message
move ahead.

LISA SKRILOFF, PRESIDENT, MULTICULTURAL MARKETING
RESOURCES

*L*isa Skriloff started her career as a bilingual elementary school teacher, but eventually left the field of education to accept a position in promotion, marketing, and advertising for the *New York Times*. Fluent in Spanish, she worked extensively in the Hispanic market, where it became clear to her that journalists were not doing a very good job of reaching multicultural audiences.

"I thought there could be more diversity," Lisa says. "It seemed as if newspaper articles about a particular industry always quoted the same people." This observation inspired Skriloff, a PR and media specialist, to found Multicultural Marketing Resources, Inc. (MMR), a public relations and marketing firm based in New York City. She represents minority- and women-owned companies, as well as the corporations that market to these groups. The goal of MMR is to raise the visibility of minority businesses by using mini–press releases to promote them to the mainstream press. She launched her innovative idea with a newsletter, *Multicultural Marketing News*, which won a Big Apple Award as best newsletter for 1997 from the Public Relations Society of America. Mayor Rudolph Giuliani praised Skriloff's publication as "an asset to our great city."

"Being in the press gives you visibility and credibility, plus it makes the phone ring with calls from potential clients and reporters," says Lisa. "For a reporter to consider doing a story about you or your company or to turn to you for a quote, they first need to know what you do and how to reach you."

GETTING ACCESS TO THE MEDIA: STAND OUT FROM THE CROWD

ATTITUDE ADJUSTMENT TIP #1

Know what you want.

Skillful manipulation of the various systems that provide access to the media can produce great results for your promotional campaign. To generate, as well as sustain, the attention you desire, it is vital to understand what different vehicles to reach the media exist, and what they can and cannot do for you or your product. Let's examine them.

Public Relations

The main function of public relations is to initiate contacts, create alliances, and build effective relationships among groups of people with compatible objectives. Facilitating communication, establishing a solid reputation, and building trust are goals of a major PR campaign. These strategies help achieve marketing objectives while creating long-term relationships that serve as the foundation of an overall promotional plan. Public relations is an ongoing process, and you must commit to this aspect of your plan.

Many activities that you are already familiar with can be valuable PR initiatives. For example, holding a small dinner party at your home to introduce a new member of your company to selected clients provides an opportunity for interaction among people with common goals. Having such a gathering provides a comfortable forum that allows for discussion, building valuable relationships in an intimate setting. This breaks down barriers, facilitating communication between the new person and those who are already on board. Such a gathering can have long-term benefits for everyone involved when it is time for negotiation, planning, and evaluation of company projects.

Publicity

Visibility, name identification, and immediate recognition are the goals of a good publicity campaign. Publicity is repetitive in nature, and an effective campaign gets your name, image, or product in front of as many people as possible, as often as possible. One goal of publicity is to sell your message to someone who sees the value in circulating your story to an even wider audience. For instance, when I sent a feature story from the newsletter of my local writers' group to my contact at the community newspaper, it was picked up and reproduced. News about my latest release found a much broader audience this way.

Another goal of publicity is to build interest, get people talking about you, and craft a positive public image. Publicity helps a target audience understand, describe, and promote the news about your venture. You want specific audiences to identify with you in a way that creates immediate attention and interest. Generally, you are at the mercy of the reporters, editors, journalists, and publishers who will decide how and where to place your news. Though it is not always easy to gauge the effects of a publicity campaign, it's an extremely effective and valuable tool that is designed to achieve both immediate and long-lasting results.

Example: The press release. Lisa Skriloff, owner of *Multicultural Marketing News,* explains that a press release is an advisory letter informing reporters of your news, or simply of the existence of your company and your area of expertise. You might send the first one to describe your company and the services you provide. It would be a single page with your logo and contact information at the top, whose purpose is to introduce you to the media. A press release is a *must* for your contacts with TV, radio, newspapers, trade publications, consumer magazines, direct-mail lists, professional, fraternal and charitable organizations. Put the most important data first. An editor needs to grasp pertinent aspects of the news very quickly to see if there is potential for follow-up. Provide additional facts and supporting data in a transitional manner to cover the who, what, when, and where of your announcement. Follow up when you have genuine news—for instance, you won an award, gained a client, established a Web site, were appointed to a board, etc. Keep the press releases coming. Stay top-of-mind with the reporters. Don't overlook seasonal or other timely angles such as Valentine's Day, Black History Month, or anniversaries of historical dates when media interest is high.

When I started doing publicity to promote *Emily, the Yellow Rose,* I decided to capitalize on opportunities for coverage during February, which is Black History Month. I did well, and got lots of reviews and feature stories in Houston local and Texas regional papers. But as February began winding down, I had to get creative. I knew the campaign could not stop on February 28. I immediately repositioned my material to snag interest during March, which is Women's History Month. Again, my story and I were in great demand as I agreed to make speeches to women's groups throughout the state, and I received great coverage in small publications targeted to women. My story of the black woman who was the Yellow Rose fit right in. As March headed into April, I had to put on my thinking cap once again and was able to take my campaign right into Texas History Month, which is April. Furthermore, April is when the Battle of San Jacinto, the central event in my book, took place. Again, I found more media outlets eager for my story. This whirlwind of activity, because it occurred in an uninterrupted block of time, created momentum that was very valuable. My name and face were everywhere—TV, radio, newspapers, schools, libraries, churches. Public interest can be fleeting. Finding a way to sustain interest over a long period of time is a challenge, but it is one that can be met!

Other ideas? If you have a financial company, offer your economic trend outlook in December, anticipating the New Year, and bridge it into tax time in April. Are you a psychologist? Offer tips for surviving the stressful holiday period and tie it into making New Year's resolutions to change old habits and start new traditions. Do whatever you can to extend the life of your news. Conduct a survey and send out the results (say, X percent of your customers plan to do Y this year), then offer a free brochure, available by contacting you.

Each press release should have your contact information at the top and some "boilerplate" information about your company at the end—a brief description that reporters can refer to, a description that you have chosen.

Make sure you are listed in the telephone company's directory information. When your company name appears in print, readers will try to find you by calling directory information. Even if you run a business from your home, consider getting a business phone and business listing so your potential clients can find you.

Once the press release is out, the reporters will call. Lisa's advice on handling these calls:

- Be prepared with an opinion or a comment that is *newsworthy*.

- Have standard responses ready for other questions that highlight your expertise, business, product, or service.

- If a reporter leaves a message on your voice-mail, return the call as soon as possible.

- Remember, reporters work on deadlines. They have most likely called others, too. Call back fast and be first.

Advertising

Advertising means *purchasing* air time, ad space, signage, or access to appropriate vehicles to place your message where it will be seen or heard by your target audience. As the buyer, you have more control over factors like content, time, location, and cost than you do with free publicity. There is a vast array of possibilities here, and the costs of promoting in this manner can vary widely depending on the outlet you choose, as well as the product, the objective, and the audience you want to reach. It is good to remember that results are often tied to the amount of money you are able and willing to spend, so do careful research and consult a professional in the advertising industry if you plan to invest in advertising. If you are launching a new product, you might decide to advertise on the radio. First you have to create your commercial, then purchase air time by contacting the sales department of your local radio station. A salesperson who sells time will provide you with different options, according to the amount of money you plan to spend, the number of times you want to run the commercial, and when it will air. Generally, the more frequently you run your ad, the lower the cost per unit.

When my book *Starlight Passage* was released in 1996, I decided to purchase advertising space in a local paper. Advertising fiction can be tricky, and my publisher had discouraged me from doing it. But I decided to go for it this time. Why? Because the edition of the paper I wanted to be in was going to be handed out free to every person who came to the Houston convention center to attend the Black Expo—thousands of members of my target audience. I met with the sales rep of the paper and got advertising costs, which I discovered I could handle. However, creating the ad was definitely beyond my budget. Undaunted, I placed a call to the advertising department of my publisher and made them an offer. If they would create camera-ready ads in a variety of sizes, I would pay for placing them. It worked out beautifully and I was able to place the ads in many cost-effective publications that I might otherwise have passed up.

Marketing

Marketing is a science that requires a clear understanding of such marketplace variables as audience demographics, geographic location, trends, competition, and timing. Forecasting the performance of a product requires the skill of professionals who have knowledge of what influences and affects consumers. Market testing, studies, surveys, expositions, and trade shows are tools used by marketing firms to predict performance levels of new products. How a commodity or service is perceived and accepted by consumers is often determined by packaging. The color and design of a package can inspire consumers to purchase your product or leave it on the shelf. Accessibility, cost, and quality-control are other factors that must be carefully and strategically considered.

If you are taking an innovative product or service to the marketplace, or are trying to access an audience that has not been adequately tapped in the past, investing some time and effort in market research is a good idea.

Here are the titles of a few books that are currently available to help you understand marketing and develop your plan:

The Market Planning Guide, by David H. Bangs, Jr. (Upstart Publishing, Chicago, 1995). This book has great charts, grafts, and worksheets, providing a step-by-step road map.

The Instant Marketing Plan, by Mark Nolan (Puma Publishing, Santa Maria, Calif., 1995). This is written in clear language and structured in an easy-to-understand format.

Marketing for Dummies, by Alexander Hiam (IDG Books, San Mateo, Calif., 1997). Everything you ever wanted to know about marketing, presented in the trademark manner of the "for dummies" books. A great resource.

Example. A fashion designer who decided to specialize in upscale tropical evening wear focused a great deal of her marketing efforts on finding out what women who travel to, or live in, warm climates want and need. By using surveys conducted among members of the target audience, as well as an assessment of the kind of clothing currently available, the designer got a better picture of where her designs would be in demand. She also wanted demographic data on income, lifestyle, and shopping trends, which would indicate where her type of clothing would be highly desirable. Professional marketing firms have such data, but her budget was limited; nevertheless she was able to get a lot of information from trade associations, chambers of commerce, departments of tourism. The business schools of area universities are also very likely to have undertaken this kind of research.

WAYS TO SPREAD THE WORD

Depending on whether your message is aimed at standard media outlets, selected organizations, associations, consumers, or industry contacts, you can use a variety of methods to deliver the information. Basic equipment that can speed your word on its way are a phone (with voice-mail and an answering machine), a fax machine, and a computer, definitely with e-mail and access to the Internet. Your press release can be delivered via standard mail, e-mail, fax, or as a video news release. A video news release is a videotaped version of your message. Send it to television stations or any other media outlet that would benefit from a visual impression of the messenger. If you send the video version, include a hard-copy version of the text. Professional speakers, actors, and musicians often use video news releases to tell their story and sell themselves more effectively.

Fax, Mail, or E-mail?

The question often arises, What is the best way to submit information to the press? My experience has shown that the answer varies widely among media professionals. Some prefer the immediacy of the fax, others like the convenience of e-mail, and many would just as soon receive their information via standard mail. I would say that the method of submission can be determined by the relationship you have with the receiver, the purpose of the message, and the urgency of the information. One word of caution about faxing press materials: There is an FCC ban on sending unsolicited material to companies where no business relationship already exists. The Telephone Consumer Production Act of 1991 contains information pertinent to fax marketing. Always inquire before sending a fax, then follow through promptly if invited to submit material by fax, and verify that it was received.

The Press Kit

Following up your press release with a press kit will augment information about your event, service, or product. This is a standard and highly effective practice to let others know what is going on. Use a basic folder with your graphics on the front. Attractive materials make a lasting impression, so try to create a package that is eye-catching, but not overdone. Depending on your business, you can be very creative. A noted romance author's press kit is a slim lace-covered box. Inside she puts a copy of her latest book, photos, a single silk rose, and standard press material, as described below. It certainly gets attention, and it works for her. That's what counts.

WHAT GOES INTO A PRESS KIT

- *The press release.*

    SAMPLE PRESS RELEASE

    Johnson Company
    P.O. Box 12345
    Anytown, U.S.A. 12345

    NEWS

    Contact: Mack Brown
    222/555–1212
    fax: 222/555–1313
    e-mail MKBRWN@Johnson.com

    **JOHNSON COMPANY ANNOUNCES NEW INTERNET
    TECHNOLOGY**

    Anytown, USA. . . . April 3, 1998. . . . Patricia Johnson, pres-
    ident and CEO of Johnson Company, a diversified internet
    web site developer, announces the market debut of a new
    product that will drastically facilitate people's access to the
    Internet.

    Speaking at the opening session of the Organization of
    Independent Website Developers (OIWD) conference in
    Orlando, Florida, Ms. Johnson stated that her company's
    product, Netweb1, will decrease the average time for access-
    ing the Internet by as much as 50 percent.

    Netweb1 is available to both home and business Internet
    subscribers and is compatible with current server systems.
    It will retail for $195.95 and will be available through most
    major computer retail outlets or directly from the Johnson
    Company over its web site: www.johnson/netweb1.com.
    Free demonstrations on using Netweb1 will be held at the
    Johnson Company booth at the OWID Conference, which
    runs through April 6 at the City Convention Center.

Founded in 1990, Johnson Company is the largest minority-owned web site provider in the United States, employing more than 200 people. It had gross revenues of $75 million in year-end 1997.

Patricia Smith Prather

Native Texan

Historian

Author

Public Speaker

Co-Editor of

P atricia Smith Prather, author, historian, preservationist and lecturer focuses her unique insight on history in her writing and presentations about the contributions of African American Texas leaders to the growth of the state.

She is author of over seventy articles about African American Texas leaders which have been published in state and national publications including *Texas Highways* and *American Visions* magazines. Prather and her work with historic preservation has been featured on television (local affiliates of ABC, NBC CBS, etc.); radio, including National Public Radio as well as daily and weekly newspapers. She has received numerous awards for community service including the Center for The Healing of Racism.

Prather is coauthor, with Jane Clements Monday, of *From Slave to Statesman: The Legacy of Joshua Houston, Servant to Sam Houston.* (University of North Texas Press, 1993). Their book has been reviewed in publications throughout Texas including the Houston Chronicle, and the Dallas Morning News. The book has also received several awards including the Violet Crown Award by the Austin Writers League and the Best Book About East Texas by the East Texas Historical Association.

Patricia Smith Prather is cofounder and Executive Director of The Texas Trailblazer Preservation Association, a nonprofit organization dedicated to preserving the important legacy of the African American presence in Texas history. Since 1992, the organization has published its **Texas Trailblazer Series**, monthly biographies with photographs of Texas pioneers. Prather is coeditor of this publication.

Patricia Smith Prather is a native Texan and graduate of Tuskegee University in Tuskegee, Alabama. She is a board member of the Harris County Historical Commission, the Heritage Society, the Jazz Education Inc., and the Buffalo Bayou Partnership. She was formerly a board member of the San Jacinto Girl Scout Council, the Houston Archaeological and Historical Commission, and the Texas Higher Education Coordinating Board.

If your organization, business, school or church would like more information about **Patricia Smith Prather:**

Contact:
P.O. Box 23320
Houston, TX 77228-3320
713-633-1125

- *Fact sheet.* Hard data on your product or service that should contain statistics and/or industry information.

1995 Romance Market Statistics

Compiled by Romance Writers of America®

Since 1992, RWA has conducted an annual study of the romance market using various magazines, catalogs, and information gathered from publishers. All major publishers were tracked, plus a few smaller ones.

- 1,796 romances were published in 1995 by 28 publishers under 54 imprints — including reissues and anthologies.

- Of the 1,796 romances published in 1995, 991 were contemporary romances; 666 were historical romances; 114 were paranormal romances; 24 were romantic suspense; and 1 was a romantic historical novel.

- Reissues rose by 10 titles in 1995 to 147, while anthologies rose to 34, an increase of 8. The largest increase was in paranormal romances, which increased by 36 titles from 1994.

- Historicals were down by 60 titles from the 1994 total, while contemporaries rose by 31 titles.

- Multicultural romances showed an increase in 1995 with 25 single title releases and 1 anthology.

- There were 390 multi-published authors of 1,050 books in 1995. Another 746 authors each had 1 book out in 1995. This makes a total of 1,136 authors published in 1995 compared to 1,049 in 1994; 1,073 in 1993; and 942 in 1992.

- One author, Madeline Baker, set a record with 21 titles released in 1995, including 5 original titles and 16 reissues.

- The most productive author of 1995 was Miranda Lee with 9 original titles from Harlequin Presents.

- Inspirational romances are still relatively new to the marketplace and so were not included in the total numbers of RWA's 1995 Romance Study. However, it should be noted that a handful of inspirational romance publishers did publish 94 books in 1995.

- Bookstores and publishers reported increased sales from romance novels in 1995.

Publisher		1995	1994	1993	1992
Harlequin	(493)				
Silhouette	(325)	866	784	813	744
Mira	(48)				
Zebra	(176)				
Pinnacle	(68)	252	260	251	200
Kensington	(8)				
Leisure		133	142	79	57
NAL		91	87	92	77
Bantam		84	106	117	116
Harper		79	88	84	47
Avon		68	80	72	68
Berkley-Jove		63	90	123	103
Pocket		44	40	35	31
Fawcett		30	38	40	39
Dell		25	29	34	42
Warner		22	10	16	18
St. Martin's		19	13	20	15
Totals		**1796**	**1790**	**1872**	**1601**

- *Biographical information sheet* on the company president: you.

ANITA RICHMOND BUNKLEY

Anita Bunkley is a novelist with a background in education. She is presently a full-time writer and an active lecturer on topics related to writing, promotion, career advancement, and issues of importance to women who lead values-based lives. Mrs. Bunkley's communication skills, both written and verbal, make her an effective and persuasive speaker.

She has been a teacher of English, French, and Spanish in both public and private schools, as well as a writer-in-residence with the University of Houston's Writers in the Schools Program. Working with the United States Embassy, Mrs. Bunkley traveled to Egypt in 1995 to present programs on the history of African-American fiction to students at Ain Shams University in Cairo and to discuss minority women in fiction with the Egyptian Women Writers Association.

In 1997 she toured with African American Women on Tour, introducing her workshop *Steppin' Out with Attitude: Sister, Sell Your Dream,* the title of a nonfiction book in progress. This work is based on Mrs. Bunkley's belief that adopting an attitude of gratitude will positively impact the way women live their lives.

Her latest release, *Balancing Act* (Dutton, July 1997), takes readers into the life of a busy career woman who refuses to compromise her values while investigating a dangerous situation that could have a dramatic impact on her family, her career, and her marriage.

The success of Mrs. Bunkley's writing career and the rapid rise of her status as an inspirational speaker who captivates the attention of goal-oriented women keeps her involved in a variety of arenas as she lectures and presents workshops to give women hope and encouragement. She networks tirelessly while promoting her novels, urging those she meets to set goals and go after their dreams. She does this with an inherent confidence that if they are willing to focus on what she refers to as the Three D's of life: Desire, Discipline, and Drive, success can be theirs, too.

For information regarding speaking engagements contact the author at P.O. Box 821248, Houston, TX 77282–1248. Ph: (281) 531-0566, Fax: (281) 531-9049. E-mail: arbun @aol.com

- *Photos, color slides, camera-ready logos.* The media outlet will need these raw materials to craft a story that fits their format and audience.

- *Other information.* Brochures, annual/internal reports, or pamphlets with comprehensive information.

- *Media materials.* Press clips, feature stories, a canned interview (ready for publication).

Page 4 • Thursday, May 1, 1997 • Southwest Sun

SUN   'We're all about YOU'

Career on the rise for author Bunkley

By HILDEGARD WARNER
Reporter

Anita Richmond Bunkley loves to read. As she went through the pages over the years, she didn't see many books with black women as the lead characters.

"I searched out books like that and since I couldn't find them, I thought I would write them," says Bunkley, an Alief resident.

Bunkley

She has since published six books, the first in 1989. With her sixth book scheduled to be on the shelves in July, the author of African-American women's fiction is discussing future story ideas with her publisher.

Bunkley, a former teacher, says she is always coming across interesting subjects.

"People send me story ideas all the time," she says. "I have a folder full of story ideas — more ideas for books that I will be able to write."

The progression from teacher to writer was natural for Bunkley, who had taught Spanish, French and English as a foreign language in Ohio before moving to Houston in 1970. She is an honors graduate of Mount Union College in Columbus.

"I liked working with language and felt the importance of speaking well and writing well," she recalls. "I have always felt very passionate about communication and encouraging students to read. I was always surrounded by books."

Bunkley's novels are a combination of history, conflict and romance.

Her first book, "Emily, the Yellow Rose," is based on the black woman romanticized by the song. "Black Gold" tells the success story of a black family in the 1920s Texas oil boom.

"Wild Embers" takes place during World War II and the heroine of "Starlight Passages" finds herself digging into her family's past secrets with the underground rail

See **CAREER**, page 4

Continued from page 1

road during the Civil War.

Her fifth novel, "Sisters," out since December, celebrates the bonds of sisterhood of three talented black writers. Elise, the main character in "Balancing Act," due out in July, struggles between defending her employer in the town where she grew up and has family ties.

Bunkley prefers to write about strong women and does not consider her stories romantic novels.

"My books touch on much larger issues. Women have to make choices. You have relationships and careers and goals, so there has to be a kind of balance," she says.

In her mid 40s, Bunkley, too, has had to balance career and family.

"Flexibility is the key," she says. Her two daughters are now grown, and she says her husband has always been supportive.

She also travels around the world to speak to readers groups and lead writing workshops. This year, she will conduct several African-American Women on Tour empowerment workshops.

Since coming to Houston, Bunkley has been active in many nonprofit groups.

She was a founding member of Woman Writers of Color and the African-American Writers Guild, a former director of volunteers for the American Red Cross, and regional director of Youth for Understanding International Exchange Program. She was a writer-in-residence at the University of Houston and has taught English as a Second Language.

- *Honors and awards received.*

- *Letters.* Of commendation, congratulations, referral.

- *Client list.*

- *Special industry-related items.* For example, a menu if you are a caterer, a book cover if you are an author.

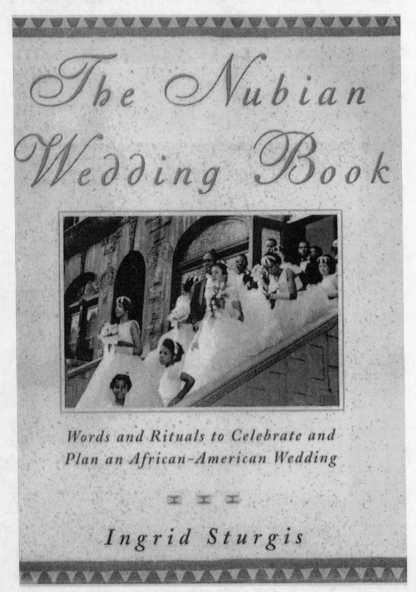

The Public Relations Firm

ATTITUDE ADJUSTMENT TIP #2

Make sure everything you do, say, or create has the
stamp of quality on it.

Denise Sharpton started her career in radio by giving
brief beauty tips for women on a local program. The listening
audience loved her and her boss quickly recognized that this
was a sister with talent and a great deal of potential. Soon,
she was promoted to news anchor, going on to become the
public affairs producer.

In 1986, she decided to strike out on her own, drawing on
her extensive media background to start her own company,
Sharp/PR. Denise's plan was to develop and implement public
relations strategies for arts and entertainment clients, but she
didn't stop there. She also planned to accept some responsibility for change in her community.

For some time it had bothered Denise to see ethnic groups
attack one another when they were really facing very similar
challenges. This radio personality–turned–public relations
executive decided to do something about it. Her firm took on
the difficult task of increasing multicultural awareness among
the residents of Dallas. Denise was disappointed when a
potential client rejected her idea to create a citywide multi-
ethnic festival, but she did not give up on her idea. Since her
client would not take on the project, she would do it herself.
Denise viewed the festival as an opportunity to cement her
place in the community, as well as showcase her agency in the
Dallas marketplace. She was well aware that the concept had
merit and could benefit the city *and* her fledgling firm.

"We need to be more culturally aware," she says. "I was
determined to find a way to highlight interesting aspects of
cultures in a festival atmosphere instead of giving seminars
and lectures." The result? She founded her own nonprofit
organization, the Multi-Ethnic Heritage Foundation, which

puts on a festival each year in downtown Dallas to highlight the entertainment, food, arts, and crafts of various cultures and ethnic groups in the city.

Opting for a unique way to garner attention and attract new clients to her firm, she also developed a marketing brochure that looks like an invitation.

"My PR agency is very selective," Denise says. "The philosophy behind the invitation concept is that we choose whom we want to do business with by inviting them to work with us. Our clients feel special, and are among a select group. This 'select appeal' has worked for us and Sharp/PR has established a reputation of being very quality-minded."

This energetic publicist, who had once dreamed of becoming a high-powered attorney, now balances the demands of her public relations firm with running her non-profit organization. Her mission is to help raise the comfort level and lower tension among the variety of people living in her city. Her attitude about sharing is evident. The Multi-Ethnic Heritage Foundation gives annual recognition to corporations and individuals who have done an outstanding job in supporting multicultural activities. In an interview with Diane Jennings for the *Dallas Morning News*, Denise said, "Free time is really scarce, but I love being an entrepreneur. I would rather create a job than work for someone else." Denise Sharpton has some tips on what to expect from a professional PR firm:

What a Professional Public Relations Agency Can Do for You

- Conduct a public relations audit. The agent conducts an audit to review the current and past PR efforts of the client to determine what has been effective. The agent wants to build on activities that worked and design others to meet the client's PR objectives. If you have no track record, the agent starts from scratch, using her knowledge of the market to design your plan.

- Provide you with a picture of their track record, with examples of agency work, including press clippings and video documentation of successful client representation.

- Provide client with a clear explanation of how services are charged and billed.

- Prepare a detailed PR plan. This outlines strategies and tactics that are related to the client's stated objective, such as increase visibility, change image, acquire new clients.

- Give expert, honest advice. The agent assists the client in learning how to deal with the media, prepare for an interview, respond to a crisis.

- Produce press material that is persuasive, creative, clever, and substantive.

- Keep the client abreast of issues/concerns that affect her industry. At the beginning of the relationship, the client and agent may have daily contact. As the plan unfolds, contact may be on an as-needed basis. However, the client should call whenever she has questions, comments, or ideas, and never forget that the agent is working for her.

- Display a high degree of integrity, conducting herself in a manner that is professional and ethical.

- Evaluate, periodically, the client's progress toward stated objectives, analyze results, make recommendations for shifts in strategy.

- Use the contacts/sources necessary to perform assignments, meet goals, build visibility, and maintain a positive image among media and the target audience.

- Be accessible to you, the client, twenty-four hours a day.

ATTITUDE ADJUSTMENT TIP #3

Go after what you want.

Postcards, Flyers, Brochures, Announcements: Your Calling Cards

You don't have to spend huge sums of money to create eye-catching promotional materials that inform *and* create a great impression. It is wise to invest in the highest-quality materials you can afford in order to reflect the value you have placed on your product—as well as your high opinion of yourself. With desktop publishing and excellent-quality photocopying technology, there is no excuse for circulating shoddy, unattractive materials. Nowadays many people are capable of creating your materials—an advertising agency, a public relations firm, or a graphic designer.

Rosalie Ramsden, owner of Ramsden Design in Houston, TX, does graphic design for individuals and companies that want to enhance their marketing communications. "I work with clients to create annual reports, brochures, newsletters, and other materials that communicate corporate identity," she says. "In order to develop a plan to meet the client's needs, I always start with an information interview. The background information I gather helps me fit the piece to the concept, choose appropriate paper stock, and decide on which photos or illustrations to use." Once all of the points listed here have been clarified, Rosalie does a design brief for her client, outlining exactly what they agree to do. Below are some marketing questions Rosalie poses to clients to help her define their needs. Can you answer them?

ROSALIE'S MARKETING QUESTIONS

- Can you succinctly describe your product or service?

- What is your advertising objective/what action or change do you want to achieve?

- Who is your target audience? Paint a portrait—age, education, income, lifestyle, etc.

- Which features of your product translate to benefits for your target audience?

- Of those, which is the single most important benefit?

- Who is your competitor?

- What is your competitor's strength?

- What weakness does your competition have?

- What evidence supports your promises to your audience? Example: statistics, testimony, guarantees.

- Are there any legal or ethical issues that affect your ability to fulfill your promises? If yes, what are they and how can they be resolved, eliminated?

If you plan to invest in professionally designed materials, take the time to study the points listed above so you will not waste your money or miss the mark with the brochures and announcements you circulate.

DIRECT CORRESPONDENCE WITH YOUR TARGET AUDIENCE

ATTITUDE ADJUSTMENT TIP #4

Keep in touch.

Smart sisters who keep in touch with their target audience via monthly, quarterly, or annual publications are using a relatively inexpensive and effective way to share news in a personal manner and provide loyal supporters with helpful information. This type of direct mail builds trust, instilling a sense of anticipation that primes an audience for the next communication. Here's what I did:

Sisters of the Word

Three years ago, after chatting on the phone about promotional activities with many of my sister-writer-friends, I decided it was time to find a better way to share our news. All of us were eager to help one another get the word out about our various book projects, but we certainly needed a more focused and efficient manner to achieve this end.

I decided to invite each interested author to write a very short column in her voice about what was going on in her life and writing career. I proposed that she share, in her unique way, whatever she wanted her fans to know—what new books to look for, where she would be touring, any prizes or awards recently received, fabulous reviews—of course!—new contracts signed, etc., along with how to get in touch with the author. The newsletter was designed strictly as a promotional tool, a safe place to brag—with no reviews or criticism allowed.

Every promotion-minded sister-writer jumped at the opportunity and sent me her chatty, upbeat submission. I was overwhelmed. Under deadline for a book at the time, I convinced my husband to edit the material, and our four-page publication, *Sisters of the Word*, was born in 1994.

The result was an economical, uncomplicated way to present information by and about black women writers. Each author is provided a master copy, urged to reproduce it, and circulate it to her mailing list of fans, librarians, and favorite booksellers. If readers want a copy, they are asked to provide a self-addressed stamped envelope.

The publication has taken off like a rocket, with hundreds of new book lovers writing each month to let us know how much they enjoy getting to know their favorite authors and learning about upcoming books—before they appear in the bookstores!

Producing this newsletter does take a commitment of time, money, and patience, but it has been a wise investment that is serving a target audience as well as the authors who participate. Through *Sisters of the Word*, I have been able to develop closer ties with my loyal fans, increase the number of readers who support me, track them by geographic location, stay in touch with booksellers, and learn what my writing colleagues are doing. I can promote my books in my own voice, feeling great about reaching my target audience in an intimate way.

After a blurb in a recent edition of *Essence* magazine, circulation of *Sisters of the Word* newsletter has jumped into the thousands. We even had to add a new column—for those "brothers of the word" who wanted to get in on the act. We sisters were happy to share!

NEWSPAPER AND MAGAZINE ARTICLES

Public relations and media professionals consider daily newspapers the number-one medium for publicity and exposure. Magazines and special-interest or trade papers and periodicals are also good spots to place your news. Perhaps you have sent your story idea or press release to the appropriate editor at your daily paper and received a negative response or no response at all. Don't give up. Competition for space is fierce, but keep your eye on current events, a hot new topic, or a recent incident of local interest. Your release might get noticed if it has an angle that ties it to upcoming events, breaking news, or important dates.

According to Luce, a press clipping service, the top-circulation papers in the country are the *Wall Street Journal, USA Today, The New York Times*, the *Los Angeles Times*, the *Washington Post*, the *New York Daily News*, and the *Chicago Tribune*. Getting coverage in these top papers is not easy, but it certainly is possible if your story is both timely and newsworthy. A flattering feature story in a high-circulation paper carries weight—it can immediately raise your visibility and be a valuable addition to your media kit.

Soon after the release of my novel *Balancing Act* in 1997, a TV reporter for our NBC affiliate, KPRC-TV, whom I had been trying to contact, approached me at a charity luncheon and said she was very interested in interviewing me for a segment of the Sunday morning news. My novel, inspired by a local fire, contained a theme related to an incident of environmental abuse that had recently brought the Reverend Jesse Jackson to town to help the angry community gain visibility for its protest. Following the television coverage, the *Houston Chronicle* reviewed my book positively, devoting a half page to the story. These were great local news happenings that worked to my advantage.

Take the initiative to investigate weekly, regional, and special-interest papers in which reporters might be waiting for exactly the type of news you have. They have to fill their column inches. Send your press materials along with photos, then follow up with a phone call. You may be very surprised at the results. Once you get initial coverage, even if it's in a small trade paper, use that article to generate more interest. Soon, a domino effect begins, with other publications taking note of your news and getting on the bandwagon to cover it.

Bonnie Gangelhoff is a free-lance journalist who has contributed to *People* and *Biography* magazines, and worked for eleven years as a feature writer for the *Houston Post*. She has written hundreds of feature stories for major dailies and specialty publications. Here's what Bonnie believes makes a good feature story:

BONNIE'S TIPS FOR FEATURE WRITING

- Have an angle that hooks the reader in the first paragraph. Journalists call this beginning the "lead"—where you either grab or lose your audience.

- Use your most attention-grabbing, interesting material.

- Use strong verbs.

- Write in the present tense.

- Avoid clichés.

- Go for an informal, chatty tone, not an academic one.

- Use adjectives sparingly. Demonstrate adjectives via the story.

- Incorporate and share facts.

- Interview credible people. Integrate your interviewees' comments in the story, and mention their places of employment and job titles.

- Include turning points in the subject's life to give the reader insight into the person's character.

If you are lucky enough to be interviewed, don't ask if you can read the story before it is printed. Approach the interview process trusting that the writer will treat you fairly. Provide adequate background information to the reporter so any controversial or touchy subject will be clarified before you start talking. Make your responses clear, to the point, and brief, to avoid the possibility of being misquoted. My words have been twisted to fit the agenda of a reporter more than once, so I have learned how to carefully consider my responses to delicate, or even loaded, questions.

My husband became my public relations manager when I was promoting my self-published book. We had no funds to pay for publicity and had to come up with creative ways to get the word out. Since he has credentials in PR as a nonfiction writer, he decided to write a feature article about me using his pen name. He sent it out to *every* small weekly paper in Texas—the ones that are hungry for any kind of news. He also sent the story to many well-known African-American papers around the country, along with a photo of me, and a review that had been written by a local reviewer. What a bonanza for me and the book's visibility when the article and my picture began popping up all over the place. I received hundreds of book orders from those small Texas towns where my book was viewed as hot news!

CYBERSPACE

The Internet and World Wide Web are valuable resources for you, both to promote yourself and to look for new audiences for your products and services. When you access cyberspace, think of entering this area as building a campaign from the grass-roots level. You will encounter a variety of individuals and companies interested in your product as well as find new places to share your message. Approach on-line promotion just as you would traditional media: When you set up a Web site or solicit a design for a Web page, include the same information that would be in a standard press kit. Those who are reading about you on-line also need answers to the who, what, when, where, and why questions; you might miss an opportunity to sell yourself if you provide inadequate information.

Finding a particular Web site or chat room to interact and communicate with others on line in cyberspace *can* be frustrating, especially for on-line novices. Time, patience, and focused searching do pay off. Once you get better at finding your way around, with the press of a button you can access areas featuring corporations, industries, entrepreneurial ventures, and communities where you can increase your visibility in a variety of venues. Information that is vital to your success is literally at your fingertips. The following is just a sampling:

- Media Distribution Services (MDS), a PR printing, mailing, and faxing service, has a free North American media guide available on its Web site: www.prplace.com

- *Community, Specialty, and Free Publications Yearbook* helps you locate publications that target your audience. For more information contact their Web site: www.mediainfo.com

The impact of marketing on the Web can be far-reaching, expanding your ability to connect with like-minded people, link with valuable services, and find new products that will make your personal promotional campaign the most important marketing tool you will ever use.

Beth Wolff was the first real estate agent in Houston to market her firm, Beth Wolff Realtors, on the Internet via a Web site. "My company deals in luxury properties and we had always been at the forefront in the real estate business, so I was eager to get on the Internet to help keep my competitive edge. When I decided to develop a Web site, I used a service provider, but in addition, my son, who was knowledgeable in how to set up a site, helped out. That was very comforting. He understood what I wanted and how I planned to use the Internet and this increased my level of confidence with the project."

Real estate is an extremely competitive industry, and Beth wanted to find a way to be up to the minute with information on hot new properties, as well as provide a comprehensive profile of her company and her staff. "Via my Web site I can promote my properties aggressively," Beth says. "The visuals are fantastic. People can browse my listings and really see what I have to offer. I can download and change information quickly so everything is up-to-date. I can also input new profiles of my agents as staff changes, and update background information on myself as well as what properties I have handled. Web marketing has made my office more efficient and better able to service my clients."

Beth serves an international market—often sending and receiving e-mail twenty-four hours a day—with dramatic visuals to showcase her luxury properties. "E-mail is great," says Beth. "Correspondence can be sent anytime and received at the other person's convenience. It is quite cost-effective, unlike faxes or other delivery systems I've used in the past. I believe Web marketing will continue to be a strong component of real estate sales. It is the most dramatic change we've experienced in this industry. Now it is unusual for my major competitors not to be on the Internet."

Professionals who design Web sites caution potential customers to research a range of consultants before contracting with someone to build your site. Getting people to your site is definitely a challenge. You must maintain your site, market it aggressively, and stay abreast of technological advances. This requires disciplined attention. Here are a few tips that may help you get started:

Action Steps

1. Speak with a knowledgeable, trustworthy source in your community who can help you become familiar with cyberspace jargon and the types of costs you can expect to incur before contacting a professional Web builder.
2. Set goals for your site and take the time to carefully consider what you expect to gain from this investment in time and money.
3. Tap the expertise of friends/family members who understand the complexities of creating a Web site.
4. Check with your current on-line service provider to see if it provides its members with a Web page, and whether you can use the page for business.
5. Consider taking a course or buying software to help you become your own Web master.

AVS On-line

Joanne Harris, an editor at the magazine *American Visions*, serves as the director of the Afro-American Culture Forum on CompuServe. "Our target audience is culturally active black adults. Everything we do is geared to creating a vibrant on-line community for them to share and network. In my position I establish policy related to on-line language usage and oversee the message and library content of the chats. In this forum we are able to feature on-line conferences with well-known achievers in the cultural arena, authors, and artists."

The American Visions Society is a membership organization devoted to exploring and preserving African-American culture. Through its magazine and on-line Internet service it unites a culturally alert and concerned black America by fostering a sense of community among subscribers. AVS On-line has created a virtual community of like-minded people interested in black culture, arts, commerce, history, lifestyles, health, science, consumer products, and much more. It is the largest on-line service designed by and for African-Americans.

Interactive Author University Network

Launched in December 1997, Interactive Author University Network is an on-line lecture series that features interactive book signings across the United States among students on a variety of college campuses. It is the brainchild of Faye Childs, the founder of Blackboard: African American Bestseller List. The Interactive Author University Network (Internet address: intau.net) puts students and their favorite authors together in an intimate way. Authors go into interactive studios in various locations across the country to have access to up to twenty different student populations at one time. In this manner, thousands of students can talk to authors as well as buy their books. (Before the students can talk to the author, they must e-mail a credit card number and charge a copy of the featured book.) This program encourages college professors to consider the featured author's book as part of the curriculum, and encourage their students to gain exposure to novels and literature beyond their textbooks.

The university student population is a huge market that Faye Childs believes has been overlooked. When she took her idea to Follett College Stores, which owns more than five hundred campus bookstores, they were immediately interested. By getting this chain of stores involved she was able to launch the first chat, which featured the mystery writer Walter Mosley. Students on the campuses of Ohio State University and New York University got to chat simultaneously with one of the best-selling black authors writing today.

The number of Internet addresses and Web sites where you can promote yourself and expand your network is increasing everyday. Go to your local library and check bookstores for new titles that will guide you to the audience you seek. Search cyberspace on a regular basis in order to discover new outlets for your message. The time you spend will be a wise investment in your personal promotional plan.

9

Tell Me More

Attitude Focus: Sharing Your Words
In the last analysis, the spoken word is still king.
                ARAM BAKSHIAN, JR., *THE AMERICAN SPEAKER*

*W*hen your talent, and the performance of and dedication
to your profession, finally attract the attention of your boss,
your peers, or the clientele you are targeting, you will probably be asked to make a presentation, lead a seminar, or conduct a meeting. Don't shy away from this opportunity.
Excellent communication skills give you a competitive edge
and are a vital component of your personal promotional campaign. Speaking before a group of people with similar interests is a natural outgrowth of heightened visibility.

In the world of bookselling, there are many ways to introduce readers to a new release, the most traditional being
book reviews in newspapers and book signings in bookstores
across the country. Feature stories, ads in trade publications,
announcements placed on the Internet, targeted mailings,
and media appearances also provide excellent opportunities
to capture the interest of potential book buyers. However, I

find that being accessible to people and speaking with them is the most effective way for me to attract new readers and strengthen ties with loyal fans.

STEP UP, SPEAK UP

Speaking well, with clarity, sincerity, and passion, can set you apart from the crowd. Advancing in your career, achieving goals in business, or successfully raising visibility for a worthwhile cause is not necessarily determined by how smart, experienced, or skilled you are, but largely by your ability to communicate your message to those in positions of influence and power.

For twelve years Reva Smith has worked in a variety of positions in the field of sales, most recently for a company that sells herbal products for healthful living. "I learned very quickly that the enthusiasm and confidence I had in my product had to become infectious. I had to be assertive, as well as persistent, in convincing others that my product would be beneficial to them. To achieve that goal, I had to be totally sold on it myself—to the point that my passion for reaching my goals would catch the attention and energy of others, just as an infectious laugh catches on."

Through time and hard work Reva became more comfortable tooting her own horn, but really wanted a more satisfying job. Writing and drawing had always come easily to her and she began to think about doing more activities that challenged her creativity.

When the Univer-Soul Circus, the only black circus in the country, came to the city where she lives, Rena attended it and thoroughly enjoyed it. In fact, she wrote a review of the circus that she hoped she would be able to publish. Soon after, while reading one of the local African-American papers, she saw an announcement that the editor was looking for free-lance writers. "I called the editor and told him that I had written a review for the Univer-Soul Circus, and if no one else had covered it, I would like for him to consider running my piece. Since I had no credentials, I used my most profes-

sional, persuasive manner, but I could tell that he was appre-
hensive. He asked me to fax my review over. I sent it right
away and was shocked when he called back to say that he
loved it. With few changes, he planned to run it that week.
Now, I have the inspiration and drive to take my writing to
new levels. The biggest obstacle I had to overcome was my
own fear. I worked through this by reminding myself that the
only difference between me and others who were living their
dreams was that they took a chance and spoke up. I can't help
but feel pride in the mere fact that my thoughts and dreams
are slowly but surely becoming a reality."

Articulating your message in a persuasive manner will
create a great impression and leave an indelible memory, initiating a positive reaction to what you say. Whether you are
speaking to an individual or a room full of people, you cannot
help but wonder what they think, expect, and will demand of
you, once they listen to your message. Each contact is unique.
What works with one person or group may bomb with
another. Each person comes to a conversation or presentation with a unique set of expectations. It's up to you to greet
them with courage and confidence.

The motivational speaker Les Brown says on his tape
Delivering a Dynamic Speech (Les Brown Unlimited, 1996),
that in an audience of ten people, three want to be informed,
three want to be entertained, three want to be motivated, and
one will not be moved, no matter what you say or do. That's a
comforting reality that I quickly embraced. It keeps me from
focusing on and worrying about that person in my audience
who is frowning or fidgeting, obviously impatient or bored. I
have learned to ignore this person and concentrate on giving
the rest of my audience my full attention. Don't get all worked
up about not pleasing everyone; just deliver the message you
were meant to give.

Seasoned speakers often admit to getting nervous before a
presentation, but they do not allow this fear to prevent them
from giving their audiences their best, most motivating
speech. Dynamite presenters who consistently deliver inspiring, informative messages may look calm on the surface, but

they have mastered the art of turning their tension into energy that works to their advantage. They permit passion to rule, releasing nervous tension by pulling the audience into their world. If you are talking about something you truly believe in, you will not be distracted by thoughts of fear or failure.

Organizational meetings, industry conferences, trade gatherings, retreats, and fund-raisers are just a few ways for you to access large numbers of people with similar interests during a short span of time. Even on a small scale, at your church or within your company, having the spotlight trained on you while you discuss a topic of mutual concern is a great way to boost your recognition factor.

If you would like to polish your speaking skills and boost your confidence about delivering a dynamite speech, here are a few suggestions:

- Become well-read. Read the daily newspaper, the African-American, Hispanic, Asian, and special-interest publications, books, and trade papers—whatever targets *your* audience. Pay attention to articles that you can discuss with coworkers and colleagues to stimulate conversation. Such stories provide anecdotal and statistical information that comes in handy in social settings and can be used when preparing your next speech.

- Take a public-speaking course. Check out continuing education programs and classes at community colleges.

- Listen to audiotapes of speakers you admire. You can find such tapes at your local library or bookstore.

- Commit to attending at least one seminar or conference a year.

- Stay in close contact with experts in your field.

- Treat business meetings, lunches, and dinners as opportunities to learn.

Whether you are leading a training session with coworkers or giving a keynote address at a national seminar, you always want your presentation to serve your objectives and *exceed* the audience's expectations.

- Surprise them.

- Make them laugh or cry.

- Involve them, but don't embarrass or mock.

- Once you know who will be in your audience, take the time to familiarize yourself with key words, phrases, and topics that will create a connection and make the audience feel comfortable.

- Strive to make each speech relevant, entertaining, and informative. It is fine to have a basic speech that can be modified for each audience. Always add something fresh if you plan to use the same speech more than once.

You want to capture and hold your audience's attention, motivating them to learn more about you, and hopefully get an invitation for a return engagement. Make every speech your best. Aim for a standing ovation. Why not?

Go with What You Know

ATTITUDE ADJUSTMENT TIP #1

Stay alert, be prepared.

I was recently invited to introduce a noted author who was scheduled to give the keynote speech at a gala celebration honoring outstanding entrepreneurs. I was happy to do this, as the author was one I had admired for years and it would be an honor to be on the same program with her. Two hours before the event, the coordinator of the organization called. She was frantic. The invited speaker would not be able to make it and she wanted to know if I could help her out by making a few remarks. Though disappointed that the author would not be there, I agreed to fill in.

As I continued dressing, I began to think about the direction of my speech, and remembered that I had spent the day editing the chapter on creative visualization for this book. I immediately ran to my office, ripped the chapter from the printer, read through it, highlighted areas pertaining to entrepreneurs, and before dashing off to the banquet, stashed a box of my books in the trunk of my car.

The coordinator was very apologetic for her last-minute request and quickly agreed to create a display of my books near the entrance to the banquet hall. The audience was a friendly, high-profile group. The mistress of ceremonies was our ABC news affiliate anchorperson, whom I knew well. Luckily, my remarks were on target and the audience was pleased. I received a standing ovation, sold all of the copies of my books, and was able to heighten my visibility among local entrepreneurs who asked to be added to my network.

ATTITUDE ADJUSTMENT TIP #2

Build on your strengths.

Tracey Tillis attended Butler University in Indianapolis with the original idea of studying music and becoming a classical pianist. However, this arts administration major soon realized that she was in the wrong field of study. She says, "I didn't want to teach music. I had set my sights on a career as a performer. I knew I was good, but in time I came to the realization that I didn't have that necessary edge to make it as a solo performer. So, I went after plan B and switched my major to journalism."

Tracey, who is a published author of romantic suspense novels, currently works in corporate communications for an insurance company in Indianapolis. She does public relations and brochure design and also writes promotions, manuals, texts, and scripts. This position allows her to combine feature writing with news writing, as well as impact the promotional aspects of the company.

"My best asset," says Tracey, "is my ability to discern what my company or client really needs from me. I have a good idea of what my strengths are as a writer, editor, and communicator. I have learned how to listen to what clients say and immediately know which of my abilities will be needed to get the job done. Speaking well is important, but I have found that listening is just as vital. Paying close attention is a wonderful talent, and quite necessary. Sisters often go into meetings presuming to know what the client wants, so they don't really hear the questions. My professional journalism training comes into play when a client speaks, and I know how to listen."

Tracey also formed a relationship with the director of adult services for the Marion County Public Library system, where she does public-service work on a regular basis. Through this connection she has done motivational speaking throughout the community. This position gives her access to a variety of people: students, senior citizens, working-class people, retirees, artists, etc. This increases her visibility greatly, opening up the market for her works of fiction.

Tracey reminds her sisters, "Stay with what you know, and never allow yourself to be rattled by a potentially hostile audience. Deliver your message professionally and good-naturedly, and don't make people feel silly or stupid. There are great opportunities for those with skills or knowledge to impart to reach a large audience via local library systems. Unfortunately, some sisters don't take advantage of these opportunities. Suspicion, lack of trust, and a general attitude of 'Get what you can for yourself' have isolated some of us from each other. It is critical for professional women to be as educated and informed as possible. We must not be threatened by each other. Every success is a reflection of the whole process and increases learning for everyone."

Practice describing yourself or your position, talent, or service in a few short sentences. If you only have a few minutes to impress the person who could quite possibly launch your project, facilitate your promotion, or give you access to potential clientele, you want to tell them something that will stick in their minds long after you are gone. What you know, your willingness to share it, your ability to organize material, and your passion for your topic can keep you at center stage. How much you benefit from this position in the spotlight will depend largely on three factors: the reason for your message, its content, and the manner of its delivery. Let's examine each one.

1. The Reason for Your Message

When asked to make a speech, stop for a moment to consider a few questions:

Are you the right person to speak on the subject? When I was asked to speak on a moment's notice at the banquet for entrepreneurs, I knew I could craft a speech appropriate for that audience. If the audience had been keyed into science or technology, I may not have agreed to step in. If your boss wants you to make a presentation on a topic that is beyond your area of expertise, proceed with caution. Arrange for a time to talk with her and discuss exactly what is expected. Don't set yourself up to fail, yet at the same time take advantage of impromptu opportunities to showcase your speaking skills and, perhaps, add to your expertise. There have been only a few times when I have turned down an invitation to speak, usually because I was not passionate enough about the topic or felt I was not qualified to address it.

Why should the audience listen to you? If you can answer this with a simple, concrete reason that has merit, this will certainly bolster your confidence, better enabling you to hook and hold the group. People are eager to listen to those who have a solid reputation and are considered credible. Audiences embrace speakers who can help them increase expertise, find solutions, create new strategies, or lead more satisfying lives. Being able to deliver such information puts your talent in demand. Introducing an audience to something new means influencing their powers of reasoning.

What results are expected? Is your objective to sell, inspire, entertain, or motivate to action? Whatever it is, keep this clearly stated objective in front of you. This will help you shape your message and keep the presentation on track. Devise a method to get feedback to measure how well you accomplished your goal.

2. The Content of Your Message

The body of a speech is the heart of the message, but not necessarily what most people remember. Studies have shown that people remember opening and closing remarks more accurately than points made in the middle. However, the middle section is the main event, so structure your speech to bridge the beginning and the end with information that will keep the audience engaged. Keep your language simple, stick to three or four main points, and present them in a way that makes them memorable. For example, have all of your points begin with the same letter or have a similar sound, like "Patience, Passion, and Practice," or "Organize, Energize, Prioritize!"

Once you have decided on the theme or topic of your speech, research the audience to be sure there is a natural fit between your message and the receivers. Seek out sources for the statistics, anecdotal stories, and facts you plan to present. This takes time and effort, but is an important part of crafting an effective message.

I usually begin my research with people I know and the books, magazines, and papers in my personal library. Then I widen my search to the public library, local experts, and the Internet. Nothing is more gratifying than having an audience rise to their feet in applause because the speaker delivered exactly what was expected or needed. Nothing is more disappointing than to sit through a speech that has not been properly targeted, leaving the audience feeling resentful. They realize that the speaker didn't care enough about them to find out what mattered.

3. The Delivery of Your Message

Even if you have rehearsed your speech many times, it most likely will not come off as practiced. That's fine. Don't worry about "forgetting" something. Your audience has no idea what you had planned to say, so they won't realize you have left something out. I often prepare note cards with key words on them to use as a guide, then totally forget to even glance at them. When finished, I am often amazed at how much of what I said simply occurred to me as I was speaking. This is what you want—to make an energetic presentation that appears totally unrehearsed.

Speaking with passion and sincerity is easily accomplished by those who are willing to learn. Make a commitment to work on acquiring stage presence, using animated gestures naturally as you speak.

Develop your voice, with the goal of becoming comfortable either pacing the stage with microphone in hand, standing behind a lectern, or talking to a group with no public address system at all. Remember, tone is just as important as content in getting and holding your audience's attention.

Being seen as well as heard greatly impacts the audience's attention span. If you are short and the lectern is tall, stand on a box. Don't start your presentation until you are physically comfortable with the arrangement. If the audience can't see you, they will never connect with you and will have little incentive to listen to your speech. Years of teaching school taught me how to project my voice to the back of a room, and I prefer not being tied to a podium or microphone unless I am addressing a very large group.

Approach the task of becoming a better speaker in the same way you would go about learning a foreign language or becoming computer literate. Turn to books, magazine articles, audio- and videotapes, and classes and seminars that deal with mastering the art of public speaking. Study the techniques of motivational masters like Les Brown, Susan Taylor, Tony Robbins, or Zig Ziegler. Pay attention to their facial expressions, physical gestures, and tone of voice.

Keep the pace brisk. Don't allow your presentation to drag. Long pauses give audience members the chance to start their own conversations, creating competition that can drown you out.

Have a good time. Include a little humor. This allows you to entertain while educating and motivating others. Express your joy with the life you are living. No one wants to listen to a grumpy, dissatisfied person. A smile of confidence automatically captures the audience's attention and heightens interest in what you are about to say.

A good speaker always demonstrates good manners. Show your appreciation by thanking the audience for listening to you. I open and close every speech with an expression of gratitude to the people who have chosen to give up a small portion of their valuable time to spend it with me. I don't take that decision lightly.

EXERCISE: BARE BONES

This is the skeleton that I use to draft a speech.

Choose one. The main purpose of my speech is:

___ to educate

___ to convince

___ to motivate

___ to entertain

___ other _____

What word best describes my audience (educators, artists, students, etc.)? _____

What topic is *currently* of interest to this group (affirmative action? date rape)?_____

Where can I get background information (magazine, newspaper, library, local TV station, the Internet)?_____

Has there been *recent* news coverage, articles, or public discussion of this topic? If so, refer to this in my opening. _____

_____

The first sentence to introduce my subject to my audience is:

_____.

List three main points I will make, expanding on my opening sentence.

1. _____.

2. _____.

3. _____.

Do I have an anecdotal story, preferably my experience, that relates to the topic? Describe. _____

What do I want the people in my audience to do with the information I provide? _____

Write a closing phrase that challenges the audience to take the action described above. _____

_____

Once your speech is written, get busy and *write your own introduction*. If the facilitator calls and asks for a résumé or a biographical piece, don't just send whatever is handy. Send the dramatic piece that you created in Chapter 1. Go back and look at the example. This showcases your background, talent, and accomplishments. Make sure it is professionally copied on good paper and send it along with a black and white photo that can be reproduced in the program.

Ask that this biographical piece be used as your formal introduction. Along with it, include any other directions you want followed during the introduction, like turning off background music or requiring that the waiters stop clearing away dirty dishes. Refuse to speak until conditions are optimal for you to be heard, otherwise you are wasting your time.

The clatter of plates or annoying background music will drown out everything you say. Remember, it's *your* time in the spotlight. Maintaining control over as many factors as possible ensures a smooth, impressive performance.

Here is a sample of a prepared introduction. Follow this guide to create your own introduction. Pay attention to the underlined words.

> This evening, Parlisha Williams, educator, gospel singer, beauty queen, and inspirational speaker will share a motivating message designed to empower our youth with purpose.
>
> Parlisha Williams represents black women across the country as the 1996–97 national Ms. Black USA Metroplex queen. This wife, mother, and role model says that winning the title has provided her the opportunity to encourage young people to stay in school, get a good education, and find purpose in their lives.
>
> She is a computer lab instructor at Wheatly Senior High School and a member of Abundant Life Church, where she teaches praise dance to the youth. Today we will learn about some of the life-changing experiences Mrs. Williams encountered during her travels around the United States as she touched the lives of hundreds of youth, giving hope and encouragement along the way.
>
> Help me welcome . . . Parlisha Williams

Added instructions to the person who will make the introduction:

Please start applauding as I walk to the podium.

Greet me by shaking my hand. No hugs, please.

Please exit the platform without passing in front of me.

Please have someone signal when there remain five minutes to finish.

Thank you for creating a positive environment for my presentation.

Tell the audience what you are going to talk about. Talk about it. Then tell them what you talked about.

TEN TIPS FOR AN EFFECTIVE SPEECH

1. After you decide on a topic, create a *dramatic title* and use it in the opening to hook your audience. Make it personal, compelling, memorable—setting the stage for what will follow.
   Example: "Turn Your Passion into a Paycheck!"
2. Develop a *mission statement*. What changes do you want your audience to experience as a result of your talk?
   Example: I want the audience to realize (using my personal story and anecdotes about other successful people) that it *is* possible to make a living doing what one loves.
3. Use no more than six *key points* on which to center your presentation. Four is better. Three is good.
   Example: (1) Assess your talent! (2) Assess your resources! (3) Assess your future!
4. There will always be surprises, but *advance preparation* allows you to handle them with ease. Find out about the room, the program, the time schedule, what is expected of you, and who else is on the program.
   Example: If you plan to use props or demonstration items in your presentation, make sure arrangements are made to facilitate this. When I talk to students, I often bring along copies of my books and pass them around as I am speaking. In advance I ask the teacher to have a table in the front of the auditorium or classroom to make a display. I don't want to waste precious class time rearranging furniture. The books do get battered and covered with fingerprints, but the students are excited about touching an author's books.

5. *Rehearse* your speech until you can deliver it with mini-
mal reference to notes. Tape it and listen to your delivery.
Your goal is to engage your audience, sweeping them
along with your passion for the topic. This cannot happen
if your head is lowered as you recite the text.

6. *Time* your speech to fit the event. Organization is the key.
No one likes a rambler, and studies show that forty-five
minutes of any speaker at one stretch is just about maximum. Twenty-five is good.

7. *Make eye contact* with people throughout the room. Try to
set a pattern, moving from the sides, to the back, to the
front of the group, giving as many people in the audience
as possible the chance to connect with you.

8. Pay attention to *audience reaction*. Are you talking too
fast? Too slow? Regulate your speech to sound natural. I
have found that the timing involved in the delivery of a
message can dramatically enhance audience attention.

9. Be conscious of your *posture*. Leaning, rocking, swaying,
hair pulling, clasping of hands, and other such manner-
ism are distracting. Rehearse in front of a mirror to catch
and get rid of any bad habits.

10. *Smile.* Even if things behind the scenes have not gone
smoothly, make the audience feel as if you really are
enjoying the opportunity to speak with them.

There are thousands of opportunities to speak before
local, regional, national, and international audiences. You
can book yourself or use a professional speakers' bureau to
represent you. If you are interested in using a speakers'
bureau, prepare an audio- or videotape of yourself in action,
and send this out, just like an audition tape, along with your
press kit. If you have a topic of interest and can make a dynamite delivery, you will most likely be able to attract the attention of the bureau. Remember, they make money each time
you speak. They are looking for talented speakers.

A recent survey conducted by Meeting Professionals/
National Speakers Association listed more than seven thousand meetings nationwide scheduled for the 1996–97 calen-

dar year. Diligent research and preparation can place you on a stage behind a podium selling your dream instead of sitting in the audience thinking about it.

ATTITUDE ADJUSTMENT TIP # 3

Make a commitment to learning.

Perpetual study keeps you involved, curious, and interesting. The more you know, the more topics you can address, heightening the possibility that you will find common ground with those who will help increase your recognition factor. There is so much information floating around in books, magazines, newspapers, and on the Internet, that staying abreast of what is happening in your field can become an insurmountable task. A real problem for busy professionals is information overload.

I try to read most of the publications targeted to African-American women, but there are new ones popping up each month. Accomplishing what I call "required reading" without allowing it to take over my life is tricky, but instead of complaining and getting frustrated, I have devised a way to manage this problem.

One strategy that helps me get through my mountain of reading material that piles up each week is to set aside publications that I plan to read, then discard or pass along to someone else. This is what I take with me on my numerous trips by plane and car. I start out with a canvas bag loaded down with newspapers, magazines, pamphlets, etc., but by the time I return home, it's empty. It's wonderful to clear a backlog of reading material and to know that I've passed along my publications to strangers and friends who have similar interests!

ATTITUDE ADJUSTMENT TIP #4

Listen to your target audience.

When you are at a conference or in a large group, you zero in on the right people, capture their attention, and hope to connect with what matters to both you and them. Your first impulse is to start talking, telling them about you, but that may not be the best approach. Practice being a more attentive listener. Pose questions in a manner that allows the other person to open up, speaking easily and naturally about what is important to her. If you are gracious and polite, such intimate chats can produce valuable information while creating a lasting impression.

When my first book came out, I spent three years traveling the country promoting and selling my self-published novel. Speaking became a regular job and I practiced my presentation until I felt very comfortable telling my story. Because my novel was self-published, it was often locked out of the major bookstore chains, and rarely got reviews in major papers. Spreading the word and hand-selling the book became my passionate mission, consuming all of my time.

I spoke at schools, churches, museums, libraries, Kiwanis and Rotary luncheons, and even at a nursing home! Anytime I could get more than two people together I considered the gathering a success. It was exhausting and often very discouraging, but I never wavered in my commitment to reaching my audience. It was also exciting and challenging, though very expensive, as I was rarely offered even travel expenses for making a presentation. I never complained. That was fine by me, all I wanted to do was sell my book. In 1994, a leading national speakers' bureau contacted me after hearing positive things about my speaking engagements. I was invited to sign with the agency. I told the contact he must have made a mistake. I wasn't in the league of their clients. The most I'd ever been paid was a couple of hundred dollars for a speech. He replied, "You will be doing much better very soon. I promise." Unconvinced, I felt I had nothing to lose, so I signed the contract. Nothing happened for months; then I was asked to make a forty-minute presentation on African-American women in fiction at a literary symposium at Texas Christian University in Fort Worth, Texas. My fee? Two thousand dollars! The engagement had been brokered by the bureau. I had never dreamed I could be paid for simply expressing my passion for something so dear to me.

There are specific organizations and institutions that represent the interests of your audience and that can provide the kind of information, statistics, and data that will help you craft formal speeches or increase your comfort level when presenting ideas in an intimate setting. See "Recommended Reading and Resources" for organizations geared toward African-American women.

10

Check Yourself

Attitude Focus: Considering Others, Consider Yourself
Your lifestyle choice
is like a drop of water in a pond.
One drop?
No, it is never just one drop.
At times, your choices descend with such powerful force
they cause waves.
SUZETTE BRIMMER, MODEL AND BUSINESSWOMAN

"*I* consider myself a humanist with a real passion for the human condition," says the model and successful entrepreneur Suzette Brimmer. "My personal mission is to be true to myself and to the people I hold dear, spreading as much joy, love, and happiness as I can." Suzette, a striking beauty who has walked the runways of Paris and the showrooms of Nieman Marcus, attributes her success as an international model to her ability to get along with a variety of people. "There has been a great deal of talk these days, especially during Oprah's book club chats, about women and their wings. My wing-giver would have to be my father. He told me in blunt, simple terms that I would have opportunities and friends he could never have had and that I would go places he had never been allowed to enter. The road was going to be *tuff,* and at times, people who I believed would support me would not. I had to stay true to myself to survive."

Determined to show him she could make it, Suzette took this message to heart as her modeling career took off and she began to interact with people from all over the world. When she and her husband decided to launch their custom uniform business, Sports Productions, Suzette's sincere interest in people was definitely an asset. Serving clients and competing for new contracts from sports teams and private schools, she lives by those words of advice from her father. Suzette gives her sisters these words of encouragement: "If you haven't had someone like a Mr. Brimmer in your life, you'd better make certain you are a Mr. Brimmer to someone else!"

DIVERSITY IS ABOUT EACH OF US

We all have skills, talents, and dreams that vary according to how we were raised, where we grew up, and the multitude of life experiences we have had. Diversity is wonderful. It helps us appreciate the differences that make each of us unique, but it can also serve as the source of great tension. There are times when perceptual differences, undefined agendas, ambiguous values, or differing organizational goals create conflict.

The energy that fuels a lively discussion, initiates a debate, or issues a challenge can foster growth and increase understanding or create division, depending on the attitude you adopt. Demonstrating a desire to engage in conflict resolution rather than in destructive argument helps foster increased tolerance for those whose ideas and opinions differ from yours.

One of the greatest joys of touring the country, as I speak to audiences and promote my books, is the opportunity to meet a variety of sisters who may differ in age, race, ethnic background, education, geographic origin, marital status, physical traits, and professional discipline, but with whom I feel totally connected. And though the bonds of race and gender certainly unite a group in sisterhood, there are still times when conflict and misunderstanding overshadow acceptance and agreement.

If you compare the accomplishments of others to what you have achieved, you may begin to think that your goals are small and insignificant. You stand back and watch other sisters get all the breaks, while you are routinely overlooked. You wonder if you are deliberately being ignored. You try to shrug off those negative emotions—but let's get real. The success of a competitor or the promotion of a coworker can initiate feelings of envy, resentment, disappointment, and failure. Be careful. These are the kinds of emotions that set the stage for conflict—conflict that could undermine your commitment to yourself.

It is important to keep your anger and envy under control. Stay focused on your own agenda and deal with internal conflict as soon as it arises. Go back and review the personal mission statement created earlier. Where are you headed? Can the emotions you are feeling be channeled toward achieving the objectives you have set yourself?

Sometimes conflict and feelings of envy arise from a work situation. Imagine that you work for a cosmetics company. You pitch your ad campaign for the new line of lipstick to the marketing team, feeling great about your work, confident that your ideas are on target. The marketing team responds positively. However, when it is decision time, you are informed that a coworker's proposal was accepted over yours. You certainly have the right to feel disappointed. Your next reaction might be resentment that your colleague is getting all the praise and glory—and the bonus money that comes with the selection. Or you are tempted to lash out, venting your disappointment to your boss. Be careful. It is a good idea to move through unpleasant situations like this with caution. Make an appointment with your superior to discuss the flaws *and merits* of your proposal. Always try to determine where you *were* on target when things go awry. Express a sincere desire to learn from the experience and stick to a businesslike approach, eliminating discussion of personal issues. Your goal is to come to terms with what has transpired and move on. But if the conflict is so great between you and your colleague, or your boss, that you are in constant turmoil, it will probably affect your work. Perhaps it is best not to remain in that environment. Consider seeking opportunities elsewhere before professional relationships deteriorate. This is not giving up, it's moving on—on to the next stage of your plan.

Let's examine several common misconceptions about conflict.

1. *It is abnormal to experience discord and friction.* Unfortunately, you can't expect harmony to exist in all situations. When things go well, we are happy, but when the water gets choppy we become anxious and usually look around for someone to blame. An unsettling turn of events can prompt finger-pointing and back stabbing, but engaging in such behavior is immature and unproductive.

    Accept the fact that there will always be people whose views and opinions differ greatly from yours, but remember, too, that if there were no conflict, new ideas would never surface.

2. *People with personality problems cause conflict.* When people of different backgrounds are brought together and a variety of objectives is being considered, it is natural for unfamiliar or unexpected reactions to occur. This has nothing to do with personality. Disagreement is virtually unavoidable when a diverse group of people interact with one another. The key is to understand that conflicting views or opinions are not a result of incompatible people, but most likely of incompatible goals.

3. *Conflict and anger are the same.* It is true that conflict can make you angry, but a much wider range of emotions surfaces when controversy erupts. Don't simplify the issue by focusing simply on anger. You may experience frustration, resentment, disappointment, rejection, or envy when

faced with obstacles that interrupt progress to your goals. The key to moving through any hostile situation is to identify all of the emotions that are influencing behavior, isolate the overriding feeling and analyze it. If your best friend won a coveted award, are you upset with the committee that made the decision, jealous of the sister who is receiving the attention, or disappointed with yourself for not doing a better job? Probably a little of each, but which emotion is strongest? Decide to handle *it* first. Put emotional reactions into proper perspective.

4. *It is a good idea to avoid conflict.* There are times when avoiding conflict is the best solution, but situations do arise when you must take a stand and fight, though I urge you to choose your fights very carefully. An intelligent discussion on points of disagreement can be productive. Approach conflict with an attitude of fair-mindedness, putting yourself in your opponent's place. When you view the situation from her perspective, can you imagine how you would react to it? Would you alter your view or propose a different solution? Examining the other person's position might even lead to a better understanding of the problem, giving you insight into your competitor's plan.

TEMPERED AGGRESSION

The writer Tracey Tillis says, "Knowing how to make your case in a way that is not confrontational or overbearing is vital. Never take *no* as a first answer if you believe you are qualified for what you are going after. Knowing how to firmly persuade a sister to open her mind and listen to you lets her see that it is only to her benefit to sample what you have to offer. You have something that will help *her.* We must learn how to be firm and convincing without being rude."

Tracey says her greatest obstacle was inspiring promotional outlets to support her when she stepped out into the literary market. "I had to overcome the cliché tag that comes with being a romance writer. Automatically there is disdain when the word 'romance' comes up in certain audiences. I found that I had to get people to listen to me. I refused to alter the kinds of books I was writing, but I have altered how I present the package directed to my audience. Going through the backdoor helps.

"If I find it necessary, I will downplay the romance angle and play up the suspense angle in my novels. Doing this has definitely garnered better press and media attention. The results? A broader range of reviews and a wider readership for my books. We must look beyond the easy niche. In marketing, we have to package and position ourselves over and over in a certain way, to a specific market, and eventually results will come around."

ATTITUDE ADJUSTMENT TIP #1

Deal with it.

EIGHT WAYS TO HANDLE CONFLICT

1. *Accommodate.* This involves showing high concern for the goals of others, making your agenda a lower priority.
2. *Compromise.* By demonstrating equal concern for both parties, you work toward a middle ground where both views can be respected.
3. *Collaborate.* If your goals are compatible with your opponent's, find points of agreement and a way to work together, creating a win-win situation.
4. *Avoid power plays.* Be cognizant of power. Use yours sparingly to avoid polarization.
5. *Offer alternatives.* It does no good to criticize unless you have a better solution.
6. *Depend on accurate, objective data* when stating your views.
7. *Behave appropriately.* Resolve conflict in the appropriate setting. A private discussion demonstrates professionalism.
8. *Limit the conflict.* Involve only those who can help. Turn

to those who can offer insight on the problem without being judgmental.

As you become more visible, you will interact with a wider range of personalities, increasing your odds of experiencing conflict. Competition and jealousy exist in every field, so remember to be aware of the far-reaching effects of every word you say. Remain mindful of others' feelings as you step out with your message. You cannot sell yourself, or your dream, if there is a personal situation or an unpleasant issue that makes you feel uncomfortable.

ATTITUDE ADJUSTMENT TIP #2

Make it a habit not to badmouth anyone. Ever.

The African-American community is much, much smaller than we tend to believe. What we say about someone today can easily come around to haunt us tomorrow. You may be moving in a variety of social and professional circles, but if they are all within your target audience, don't be naïve: These worlds can and will connect.

When the Waldenbooks chain refused to carry my self-published book, I was disappointed and hurt. The store managers assured me it was corporate policy not to carry small-press books and the decision had nothing to do with the book itself. For months, I kept trying to get them to make an exception, but the decision was final. No sale. During this time I could have said hurtful, mean things about the bookstore chain that was locking me out, but I did just the opposite. I strongly encouraged all of my friends to shop at Waldenbooks and after making their purchases to inquire about my novel, *Emily, the Yellow Rose*. Nearly a year passed. One day I got a call from the manager of a Waldenbooks in Houston. The demand was so strong for my novel, she had to have it. That first order opened up the entire chain, and soon other chains and distributors were placing orders, too. Now, whenever I walk into a Waldenbooks outlet for a book signing, I just smile and remember when.

ATTITUDE ADJUSTMENT TIP #3

Make it a rule never to burn bridges.

Success is a journey, not a destination, and the road is neither straight nor easy to follow. As you move from one stage of your career to the next, you will touch many lives. Whether the people you encounter play significant or minor roles in helping you accomplish your life's mission, each one makes a contribution that shapes what you become. There are valuable lessons to learn from both good and bad experiences that foster your growth as a mature individual. My ability to actively support the Waldenbooks chain, when I was so angry because they would not carry my self-published book, is an example. I knew better than to burn bridges with those valuable bookstores—contacts and support I knew I would need when I did get published by a major house.

LIVE THE MESSAGE YOU DELIVER

ATTITUDE ADJUSTMENT TIP #4

Resolve uncomfortable issues.

Reach out to repair an estranged relationship and make peace with the past. Even if the person with whom you have experienced conflict does not accept your overture, make it. Allowing an unfortunate situation to simmer keeps the conflict alive, draining mental and emotional energy. Deal with it in a manner that allows you to put it behind you with a clear conscience, so you can concentrate on living your life as an exclamation, not an explanation.

People who are good role models accept the fact that they are expected to live by the high moral, ethical, and professional standards that the public expects of successful people. These standards include honesty, dependability, fairness, and compassion. Such people understand the importance of following established guidelines related to etiquette, protocol, and acceptable social behavior.

If this sounds like a tough set of standards to live up to, you're right. It *is* tough being held up as an example, but that's what comes with the territory if you expect to influence someone else's life. Just think of all the good you will accomplish by leading a lifestyle that makes you, your sisters, and brothers shine with pride.

STAR QUALITY

If your mother told you to sit up straight, keep your elbows off the table, not to speak with food in your mouth, to write thank-you notes, and to set a proper table, consider yourself lucky. Sisters who have been taught proper etiquette possess the social skills that work to their advantage.

It has been estimated that close to 85 percent of all business deals are negotiated over lunch or dinner. Whether you are trying to sell a potential client on your product, pitch an idea to your boss, or enlist the services of an expert, it is vital to understand the power of appearance and proper etiquette. No matter how many degrees you have or how much money you make, your ability to use the tools of protocol and good manners to your advantage is a factor that can make or break your career. Moving up, stepping out, and entering new professional and social circles means entering arenas where certain dress codes and behaviors are expected. If you don't take the necessity of playing by the rules seriously, you may soon be out of the game. But it's not difficult to acquire confidence in the way you handle yourself in public. Here are a few things you can do to keep from making the kinds of etiquette faux pas that could embarrass and haunt you forever.

Action Steps

1. Invest in a comprehensive etiquette manual such as *Etiquette*, by Emily Post, or *Basic Black* by Karen Hudson and Karen Grisby. Read the book! Use it as a reference.
2. Browse in the fine china and silver department of an upscale department store. Ask a salesperson to explain the various glasses, knives, forks, etc. that make up a place setting.
3. Contact a local charm school and consider taking a class.
4. Spend an afternoon with a family member or a friend who practices good social graces.
5. Observe and imitate the behavior of others at social functions.
6. Be gracious to those who are interested in you.
7. Use humor, if appropriate, to diffuse an embarrassing situation.

A FEW MORE HELPFUL HINTS

- Stand when important people enter a room.

- Be cognizant of your posture at the table.

- Follow the lead of your hostess.

- Use eating utensils in the order of arrangement, from the outside in.

- Be relaxed, gracious, and participate in the conversation.

- Always send a thank-you note to your hostess.

MIRROR IMAGE

ATTITUDE ADJUSTMENT TIP #5

Be comfortable with the image that best suits your personality, service, and message.

For all women, and especially African-American women, their hair, skin, and dress play a major role in defining their very unique and personal images. Our sense of fashion has been influenced by a multitude of things: our parents, our social and economic status, education, career choices, personality traits, as well as cultural and geographic origin. The emotions tied to choices in dress and makeup reflect the experiences we have had, as well as those we anticipate having. The image you choose to project is a personal decision. Many options exist. Whether you prefer a look that is classically conservative, elegantly casual, or one that strongly defines your cultural and ethnic background, it is important to find a style in which you feel comfortable. The following tips can help you make good style and fashion decisions.

- Adopt a look that reflects who you are.

- Please yourself first.

- Stop worrying about what "someone else" will say or think.

- Don't apologize for your choices.

If you choose to wear relaxed hair instead of braids and twists, that is your prerogative. If conservative suits are more your style than traditional African dress, that's your decision. What is important to remember is that good grooming always prevails.

I recently read a study that said women who wear casual clothing are regarded as less professional, are not taken seriously, and earn less money than those who dress in a more traditional manner. That may be true in general, but I think it is valuable to take work environment, geographic location, cultural heritage, and the way a sister wants her audience to perceive her into consideration, too.

A recent newspaper article detailed the results of a survey done by Sears to determine what kind of clothing "ethnic" women wear most ("Sears Clothing Line Targets Ethnic

Buyers," *Houston Chronicle,* Jan. 16, 1997). This study was initiated to increase the department store's customer base of women who desired a creative, "global" look and had not been able to find it. According to the report, African-American women wear more brand-name clothes and prints than white women and usually opt for a coordinated "head-to-toe" look. I am sure some sisters will agree, others won't. It just points out that there are no hard and fast rules about image.

John T. Molloy, in *New Women's Dress for Success* (Warner), says that the way a woman dresses won't ensure her success, but dressing poorly will almost always ensure that she will fail. Let good taste be your guide.

Set aside some time to seriously analyze your wardrobe to determine whether you are projecting the image that will enhance the odds of your meeting your objectives. Zero in on the kind of impression you want to make and why. Your profession, lifestyle, and social activities all contribute to your sense of style and impact your choices in clothing.

Buying clothes that will help you go after your dreams is an investment that should be taken seriously, but don't go into unnecessary debt to put on a front. I guarantee you— *nobody* needs to know that the fabulous power suit you are wearing cost $39.99 at T. J. Maxx. Protect your sources: If you borrowed your best friend's dress to arrive in style at an important event, keep it to yourself.

If you lack the necessary interest or background in wardrobe building to create the image you envision, consult a sister who dresses the way you'd like to dress, engage the services of a professional shopper, or let the salesperson in your favorite store assist in pulling together the look you want.

Generally speaking, going for conservative, high-quality clothing in basic colors that can be accessorized in a variety of ways will always be a wise choice. You never want to be thought of as boring, gaudy, cheap, or flashy, so take your cues from the coworkers and colleagues with whom you interact on a regular basis.

EXERCISE

To better define your image, enlist the help of a few sisters you trust. Ask them to answer these questions honestly:

1. What one word represents the essence of my personality?
2. If I were cast in a movie, what role would I best play?
3. What do you think I value most?
4. How is my career choice reflected in the way I look?
5. What one thing about my appearance, that I can control, should I change?
6. Why?

YOUR ADDRESS IS PART OF YOUR IMAGE

"The perception people have of you and your business often comes from your location," says Elizabeth Martin, the CEO of E. L. Martin & Co., Inc., a commercial real estate firm in New York City that she founded in 1993. "In a savvy real estate market it is vital to know what benefits come from having a certain address. My mission is to provide quality service as well as educate clients on the importance of where they locate their businesses." Elizabeth advises professionals not to underestimate how much the address and location of a business can negatively or positively impact a customer's decision to visit your store or use your services.

Most major cities have areas that are defined by high concentrations of various ethnic and racial groups. Often, African-Americans, Hispanics, or Asians place their businesses in these areas in order to reach their target market. Others opt for mainstream locations, aiming for a crossover clientele. Which is best? That depends on many variables. It is a good idea to use the services of a real estate firm, like E. L. Martin, to help you make such tough decisions. However, finding culturally diverse real estate firms to guide you is not easy.

"I got into commercial real estate for two reasons," says Elizabeth Martin. "First, I was intrigued by the industry.

Second, I realized that there were not many minorities dealing with commercial property. I saw a niche that needed to be filled. I don't solely target African-Americans, but because of who I am, a large part of my clients are black. I feel blessed to serve them, and word of mouth brings new referrals every day. Timing is great for my business. It would have been very different if I had started this ten years ago."

This high-energy sister is very busy helping African-American businesses find the perfect location in New York. She started her own company with $25,000 of personal savings because she wanted more flexibility in her life. In 1996, her company completed transactions worth $5 million. When *Black Enterprise* magazine heard about her, she was invited to participate in a full-page ad for AT&T featuring her company as a satisfied customer. The attention-grabbing headline was "Donald Trump . . . Move Over." *Black Enterprise* thought the ad would create good synergy, since they had also done a feature story on her. This was great promotion for her firm. "It was a little different way to get noticed without hitting people over the head," says Elizabeth, laughing. "It is so important to continually build on PR. It is a full-time job."

This busy CEO knows that people are curious about the commercial real estate industry because they hear about great sums of money being made. "But," she cautions, "the person who seriously wants to enter this field needs to have a certain amount of financial stability to sustain herself between deals." Elizabeth's goal is to retain talented people on her staff and help them grow. As they become successful, the firm becomes successful. "I want my salespeople to make hundreds of thousands of dollars. I strive to create an environment where people can take chances with new ideas. You have to be a self-motivator, an innovator. You can't be afraid of rejection or take it to heart. Above all, you must enjoy sales—you are selling all the time. Each person I meet is a potential client."

Here are some suggestions to find information about realtors in your area who can best meet your needs:

- Contact the Chamber of Commerce.

- Contact the local association of realtors.

- Go on-line and check Web sites of various real estate agencies.

- Talk to business owners in the area you have targeted. Ask for real estate referrals—who sold them their property, who they work with to locate space, etc.

Part II Worksheet

Assessment Questions

1. What's wrong with my life as it is? _____

2. What's right with it? _____

3. Have I been complacent about negative habits/situations/ influences too long? _____

4. Am I spiritually grounded? _____

5. Do I maintain a connection with a higher source to fuel my inner strength? _____

6. Am I a forgiving person? _____

7. Do I feel guilty if I put my needs first? _____

8. Do I procrastinate and make excuses about my lack of progress? _____

9. Am I organized in my personal and professional lives? ___

_____

10. Am I self-disciplined or do I depend on others to keep me focused? _____

11. Do I pay attention to how my words and actions will be

perceived by others? _____

12. Do I consider myself a good role model?_____

Action Steps

1. Write down the negative habits/influences/situations that bother you most. _____

2. List what you can do to eliminate them. _____

3. Write down the names of people/resources that can help you accomplish this. _____

4. Set dates to call or visit with them. _____

5. List the tools you need to get organized. _____

6. Check your budget and make a time line for acquiring these tools._____

7. Clear away unnecessary clutter in your home/office.

8. Adopt this motto: "Never pick up a piece of paper more than once." Either act on it or throw it away.

9. Track your progress by using a to-do list.

10. Value your time. List the people who get you off-track.___

   _____

11. What grudges are you holding? Release them now. _____

   _____

PART 3

Drive

My life has been about survival. Along the way I became an artist.

LENA HORNE, ACTRESS AND SINGER

The Relative Importance of Things

Nancy Wilson

Singer and actress

*E*very sister should have her own personal sense of how to keep a strong perspective on all aspects of her life, including herself, her family, her career, and the general public. Family and career are the great equalizers of our life force, keeping us grounded and focused.

From the very beginning of my singing career to today, with all of the great success I've been so honored to receive and achieve, I have always maintained a single vision, focusing inner strength on properly balancing all of the responsibilities and emotional connections I create. In my quest for happiness, achievement, and success as a woman, a mother, a businessperson, a performer, and an active philanthropist, I have become a conduit for inspiring and helping others along the way. This has been possible because of my ability to keep things in perspective.

Never have I let struggle or disappointment knock me to my knees. I have always turned it around, letting it teach me the lessons that life *will* and *can* teach you. When you listen to your heart and dig deep into your own well of faith, hope, and spiritual strength, you become self-reliant, always sharing, never excluding others.

The music business, like any other business, has its negative side. But in any industry or situation, if you dwell on negative energy, that is exactly what you will receive. "To thine own self be true" is important to remember. If you can't be true to yourself from the very beginning, you are in trouble. Fantasy is for movies, plays, and stories. I firmly believe that if we lived by, and spread, more of the wisdom learned at our parents' and grandparents' knees, there would be less illiteracy and more sense of self, strengthening our commitment to community.

Most of us don't know our neighbors. We have lost touch with siblings, cousins, nieces, nephews, uncles, and aunts because we are so wrapped up in what we are doing, too busy to take time to reach out. Friendships, associations, family, career, employees, and the material I perform are all important to me—they help me keep perspective. What I sing is a reflection of who I am. What I wear, what I say, and where I choose to go are also reflections of my personality. I am at one with my God.

Sisters, look to yourselves for guidance. Don't blame others for setbacks. Set attainable goals and put forth positive thoughts and deeds that will keep you driving forward. What you get back will amaze you. Know when to say NO and mean it. Know when to say NOT FOR ME and execute it. Say YES to the positive—it will be the driving force that benefits you *and* your sisters.

11
Work It, Girl!

Attitude Focus: Problem Solving

*I*t is five o'clock and you are clearing your desk, ready to call it a day. The phone rings. Reluctantly you answer, one eye on the clock because you have three kids to pick up from two different places and a stop to make at the grocery store before heading home to fix dinner, throwing in a load of laundry, and making the seven P.M. committee meeting at your son's school.

Your supervisor is on the line, and there's a problem. The high-profile speaker you managed to book for the company-wide meeting tomorrow just canceled. You have less than twenty-four hours to find a replacement.

In another scenario, you arrive at a trade show loaded down with promotional materials, ready to set up your booth, sell your product, and toot your horn. When you open the boxes that had been sent directly from the manufacturer to the convention center, you discover that the wrong order has been shipped. Panic sets in. You spent thousands of dollars for exhibition fees, plane fare, and promotional materials. What are you going to do now?

Or, you open the newspaper and read that your competitor has made negative comments and unfounded charges against you, your service, and product. This unflattering media coverage will affect sales and definitely have a negative impact on the reputation you worked so hard to establish. How can you ever recover?

Interruptions, mistakes, and emotionally draining events will always come along and threaten to sabotage your progress. When nasty situations strike, try not to get discouraged or let anger take over. Losing your temper, shouting, threatening, or placing blame on others, accomplishes little. What you need to do is focus on solving the problem. Here are a few suggestions that can help you cope when it seems as if everything is going wrong.

- Demonstrate to people involved in the problem that you are in control.

  In the first situation, you have to find a new speaker. My suggestion is run to your Rolodex and see who has the proper credentials, and whom you know well enough, to ask to make a presentation. I am called on *quite often* by sister friends who are in a pinch for a program speaker. Because of our friendship it is difficult to leave them hanging, so I usually step in if I can. For me, the benefits outweigh any imposition—I get the chance to meet a new audience and when I need advice or assistance, these same friends don't hesitate to help me out.

- Assess the situation and determine how the problem affects your short-term goals. Make adjustments in the immediate situation to get through the crisis stage.

  In the second scenario, you are caught without your promotional materials. This happened to me when I found myself with no books or promotional materials to pass out at a trade show. I immediately called a local bookstore and persuaded the owner to lend me a few books to create a display. Her assistant even brought them over—which was a major benefit of my having developed a relationship with the bookstore owner over the years. In the conference center's office, I photocopied the single handout that I had luckily brought with me (paying way too much for several hundred copies). If you don't have an original of your promotional piece, design something simple and effective on the spot. It can be costly to have things copied on-site or sent by messenger or overnighted to you in situations like this, but it's better than wasting the money you have invested in the event and losing the chance to promote yourself.

- Turn to the appropriate people for information and assistance, involving those who have a role in resolving the situation.

    In the third scenario, you received negative press. Discuss this issue with someone who can give you professional advice. Unless libel, slander, or some other legal issue is involved, it is probably best to wait this one out, letting your good reputation and track record speak for itself. Be sure to document conversations and actions related to the incident. This helps keep communication clear, progress focused, and everyone moving toward a resolution. These notes can also serve as a reference for dealing with similar problems in the future.

ATTITUDE ADJUSTMENT TIP #1

Don't turn tail and run when faced with a problem.

Sharon Michael started out in 1977 as a consultant for small commercial customers in their dealings with the power industry, which allowed her to learn everything she could about the industry. "I was always being thrown into sink or swim situations," says this superachiever who became the first African-American manager at Houston Lighting and Power; she now holds the title of vice president at the company, one of the largest power companies in the nation.

"I had few mentors when I started in this business twenty years ago," Sharon says, "and those who did try to help me find my way were usually white men. I knew I was the token African-American at that time, but I decided to use this to my advantage. I felt discouraged and cried a lot, almost quitting more than once, but job stability was important to me, so I stuck it out. When things got rough, I suddenly woke up and realized I would not play into what management wanted— which was for me to quit."

Early in her career, when a promotion Sharon had fully expected did not materialize, she went directly to her superior and asked why. He told her she didn't have good writing skills. This was puzzling to Sharon, who had never been asked, or required, to write much more than interoffice memos. Immediately, she volunteered to write the next annual report to demonstrate her writing ability. Shortly after the report was completed, she got her promotion.

This hard-working sister learned very quickly that doing a good job was not enough. It was vital that she play the game—use politics to get what she wanted.

"I decided to become more visible among those who were deciding my future," Sharon says. "My white coworkers and their managers often socialized after work, and though I was invited to join them, I never accepted their invitations. Suddenly, I realized that they were probably talking about me while I wasn't there. I made up my mind to be present if I was going to be discussed, and began joining them after work. It was one of the best decisions I ever made. Because my visibility was increased, they got to know me better and began to see how I could be an asset to the company."

Here are a few problem-solving tips from Sharon on making it in the corporate world:

- Look at the larger picture. See the company's vision and where you fit in. If you can't see that, maybe you are in the wrong place.

- Speak for yourself. Don't let others carry your message.

- Turn a problem into a personal challenge.

- Ask questions.

- Demand answers.

- Diversify your social groups and become more inclusive.

- Let those in power know what you want.

- Get acquainted with those who know what's going on, but have little power, such as cleaning people, or mail-room staff.

ASSUMING RESPONSIBILITY

Problem solving requires abiding faith and unflagging optimism. I believe there *is* a solution to every problem, though it may not be immediately visible. As you become better known and recognized in the workplace, community, or marketplace, complicated issues will arise that test your commitment and your self-confidence. Pressure increases on sisters who are making things happen. Actors, authors, musicians, and other artists who are always striving to make their next movie, book, or recording better than the last also must be able to deal with painful setbacks that could easily derail a career.

Be patient, observant, cautious. Every problem does not require immediate action, so break the issue down into manageable tasks. Chip away at what may seem to be an insurmountable obstacle in order to keep the momentum going and the enthusiasm high. Your coworkers will see that you are not daunted or defeated by the problem and their morale will improve. Low morale among your coworkers can take a toll on you.

ATTITUDE ADJUSTMENT TIP #2

Don't dwell on the problem.

Attracting positive attention is flattering. Increased name and face recognition draws you deeper into the lives of those you want to access, influence, or impress—but this also makes *you* more accessible. As you become more familiar, more people will turn to you for answers. As you *step out* to accomplish the objectives of your overall plan, you are sure to *step on* someone's toes. When delicate situations surface, give them your immediate and honest attention.

"When I have a problem, the first thing I do is fast and pray," says Cathy Hughes, CEO of Radio One, Inc., a conglomerate of radio stations that fill the air waves with talk and music from Baltimore to Washington, D.C., to Atlanta. To handle the kinds of problems that come with running a multi-million-dollar corporation, Cathy relies on an inner strength that never fails. "I do not say that I look to God for the answers," says Cathy. "Instead, I look to God to open me up to find answers. Remember, God helps those who help themselves. Too often we concentrate on the problem instead of concentrating on identifying the solution. We fret and worry and discuss it too much. Once I know the problem, I don't need to keep replaying it in my mind or keep thinking about it. I need to get past it. I try not to discuss it any more than necessary. Rehashing the issue just gets me emotionally upset all over again. I refuse to relive the fear attached to whatever difficulty I am facing. My solution is to start researching and looking for people who have had the same problem—reading everything I can about them to see how they handled it."

It is important not to panic if unexpected situations occur that interrupt your progress. Illness, a death in the family, a tragic accident, or a severe financial setback can trigger emotional reactions that will wipe you out if you are not careful. You could pay a very big price for allowing yourself to deviate from the concrete reality of your day-to-day routine. This does not mean that you should suppress your emotions or refrain from expressing sympathy when someone close has suffered misfortune, but you do not want to get stuck in an emotional state that could insidiously erode your perspective.

Action Steps

1. Isolate yourself in order to think calmly about the problem.
2. Focus on the desired outcome.
3. Make a conscious effort to remain optimistic.
4. Determine where you can most quickly and positively impact the situation.
5. Write down three steps that you can take to move *closer* to the desired outcome.
6. Try to stick to your normal routine while dealing with the problem.
7. Tell yourself you can handle it.

ATTITUDE ADJUSTMENT TIP #4

Do some strategic planning.

Going on a multicity book tour almost ensures that stressful times lie ahead. I try to anticipate what problems may pop up and what I will need to handle them by preparing, as much as possible, for unexpected situations.

I showed up at a bookstore in Ohio for a signing a few years ago, only to find that my books had not arrived. The bookseller was very apologetic, and began telling people that the event was canceled because there were no books. I stopped him right away. Yes, I was disappointed, but not ready to turn tail and run. After all, the objective of the gathering was to sell books—now or later, I surmised.

I quickly decided to create an opportunity to chat intimately with my fans, taking time to listen to their comments, not only about my books, but about other authors they enjoyed reading. Everybody stayed. The crowd grew as casual shoppers in the store drifted over. We held a lively book discussion and I learned a lot from those avid readers that afternoon. I know that this exchange brought me closer to my fans and brought new ones, too. The people left with smiles on their faces, instead of frowns. Instead of feeling alienated and angry, they felt pleased to have been able to share their thoughts on a topic that obviously interested them. Two years later, a woman showed up at a book signing in Chicago and promptly reminded me that she had been among those who didn't get a book that day, but she brought along the title I had planned to sign and, laughing, said it had been worth the wait.

ANTICIPATION, PREPARATION, ORGANIZATION

Whether I am working on a new book, preparing for a dinner party, or organizing a community project, I always create a time-line and planning schedule to keep me on track, along with a running to-do list. For example, if you are the publicity chairwoman for the annual Career Day fair at your church, after you have delegated tasks to be done by others, divide your schedule into time-related sections that detail *your* responsibilities. Use the sample below as a model.

PLANNING SCHEDULE—MY RESPONSIBILITIES

- *Eight weeks prior to event:* Distribute posters and flyers to sponsors, committee members, and community outlets. Get a feature story to the editor of church newsletter.

- *Seven weeks:* Get letter from pastor to send to all members encouraging support and attendance.

- *Six weeks:* Draw up list of sponsors, committee members, participants, and financial contributors that will be included in the program. Give to program chair by end of week.

- *Five weeks:* Prepare press releases and press packets. Check on progress of signage for event location.

- *Four weeks:* Send invitations. Send press kits to community papers, targeting editors of religious and youth sections.

- *Three weeks:* Follow up with members of organizations

who are involved, all committee chairs, continue to solicit sponsors and other support.

- *Two weeks:* Follow up with media to secure TV, radio spots on local stations.

- *One week up to day of event:* Call final meeting of all committee chairpersons. Go over responsibilities for the day of the event, troubleshooting tricky areas. Make sure outside signs go up, coordinate requests for media interviews and the logistics involved, track press received so far.

WATCHFUL EYES

You want the promotion. You want the recognition. You want the prize. You want your phone to ring. You want your business profiled in the newspaper. You hope to be interviewed on TV. You plan to shine in your role as leader, artist, or community organizer. You expect your plans to unfold as you've dreamed. But most of all you want to be thought of as reliable and trustworthy, a person who truly cares.

As more people learn about you—your talent, service, or expertise—you will receive more scrutiny. However, as accelerated activity brings you in contact with a wider range of personalities, the odds are increased that a segment of your target audience will misunderstand your message.

Your being in the spotlight inspires supervisors, coworkers, colleagues, members of your community, and family to consider you a role model. People will increasingly turn to you for advice, answers, and support for their causes. When the responsibility seems too heavy to bear, remember, *you* are the one who sought the attention, therefore *you* are the one expected to respond in a positive way.

If you have ever been audited or sued, had your behavior questioned, or engaged in a confrontational discussion with a colleague or superior, you know the devastating toll such negative encounters can take on your self-confidence and sense of purpose. Don't let the difficult times overwhelm you or prevent you from selling your dream.

ATTITUDE ADJUSTMENT TIP #3

Get mentally prepared.

Accept difficult times as part of the deal. Just as movie stars and sports celebrities know their every move will be watched and tracked, you, too, must realize that others are watching you closely, even waiting for you to stumble. To keep frustration levels as low as possible, adopt a mature attitude about the responsibilities that come with recognition and remember to balance the demands that others will make on you with what you need for yourself, to survive and thrive.

ATTITUDE ADJUSTMENT TIP #4

Don't be vulnerable.

Protecting your reputation requires vigilance. Crafting a career requires hard work. Here are some tips to help you avoid mismanaging either one.

1. *Document your activities.* This is a valuable way to protect your reputation as well as your livelihood. Advance preparation translates into paying attention to details at the start of a project.

   - Obtain written confirmations, document appointments and conversations on your calendar.

   - Keep receipts and correspondence in a separate folder for each activity.

   - Carefully read all contracts and agreements.

   - Get legal advice if the terms are not clear.

These steps can prevent nasty surprises that could cause problems down the road.

2. *Find out what else is going on.* What's on the drawing board within your company/community/industry that could negatively impact your plans?

   • Scope out potential problems by checking with key people who are in the know.

   • Contact the Chamber of Commerce or the department of tourism in your city. Find out what engagements will affect interest in or attendance at your activity.

3. *Measure progress on problems.* Resolving a problem may take time, but step by step you will get there. Create a tracking system to stay on top of what has happened so far. For example, list dates of discussions with those involved. Describe the results of these meetings. List what actions were taken by whom and when. Create checklists or use graphs and charts on bulletin boards to remind yourself how far you have come and where you are headed. Computer files or even index cards will also provide visual updates.

4. *Consult.* Make a file of professional contacts who are experts in various fields. Turn to those with whom you feel comfortable. I have sister friends who are computer whizzes, legal experts, realtors, politicians, community activists, medical professionals, educators, etc., who will give me an honest assessment of where I stand on a complicated issue. I call on them a lot for input when I am doing a book. They love to help me out.

5. *Vent.* Make a phone call to a close sister friend who perhaps has been through what you are experiencing. Nothing is more helpful than discussing a problem with someone who can empathize with what you are facing.

Openly expressing your disappointment or frustration can definitely renew your faith in yourself. Listen carefully to your sister. If you truly trust and value her opinion you will let her help you explore the upside and the downside of a problem. Play the devil's advocate: "What is the worst thing that could happen if I take certain steps? What is the best?"

ATTITUDE ADJUSTMENT TIP #5

Separate family obligations from professional responsibilities.

Black women are often accused of allowing personal relationships and professional matters to get entangled, causing problems that negatively affect their chances for advancement. Sometimes it is extremely difficult to balance our commitment to both, but you can undermine your career by using business hours to deal with family problems, spending too much time on personal issues, and shunning assignments that could boost your visibility.

There is so much going on in our lives that we can easily confuse our priorities. We must make difficult choices and hard decisions every day. When you make a commitment, whether to a supervisor, a member of your target audience, or a colleague, your first obligation is to honor it without complaint or resentment, even if it means putting personal matters temporarily on the back burner. If your friends and family really want to see you sell your dreams, they will be patient while your time and energy are directed to activities that can take you closer to your goals.

TEAM EFFORT

There will be times when an active exchange of a variety of ideas is required to solve a problem or take a project to a new level. Effective utilization of such a pool of knowledge takes skill and preparation. Holding a meeting is a common way of getting input, solving problems, exchanging opinions, sharing concerns, and clarifying issues. In order to accomplish the goal of your meeting, be sure to follow a few rules.

RULES FOR SUCCESSFUL MEETINGS

1. Decide on the purpose of the meeting.
2. Do background research on the topic.
3. Set the agenda with input from appropriate parties.
4. Let attendees know in advance what will be expected of them.
5. Give those involved a clear understanding of the objectives.
6. Distribute advance copies of the agenda.
7. Start on time.
8. In the meeting, keep the discussion moving and stay in control.
9. End on time.
10. Do an evaluation of the meeting when it is over.

Structure of Sample Agenda

Name of group: Recruitment Committee members: Bill, Eric, Helen, Tim

Called by: Anita Bunkley

Date: January 3, 1998

Place: Main Towers, 3rd floor, the Blue Room

Time: 6:00 P.M. to 8:00 P.M.

Purpose: To evaluate recruitment activities of the last quarter.

Our objectives

Announce our membership drive

Develop a new brochure that describes our mission

To recruit twenty-five new members by April 1, 1998

Materials to bring: Your Phase Three Handbook, your activity report, three new sources to target

	ACTION/BY WHOM?	DEADLINE?
Agenda Item #1	_____	_____
Agenda Item #2	_____	_____
Agenda Item #3	_____	_____
Follow up:	_____	_____

Next meeting date: February 25, 1998, Main Towers, 3rd floor, the Blue Room

You can benefit from participating in a well-run meeting in several ways. As a leader you will gain experience expressing yourself and will have a forum in which to further develop your ideas. Chairing a meeting lets you demonstrate your leadership skills while promoting your objectives. As the group leader, you will be able to test the loyalty and assess the commitment of those involved in finding solutions to the problem.

As an attendee, you are able to carefully observe and analyze a group leader in action. Take notes. Identify traits you admire. Were there actions that made you uncomfortable? Add effective leaders to your talent pool by getting to know them better. Interacting with successful peers in a meeting allows you to gain insight into their attitudes toward shared objectives while highlighting your commitment.

EXERCISE: EVALUATING A MEETING

Think of the last meeting you attended. How did you feel about it? Here is a way to determine whether the meeting was effective for you. Complete the following:

For me, the following objectives were accomplished:

The most satisfying aspect of the meeting was _____.

The least satisfying aspect was _____.

After the meeting I wished _____.

At the next meeting I wish _____.

If I had chaired the meeting, I would have _____.

IN THE DRIVER'S SEAT

What motivates you to keep going, circumventing all the traps that are waiting to drag you off-course? What is the source of the fuel that goes into your engine? Do you have something to prove? To whom and why? Is there a situation you are desperate to escape? Is there a debt—emotional, personal or financial—that you feel compelled to repay? What drives you?

People who are focused on success bounce back after devastating setbacks. They take up the gauntlet and charge forward again and again after experiencing disappointment, obviously inspired. If problems arise and unexpected disaster strikes, they immediately refocus and start over without ever considering throwing in the towel.

Each of you has a unique reason for wanting to use a personal promotional campaign to touch the individuals or audience that you believe will have a major impact on your future. Whether you are motivated by a closely held, private matter or a publicly stated goal, it is important to have a solid understanding of exactly what is driving your quest for recognition.

I've read hundreds of biographies about successful people; I've watched hours of television programs chronicling the historical and contemporary movers and shakers in this world; I've met and talked with quite a few celebrities; and I have come to the conclusion that the single most common characteristic of these high achievers is persistence.

"Perseverance cleared the path to help me meet my goals," says Helen Callier, a sister who was determined to find a way to integrate her love of poetry with her technical background. An engineer in the corporate world, Helen boldly "engineered" a unique artistic situation to put the spotlight on her poetic works. By collaborating with the nationally known artist LaShun Beal, she launched an innovative series of affordable, colorful ceramic tiles entitled *Spiritual Works*. By combining Beal's artwork with her own expressive passages, Helen has been able to touch a wider audience and create opportunities for art lovers to access works by a talented brother whose images fit Helen's words like music to lyrics. She says, "Persevering with this project enabled me to pursue more opportunities to share my poetry, rise before the sun to meet a deadline, to give one more reading, and to continue improving my craft. Drive is the input-output device that allows me to continue serving my audience."

12

That's a Lot of Money!

Attitude Focus: Managing for Wealth
Money has power. For centuries we have empowered other folks by making them rich. Now it's time we committed ourselves to creating wealth for us.

SUSAN TAYLOR, EDITOR-IN-CHIEF, *ESSENCE*

ATTITUDE ADJUSTMENT TIP #1

Shun the "poverty is virtue" mentality.

The right to accumulate wealth was historically denied to black people. Keeping slaves illiterate while restricting their mobility was an effective way of denying access to information and awareness of opportunities that could inspire them to improve their economic situations. Even after slavery, many blacks feared being too successful because a wealthy Negro, with too many material possessions, was often the target of envious, resentful whites. When African-Americans had

had enough of their status as second-class citizens, demonstrations erupted and riots broke out in the 1960s as they rebelled against the barriers to financial progress and economic security under which they had suffered so long. This tragic legacy of economic oppression has had a profound impact on successive generations, creating complicated attitudes and beliefs about acquiring, managing, and sharing wealth. Attitudes of making do, of not asking for or expecting too much, and of being thankful for any small improvement in one's financial status influenced the thinking of generations of African-Americans who felt financial success was out of their reach.

I firmly believe, no matter what your circumstances, that financial gain can and should be yours if you are willing to go after it. African-Americans have always been resourceful, using nontraditional methods to get what they needed. Word of mouth within the black community was, and still is, the strongest, most reliable messenger. Just ask. Someone is waiting to give you a hand.

Planning for Wealth

> If your expenses are higher than your income, it doesn't take a rocket scientist to show that you're not going to make it.
>
> *Loida Lewis, CEO, Beatrice Foods*

Adequate funding is important to the success of any business, creative venture, or promotional campaign, but it is just as important not to let financial considerations drive all of your decisions. Spending more does not necessarily mean attracting more customers or widening your audience, while spending less does not automatically mean that your venture will fail.

A study conducted by the Gallup Organization showed that the number one New Year's resolution of Americans was not losing weight or stopping smoking, but managing finances better. We know the drill: Make a budget, stick to it, cut up your credit cards, pay yourself first with regular savings, pay cash for everything, etc. But how many times have you pledged to get out of debt, to stop using plastic to make ends meet, and to save enough money to quit your day job and launch your own business? How long has your dream been deferred because of insufficient financial resources? Probably longer than you wish to admit.

Wanting to improve your financial standing is natural. Poverty is not a virtue and the desire to be wealthy should make you happy, not make you feel ashamed. For too long, African-American women bought into the theory that they should be content with whatever financial gain they were able to make, no matter how small. Such a mind-set made it easy for them to settle, to forgo grandiose dreams, and become content with less than they deserved. And if a windfall or an improvement in financial standing did come along, sisters often felt uneasy, even guilty about admitting their good fortune. Generations of poverty and lowered standards of living have created deep-seated mental barriers. Many African-Americans have a hard time believing that great wealth is not only achievable, but *deserved*.

Times are changing, though. Black women are entering the marketplace with aggressive enthusiasm, altering the economic landscape to make it more reflective of the consumer base that supports mainstream business. The National Foundation for Women Business Owners (NFWBO) announced in a report that the number of businesses owned by women of color is growing three times faster than the overall rate of business growth in the United States. The study, sponsored by IBM, reported that between 1987 and 1996 the number of Hispanic women–owned firms more than tripled, the number of Asian-American/Indian companies also tripled, and African-American women–owned firms more than doubled.

"One in eight of the nearly eight million women-owned companies in the nation is owned by a woman of color," states Susan Peterson, the NFWBO chair. "These women entrepreneurs differ from their male counterparts in many ways, including how they manage, make decisions, select vendors, and use credit. It is increasingly valuable for all businesses to understand and benefit from these differences."

INVESTING IN YOU!

The monetary investment required to build identity in the marketplace varies considerably, depending on your objectives. You may be able to accomplish your goals by spending very little money. If you have a home-based enterprise handcrafting black dolls and are targeting a local or regional market, you certainly will not have the same type of expenses as would a sister who owns several soul-food restaurants throughout the state. The restaurateur may need to spend thousands of dollars to facilitate access to the media and her clientele, while the doll maker may spend several hundred. Having experts write promotional text, design materials, and book speaking engagements can be costly, but sometimes it is the best route to take.

Developing Your Plan

Make a wish list, prioritizing promotional activities according to what needs to be done first. Concentrate on the ten most important expenditures and set a dollar amount for each one. You must be realistic—don't try to cut corners so sharply that you fail to meet objectives. If anything, err on the side of overestimating; then your budget will remain more fluid. Determine what sacrifices/adjustments you can make to increase available cash.

If you decide to borrow money, bear in mind that financial institutions require collateral. Without sufficient collateral it is going to be difficult to borrow funds. Many people mortgage their homes or borrow against retirement funds to launch a business or infuse capital into an ongoing venture. Before making such a move, you should talk to a professional—contact the Small Business Administration (SBA) and gather all the information available on the success rate of your type of business. Request names of former clients to contact for references.

At the time when I self-published my book, in 1989, the SBA did not make loans to publishers because the industry was considered too risky. I had to use my own savings and family loans for help. Now I am glad I didn't have to go into debt, because as the book sold and money came in, I was able to move to the next stage of my plan and keep the promotional plan going.

If you are thinking of using your home as collateral for a loan, talk to a loan officer at your bank or a financial planner to determine whether this really is the best route to take. Make sure you can live with the consequences if your business flounders and your note is called in by the bank. An option that works for many is to get a revolving line of credit and draw on it as needed. This keeps you from going into heavy debt all at once.

Savings, bonds, loans or gifts from family, acquiring a partner, and credit cards are other resources to tap. The film-maker Spike Lee said a great deal of his first film was financed on his credit cards.

Perhaps you don't need all of your projected expense money at once. Map out a six-month to one-year calendar of projected expenditures related to promotional activities. For example, in the early stages you will need to focus on costs related to the design and production of your promotional materials: brochures, fliers, professional photos, press materials, setting up a Web site, making television or radio commercials, creating print ads and other visuals.

The next stage is the dissemination of your materials: postage, delivery costs, telephone, fax, fees to professionals providing public relations services, travel costs to spread the word. You may also need to provide samples or promotional copies of your product. A big expense in the book business is the cost of review copies that must go out to the media and reviewers in order to promote the book.

Once you have developed this six-month-to-a-year plan, share it with those involved in your project and keep it in front of you. Track expenditures by making notes on your calendar, and keep receipts, invoices, and copies of written/faxed financial communications. All of this will be needed at tax time, so get in the habit of keeping good records.

Take it a day at a time. Although we must think of the long haul, I have found that doing what I can with what I have at the time usually keeps the promotional plan moving forward, and I find that I can get really creative when things get tight. Don't forget to congratulate yourself whenever you come in under budget on a specific line item. Allocate those savings to the next objective and keep on pushing forward.

Working with a Financial Adviser

Laying open the pages of your financial history can be a scary thought, but if you have difficulty sticking to a budget, perhaps you could use some guidance. If you decide to take the plunge and enlist the help of a professional service, it is a good idea to refer to trade associations like the Institute of Certified Financial Planners or the National Association of Personal Financial Advisors (NAPFA) to find someone to work with you. These associations maintain directories of qualified professionals who work in financial planning.

You can also talk to friends in financial situations similar to yours, or seek referrals from your bank, attorney, broker, or CPA. When you get the name of a financial planner, ask questions and determine her experience and rate of compensation. No educational or experience qualifications are required for registration with the Security and Exchange Commission to work as an investment adviser.

Financial advisers earn their money in basically two ways, fees and commissions, and you will be charged by the hour or asked to pay a flat rate for consultation and planning advice. The cost of a standard fee-only plan can start at $1,800 to $2,500.

Before you sit down with an adviser, familiarize yourself with the language and terminology used in discussing finances. An excellent resource to help you accomplish this is *The*

Business Words You Should Know: 1500 Essential Words to Build Vocabulary Needed in the Business World Today, by Brian Tracey (Adams Media Corporation, 1997). Typical terms in your budget and marketing plan might include the following:

- *Merchandising costs.* What will it take to get the product to the market?

- *Percentage of projected sales.* What is the anticipated monetary return on each unit?

- *Cost per task vs. return.* What is the ratio of cost of labor, packaging, distribution, and advertising to the amount received on each unit?

- *Estimated payback time frames.* How long until costs are recouped? Profit realized?

- *Methodology for measuring return.* How to calculate net profit or loss.

Before you consult a financial adviser, know what to expect from the services of a professional. Prioritizing your financial goals will help your sessions go more smoothly and will help you get the most from the money you invest in this service. You can get a list of fee-only planners from NAPFA by calling 800–366–2732.

Determining Your Net Worth

You'll also need to determine your net worth in order to have a firm idea of how much money you can risk. Here is how to do it:

1. *List your assets.* Cash, stocks, bonds, certificates of deposit, insurance policies, the value of your home, car, jewelry, personal property—anything that can be converted to cash.
2. *List your liabilities.* Debts such as the mortgage on your

home, the balance on your car loan, credit card debt, out-standing personal or business loans.

3. *Subtract your liabilities from your assets.* For example, your assets are worth $200,000. Your debts are $75,000. Your net worth is $125,000.

Other Steps to Take

Take stock of your resources. What changes can you make to better utilize what you already have?

Create a short-term and long-term budget for promotional activities.

Seek appropriate financial support from banks, financial institutions, and government lending programs.

Get a good book such as *The Sixty-Minute Financial Planner,* by Dana Shilling (Prentice Hall, 1997), on how to create a financial plan. Follow the guidelines given.

Contact the Small Business Administration, the Internal Revenue Service, or other government agencies that assist the public with financial planning. Ask your local IRS office to send you information on the tax implications of the business you are contemplating starting. Find out about state tax laws as well.

Seek free materials and services through nonprofit agencies like Consumer Credit Counseling (consult your local phone directory for the number), which are designed to help people learn how to budget.

Take a short course on financial planning at a community college.

Keep good records so you can provide the data required on loan applications and financial statements.

Separate business and personal funds.

Get to know your local banker. Having a good relationship

with someone at a financial institution who knows you and what you are about is extremely valuable.

GETTING WHAT YOU PAY FOR

It is true that in order to make money you must spend money. How much depends on you. Career paths change, new products are developed, and new causes arise that demand your support. Accessing new members of your target audience is an ongoing process that ebbs and flows. Some years you will spend heavily, other years will be lighter. Launching a new product generally takes more focused publicity and promotional dollars than servicing existing accounts. Keep a careful watch on the cycle of your expenditures to facilitate long-range planning.

In a recent edition of *Tactics*, a monthly publication that focuses on news, trends, and how-to information for public relations people, an innovative publicity strategy of a cellular phone company was highlighted. In place of the standard press kit, the company sent out palm-sized kits that included mini–cellular phones. Reporters were given a phone number to call and get free air time. The kits also included the press release, fact sheet, and a computer disk with additional information. Though the total budget for the media release was $75,000, it generated over 40 million media impressions!

Okay, I understand that your promotional plans may not be as grand as this, but it is very important to remember that you need to be creative in order to make your audience pay attention.

In her job as promotions director for a local radio station, Sarah Wong St. John was presented with the challenge of putting together an exciting, creative promotional campaign for a valued client, a Mazda dealership that was anxious to stand out from its competitors. Sarah's first idea was to put a windowless Mazda on the parking lot of the dealership, invite the public to come out and take a swing at it with a baseball bat or sledgehammer. The on-air announcement encouraged listeners to take out their frustrations by beating the car. It

would cost one dollar to engage in the bash, with money
going to a local charity. The event was a "smashing" success.
Her client was so impressed he called Sarah the next week
with a request that they repeat the event, but with some kind
of a twist this time. Sarah got busy thinking and concocted
this plan:

"I invited three charities to put together teams of big mus-
cular people like weightlifters and football players. Next, I
went to a piano dealer, also one of our clients, and asked for
three pianos that were beyond repair. I wanted them delivered to the Mazda dealership parking lot on a Saturday morning. For doing this, I guaranteed the piano dealer on-air promotional mention the day of the event—basically I was
offering commercial time of value equal to the pianos. Next, I
had the car dealership build me a high wall with a twelve-
inch hole near the top. On the wall I plastered tons of radio
station signage. I invited the press to come out. Each charity
team got one piano to bust up, the goal being to break the
piano down into pieces small enough to put through the hole
and the fastest charity team to do this would win a monetary
donation."

The radio station roped off a big area on the parking lot,
encouraged the charities to invite supporters to come out and
cheer, and announced that the Mazda dealership would give
$1,000 for the fastest team, $500 for second place, and a $250
charitable donation for the team that brought out the most
supporters.

The fastest team broke down its piano and stuffed it
through the hole in the wall in fourteen minutes flat. The
excited crowd cheered and roared, its enthusiasm coming
across on live radio coverage. Smashing the pianos and the
cheering crowds all made for a wonderful media event.

"We got fantastic coverage on all of the TV stations," says
Sarah. "It was wild—the ultimate fun radio commercial. Most
of all, it turned out to be a win-win situation for everyone
involved. The monetary investment on the part of the radio
station was very small. All of the clients benefited, leaving
them happy and anxious to continue advertising with us.

After all, this is the bottom line of sales promotion. I don't want clients to buy air time just for today. I want them to become friends and loyal advertisers with my station for the long run."

ATTITUDE ADJUSTMENT TIP #2

Be willing to change.

Our relationship with money is extremely personal and is largely determined by the way we grew up. We have been influenced a great deal by our parents' values and how they handled financial matters. If you grew up in a household where every penny was allocated before it was even earned, you may be very conservative about the way you handle cash. Some people have trouble spending money for anything other than necessities, while others splurge with little restraint, using money to satisfy emotional needs.

Meeting professional goals often involves going into debt. You will need to make an investment in the materials and tools that support your effort to step out. Printing, postage, distribution costs, telephone/communication expenses, a computer, a fax machine, a cellular phone may be necessary for you to meet your objectives. Your wardrobe, professional dues, conference fees, and travel expenses are also routine expenditures related to enhancing visibility. Within these main categories there can be a vast array of additional items that can take little bites out of your promotional budget.

It is always wise to compare costs and get written estimates when starting any project. Shop around, look for special rates or deals that can get you where you want to go. Spend only what you can afford. Don't go into unreasonable debt to impress anyone. It is a good idea to find out what your competition is doing, but don't base your activities on besting someone else. Do what you can. Hang in there. Turn that corner, and the market will begin to notice you.

"When I was going after my first million-dollar loan, I was

terrified," admits radio executive Cathy Hughes, who set out to expand her media empire. "The terms of the loan were frightening. I did not understand why the bank was asking for everything I owned. They wanted my house, my cash, even—it felt like—my firstborn child as security! I didn't know anyone who had ever borrowed a million dollars, so I had no one to turn to for advice. I was worried to death, but I wanted that money to expand my broadcast base. During this stressful time, while driving down Connecticut Avenue in Washington, D.C., I spotted J. Bruce Llewellyn, the chairman and CEO of Philadelphia Coca-Cola Bottling, Inc., walking down the street. I had only read about him in newspapers and magazines, but I knew this man was very comfortable making multimillion-dollar deals. I honked my horn, pulled over to the curb, and hopped out of my car, leaving my keys in it, engine running. Consumed with the need to get advice from Mr. Llewellyn, I chased him down. He must have thought I was nuts, but after he regained his composure and listened, he realized that I was a young entrepreneur who needed his help. He walked me back to my car and spent about fifteen minutes with me, explaining how banks function and what to expect.

"He asked me, 'Do you know anybody who could lend you a million dollars?' I said no. He pressed on, 'If you were about to lend somebody a million dollars, wouldn't *you* want their house?' Then he walked me through the loan process in reverse so that I could see where the bank was coming from. He listened to my business plan and assured me I was going to be okay. I got the loan, and today, from time to time, Mr. Llewellyn calls to check in on me and see how I am doing. When I needed advice in those early days, he was there for me, just as he is today."

Polish Skills via Conferences and Seminars

If you are in a supervisory position or on the fast track to upper management within your company, a major segment of your budget should be directed toward training and professional development. Yes, conference attendance can be costly, even if your company is picking up most of the tab, but don't cringe at the thought of spending thousands of your own dollars to join a gathering of like-minded professionals. Instead, focus on the end result that such exposure can provide. If you are self-employed, these costs are tax-deductible.

Each year, decide which conferences will best serve *you* and your company's objectives. Talk to others who have attended in the past to determine whether going will be worthwhile.

Scrutinize the Program

- Who are the workshop leaders and speakers?

- Are they people who are willing to act as mentors?

- Can you include them in your professional network?

- What can they offer that you cannot access locally?

- Who are the participants likely to be?

- Are they members of your target audience?

- Can they be instrumental in enhancing your career path or business?

- Is the conference location one in which you can do independent promotion or networking, making the most of the time and money you spend?

- Is the hotel a full-service hotel with fax, computer lines, and other amenities so that you can stay in touch with your office or continue working on a project?

If you decide to attend a conference, go with the intention of participating fully, getting maximum results for your expenditure.

When I go to a conference, I always take lots of business cards, appropriate promotional materials, and even a few press kits. Steppin' out with attitude can be extremely labor-intensive, requiring me to continually come up with creative tactics to generate the most return from each dollar I spend. It is vital to have attractive, easy-to-read, professional-looking promotional materials, but that doesn't mean you have to go for broke with four-color brochures and fancy designs. Publicity photos, business cards, stationery, press kit supplies, and marketing information are a big part of your budget, so be practical. If paying for some of these items seems to be beyond your budget, there are other ways you can get them:

- Barter.

- Offer in-kind services in return for the item you need.

- Engage in time-sharing.

- Do volunteer or community-based work to access products, services, equipment.

When I needed artwork for a logo for an organization I was working with, I approached a local art school and found a student who was very talented, excited, and capable of designing the logo for us in exchange for the exposure she would get. Seek talented people who are hungry. Give them an opportunity to shine.

On the Road

When estimating out your promotional costs, remember to factor in the cost of a good set of luggage, clothing that travels well, and the services of professionals for personal grooming (hair, nails, skin). Attention to grooming reflects the importance you give to creating a positive impression, an important visibility factor. Purchase the highest-quality items you can afford, but don't worry about buying designer names or trendy brands. My luggage comes from J. C. Penney and I receive many compliments on it whenever I travel, plus it has held up very well during all of my trips—including arduous international treks to Spain, Egypt, and China. Personal organizers, briefcases, laptop computers, and small electronics that make you more efficient must hold up under continuous use, so invest in the best you can find.

In many professions, extensive travel is the only way to get your name on the lips of those in power. Good-quality but also comfortable clothing is a must if you are in the spotlight. Moving up in professional circles doesn't mean keeping up with others, but it does mean maintaining the kinds of standards that generate a competitive advantage. With care and attention, you will learn to make good choices, creating a great impression within your budget.

A POSITIVE FORCE

Smack dab in the middle of a huge suburban mall in Houston, Texas, is BabyPace, the only "Hallmark-type" store for African-Americans in the city. The inventory, carefully selected by the owner, Darleane Pace, includes black figurines, dolls, books, cards, and unusual gift items from around the world. "I always wanted to own a business and to do something for my community that would stand out," says Darleane, a spirited entrepreneur with a mission to give black people positive images of themselves. "When I was young, there were no Mother's Day or Christmas cards with people who looked like my family. I was determined to change that."

Darleane comes from an entrepreneurial family that has owned a plumbing business for forty-two years. After graduating from college in 1987, she worked for Dun & Bradstreet in Los Angeles as a business analyst. Her job was to analyze efficiency as well as solvency, read financial statements, and assess the credibility of Fortune 500 companies. This gave her an opportunity to analyze the ethnic market, a fast-growing portion of the consumer base that she knew was underserved. This was also very good training in the financial aspects of running a business.

In 1992 she launched BabyPace, at that time selling at trade shows and professional conferences. At first she worked out of her home; then she tried a mail-order catalogue, but that didn't work very well. She tried the Internet and discovered that it was not profitable for her. Darleane says, "Less than thirty percent of African-Americans go on-line to buy things. For us, shopping is a social event. We want to spend time with friends. This goes back to how black people value time."

Finally, Darleane decided to open her store in a mall. When she sought funding, banks quickly turned her down. "They considered my concept risky," she says. "Putting my store in the mainstream mall was considered a novelty and there were no statistics or trends for them to analyze. Those white men were afraid to give me a loan." She studied demographics of the city to find the area populated by her ideal customer. "At First Colony Mall, the consumer profile matched my objectives," she says. "I wanted to place the store in the mall, instead of the community at large, in order to gain maximum visibility and provide easy access for my customer base."

In order to get the kind of funding she needed, Darleane knew she had to find a creative way of getting what she wanted. This is what she did. "I applied for a substantial amount from the Small Business Administration. When they called to tell me I had been granted what I considered pennies, I knew something had to give. I decided to become really visible. I made a personal call to my SBA loan officer's boss. It was a conference call with myself and my accountant. I talked from my heart on why I deserved the loan. I told the SBA supervisor that I had two degrees, I was from a family of entrepreneurs, I had worked for Dun & Bradstreet, and I also schooled him on why it was important that he grant *me* more money. I was not just a name on a loan application. I had to get really personal. I told him I am a black woman who does not want to depend on the system for a livelihood. I have the ability to train other young women in business to keep them out of the system, as well. Please, help us!"

The supervisor called Darleane back two hours later and told her she would get $21,000 more than she had applied for. BabyPace was born! Darleane Pace was a sister smart enough to know that her background alone would not sell her dream. She had to let those in power know who she was, what her goals were, and where she fit into a much larger picture.

With help from her parents and the Small Business Administration, she eventually opened her store in the mall on the day after Thanksgiving, one of the busiest shopping days of the year. Once open, Darleane didn't change her mission—to expose people, especially African-Americans, to beautiful black products. Darleane says that her best asset is her personality and her honesty. She says she is a regular person with a sincere desire to help others. Sales are motivated by her customers' trust in her.

"We are descendants of kings and queens. We need to feel good about ourselves, see ourselves as beautiful. My gift items relate to that. I want to give back to the community and to train young girls to be self-sufficient, providing exposure and options for them. Blacks need to teach young people to consider owning their own business as a real possibility. One of my favorite books is *Sister CEO* by Cheryl Broussard. Reading this book gave me the power and courage to call myself a CEO. Traditionally we have not done this, but I am a sister CEO who is just as important as the head of IBM."

With minimum advertising Darleane Pace has managed to surpass her financial goals and is planning to expand. Here are a few of the community-focused promotional activities that helped spread the word about her shop:

- She hosted Felicia (Mrs. Warren) Moon in the store to read children's books. This brought parents in, too.

- She snagged the motivational speaker Les Brown to do a book signing, a major coup that paid off handsomely.

- During Black History Month, Darleane held special events every weekend.

- American Express came in and conducted a financial planning seminar for black professionals.

- The Links, a socially conscious sister group, came to the

store on Take Your Daughter to Work Day and sponsored a personal-development and self-esteem seminar.

- Darleane held a black puppet show in the store.

- She regularly spotlights local artists and authors (like me), creating a festive ambience in the store.

"I've had tremendous response," Darleane says. "The black community is a four-hundred-billion-dollar consumer and I am glad to be a part of this resurgence in ethnic pride."

WHEN YOU NEED TO GO TO THE BANK

Angela Caraway, who works in the executive banking department of Nations Bank, recommends that you have the following items available *before you go to the bank* to apply for a loan:

- Tax returns for the past two to three years.

- A personal financial statement worksheet showing personal net worth, based on your liabilities and assets.

- Your business plan, including a mission statement, goals, and financial projections for one year. See "Recommended Reading and Resources" for books and sources to guide you in creating a business plan.

- The planned legal form of your business, e.g., corporation, sole proprietorship, professional association, nonprofit organization.

- Breakdown of how funds are to be allocated.

- Cash-flow worksheet.

- Sources for repayment of loans.

- Debt-to-income ratio. A bank will not lend to you if the loan means you would spend more than 30 percent of your income to pay debts.

Banks consider a variety of conditions when deciding whether or not to lend money.

- *Credit history and character.* Are you an honest person? Does your credit report reflect your sense of responsibility?

- *Collateral.* What can you put up to ensure repayment of the loan?

- *Experience.* Are you capable of running the business you propose?

- *Equity.* How much of your own money are you willing to put up?

- *Potential growth.* Is your industry on the upswing or beginning to fade?

Be prepared to supply all of the information requested in order to satisfy the loan officer's requirements.

LOW-COST PROMOTION

There are many ways to promote your service or product that cost very little and produce great results. Spend some time and energy doing a little research. Start with local outlets that cost nothing and are designed to serve the community. Here are just a few possibilities that don't cost much that will get you started.

- Word-of-mouth. Grass-roots efforts are highly effective if you continually work at it. Engage your family, close friends, and coworkers, asking them to spread the word.

- Use posters, fliers at bus stops and on lampposts, and postings on bulletin boards in places where your target audience gathers.

- Place notices and announcements in community, religious, university, and special-interest publications.

- Offer to speak at meetings of groups that share your interests.

- Write articles for newsletters of local chapters of national organizations.

- Appear at fairs, bazaars, expos, and seasonal events.

- Volunteer at schools, churches, social service organizations, and on career days.

- Inform owners of bookstores and specialty shops of your product/service.

- Conduct free seminars, workshops, informal chats—anywhere you are invited.

- Write a column or feature story for audience-targeted publications.

- Create your own newsletter and distribute it free.

- Make on-line postings in appropriate Web sites.

- Join social organizations that have regular functions that provide opportunities to network.

- Always carry business cards and brochures that explain what you do. Hand them out!

- Join forces with a sister who has a business that is similar to yours but not in direct competition. Pool your resources to place an ad, pay for exhibit space, or travel together to a conference.

ATTITUDE ADJUSTMENT TIP #3

Perception is everything.

Act and live as if you have already "arrived." Stop complaining about being broke and talking about what you *can't* afford. It's a bad habit that wears thin very fast. Nothing is more of a turnoff than someone who "poor-mouths" all the time. Make a personal commitment to shatter the stereotype that all African-Americans have financial problems. *We don't.* Neither did all of us come out of the ghetto or just get off welfare.

When money is scarce or even nonexistent, put on your creative thinking cap, keep a smile on your face, and concentrate on finding alternative methods of getting what you need. Don't lie about your resources, but do not volunteer unsolicited information. A successful image speaks volumes for you, and a positive attitude inspires positive reactions.

You've captured the spotlight. You are pleased with the delivery and results of your efforts. Your dream is coming true. But you want your hard work to pay off financially, right? If the money you dreamed of earning is not materializing as you'd hoped, don't panic. It will come, I assure you, though success certainly cannot be measured simply in dollars and cents. Examine your definition of wealth. It may now be very different from what you first thought.

INFORMATION ON SECURING FINANCING

Small Business Administration, Office of Women's Business Ownership, 800–8ASK-SBA.

Web address: www.sbaonline.sba.gov/womeninbusiness

Directory of Venture Capital: 630 Venture Capital Firms, by Catherine E. Lester and Thomas D. Harnish (John Wiley, 1996).

Women's World Banking, 212–768–8513.
E-mail address: wwb@igc.abc.org

Women's Collateral Worldwide, Inc., 215–564–2800.

13

Common Ground

Attitude Focus: Creating Connections That Work
Nothing outshines a woman who dares to be herself.

ANGLE S. BUSH

*I*t is estimated that over 30 million business cards are exchanged every day. As the most common form of self-promotion, a business card is the easiest and least expensive way to make your presence known and make sure you can be found. Can you remember the color or design of a sister's card as soon as you hear her name? It happens to me quite often. When I am searching my Rolodex for a particular contact, I easily zero in on the cards that made a statement and left an impression.

The business cards you circulate become an extension of your image, so take care to design one that reflects the identity you desire. Also, please keep a *fresh* supply with you and easily accessible at all times. Nothing is more exasperating (and unprofessional) than the sister who fumbles around in her purse trying to dig out a card, and when she finally finds one, it is a smudged, dog-eared scrap of paper. This is a sign that this sister does not take the art of networking very seriously.

ASK!

In every networking situation, circulate among the group with the supreme confidence that you belong, you can relate to those present, and you have something of importance to offer. Don't be afraid to ask questions if you are in unfamiliar territory. Most people want you to feel comfortable, so don't be afraid to ask for help!

ATTITUDE ADJUSTMENT TIP #1

Don't let the unknown frighten you.

I've stayed in five-star hotels around the world and been wined and dined by foreign dignitaries. I've partied with movie stars, joked with celebrity authors, and been honored right alongside wealthy socialites. I consider these kinds of opportunities as wonderful adventures that broaden my understanding of others and heighten my belief that we are human first and share common desires of wanting to feel needed and valued. In unfamiliar territory, relax, be observant, and learn from those around you.

In November 1989, the one thousand copies of my self-published book, *Emily, the Yellow Rose,* were finally delivered to my home. This was a day I had looked forward to for so long, but instead of rejoicing after the books arrived, I began to panic. The enormity of my project was suddenly very real. What in the world had I been thinking of to take on such a monumental task? I knew I had to get busy and sell those books fast to avert a financial and emotional disaster.

I contacted local African-American booksellers, who were very happy to place my novel on their shelves. However, I wanted to get into the mainstream bookstores, too, because I knew my book had great crossover potential, especially among Texans. I have to admit, I was hesitant about approaching the white booksellers with my African-American romantic tale.

I recalled the offer of Barbara, a good friend and colleague who was then co-owner of a bookstore in an exclusive mostly white area of Houston called River Oaks. This is the upscale neighborhood of mansions where former President Bush and Mrs. Bush now reside, not a place that reflects a multicultural residency. I had met Barbara through my membership in the River Oaks Business Women's Exchange Club, where at the time I was the only African-American member. It is a wonderful organization of local businesswomen who help each other do better business. When Barbara learned about my book, she read the manuscript, loved the story, and expressed interest in carrying it in her bookstore. I figured I had nothing to lose by reminding her of her offer, so I called and told her the books were in. She graciously agreed to place six copies in the front window of the River Oaks Bookstore. If they sold, she said she'd mail me a check. If they didn't, I could pick up the books!

I didn't feel very hopeful after leaving her store. After all, how many copies of my African-American historical novel did I really think she'd sell? I decided to view her gesture as one of support, and was glad to have one more placement for my work. But as I drove away, I began to consider how valuable Barbara's support really was and I began to calculate how to use this placement to better my chances of distributing my book.

A few streets over, I stopped in at another independent bookstore, went in, and introduced myself to the manager, a white male. His reception to my pitch was definitely cool. I could tell he was not enthusiastic about carrying my ethnic tale. He said he knew what his clientele liked and doubted he'd be able to move any copies. I rushed to tell him that the River Oaks Bookstore was carrying my novel and had placed it in the window. His expression changed. He was obviously surprised and immediately decided to take twelve copies on consignment. I left there feeling much more confident about my marketing tactics and headed into another store.

That day, the interest and enthusiasm I was able to generate got the momentum rolling as I confidently worked my way across Houston, citing the names of the independent bookstores now carrying my book. Piggybacking the commitment of each successive bookseller onto the next provided fuel to help me sell myself and my product with confidence. By the end of the day, my trunk was nearly empty and I had conquered my fear of entering unknown territory.

After meeting me, booksellers began to inquire about scheduling in-store book signings and speaking engagements. They were fascinated and impressed with my ability to market myself and wanted to do all they could to help me succeed. Plus, the book was selling well! One month after my initial store visit, all one thousand copies had been sold and I had orders for hundreds more! Soon, write-ups in the local papers and interviews on community TV shows helped spread the word. Over the next three years, thousands of books were sold this way.

It is important to value your colleagues' ability to help spread the word, even if they are not of your background or race. While they support you, you are supporting them. Don't overlook the resources that are easily within your reach.

TALK!

ATTITUDE ADJUSTMENT TIP #2

Work the room!

Recently I was the keynote speaker for a luncheon honoring the contestants in the Ms. Black Metroplex USA competition. Since I was speaking to women who had already proved that they knew how to step out and highlight their skills and talent, I talked about my belief that having an attitude of gratitude can create momentum and positively impact the success of one's personal promotional campaign. I did not talk about books or my writing career, but focused on inspirational stories to illustrate my point.

During the reception that followed, a young lady from the West Coast came up to me and said that she had read a review of my latest book, *Balancing Act*, in the *San Francisco Chronicle* and had seen it in the bookstores, but so far had not been motivated to purchase it. But she admitted that after hearing me speak and learning about my commitment to personal growth and my passion for excellence, she could not wait to get it. This is a typical reaction to my presentations. I am sure there were other sisters at the luncheon whom I inspired to check out my novels. Speaking before groups is a very high priority and it pays off in ways I may never realize.

If you approach receptions, seminars, happy hours, and mixers as more than opportunities to listen to a lecture, nibble hors d'oeuvres, and sip white wine, you will increase your chances of broadening your field of valuable contacts.

I am convinced that the "six degrees of separation" theory is true. According to this theory, any two people in the world are connected by a chain of no more than six people who know each other or whose lives intersect in some way. Without fail, if I talk to someone long enough, we eventually exchange sufficient information to discover common interests. Religious, fraternal, community, and educational affiliations can serve as starting points in a conversation that can lead to establishing the type of bond that brings social or professional circles closer.

I faithfully attend our public library's used-book sale every year. Last year, I was surprised to see Dawn, the real estate agent who had negotiated the deal on my house ten years ago, working the book sale as a volunteer. Dawn is an energetic woman with whom I had enjoyed touring homes for almost a year as my husband and I searched for the perfect house. She was so glad to see me, and said that she had been following my writing career in the papers. She expressed her delight with my success as an author and quickly informed me that she was president of a nationally recognized service organization that held book discussions once a month at her home. Her club had just been discussing one of my books for its next selection!

It hit me that I had never considered getting to know Dawn personally while we were house-hunting together. I had sat in the front seat of her car for many long hours riding around town without learning about her interests beyond selling real estate. I was flattered that her group wanted me to visit them, and accepted her invitation to attend a meeting where the members discussed *Black Gold*. It turned out to be a fantastic evening of lively interaction with a variety of women, broadening my network and initiating invitations to attend similar meetings throughout the city.

This experience was an eye-opener that taught me a valuable lesson: Don't allow the professional face a sister shows the world to define the scope of her life. If you block your mind to what someone is beyond her role as a manager, homemaker, administrator, nurse, teacher, author, or politician, you cheat yourself of an opportunity to find out what she values, does outside of work, likes to read, and finds enjoyable. Get to know your sisters better. They are truly multifaceted.

EXERCISE

1. Go through your Rolodex or address book and make a list of *friends*, people you would not hesitate to call at home anytime—on the weekend, early morning, late at night. These are the foot soldiers in your campaign.
2. Make another list of acquaintances you would feel comfortable calling by first name if you called them at their office during business hours. These are supporters in your campaign. They will help if it is possible and convenient for them.
3. Make a third list of those you do not know well, but who you feel are potentially valuable. They represent growth and expansion for your network.

4. Beside each name, write as much of the following as possible:

    *   Profession/area of expertise—attorney, graphic designer, computer programmer, university professor, etc.

    *   Memberships/professional organizations—Black Lawyers Association, Black Journalists, Women in Television and Radio.

    *   Hobbies—tennis, gardening, collecting antique books.

    *   Religious affiliation.

    *   Memberships in social or fraternal organizations— Alpha Kappa Alpha, NAACP, Girl Scouts, Red Cross, Coalition of 100 Black Women.

    *   Skills/talents—organizing parties, cooking, flower arranging, writing, singing.

As you look at your lists, you may realize that you have taken your friends and colleagues for granted, failing to learn important things about people with whom you interact on a regular basis. With some creative planning, I am sure you can find ways to better utilize *and serve* the network you uncover through this exercise.

Last year, while waiting for a taxi in front of a hotel in Dallas, I was chatting with a sister after coming out of a meeting. We talked about how great the presentation had been and exchanged business cards. She worked as a manager for a computer company. I told her I was an author, but my cab arrived before I could tell her much more. We parted, promising to stay in touch.

By the time I got home to Houston, I had forgotten the conversation. But the sister had already faxed me, letting me know that she had gone directly to the bookstore when she got home, asked the bookseller to recommend one of my books, and had selected *Starlight Passage* to be featured that week in her sisters' reading and discussion group. You never know what a casual conversation will produce.

ATTITUDE ADJUSTMENT TIP #3
Learn the lingo of your profession.

"Learning the language of your industry is very, very important if you want to attract the kinds of people you will need to accomplish objectives," says Vanesse Lloyd-Sgambati, literary consultant and owner of The Literary, a promotion and marketing firm that specializes in enhancing the visibility of African-American authors. Vanesse began her career in Rome, where she worked for an English-language radio station called the Voice of the Daily American; her job was hosting the program *In the News*. When the station owner asked her to write a fashion/gossip column for his newspaper, she jumped at the chance, gaining extensive experience as a journalist, which she planned to put to good use on her return to the States.

"Once I was back home, I began working in radio on a magazine-format show called *PM Magazine*, booking a lot of authors," says Vanesse. "When the show was canceled, many of the publicists at the publishing houses continued to call, asking me to help them out with promotion for their authors. I said, sure—if you can pay me. These connections led to my starting my own company to do book events. Because of my experience and journalism background, I survived and am celebrating my fifth anniversary in business. Many of my colleagues who started out when I did are not doing well, but I believe that my business continued to increase because I never took on more than I could handle. I learned the language within the network I was accessing. If you don't know the language, you will not succeed. I have worked in radio, television, and print. I know how to communicate with key players to get the publicity I need for my clients. Keeping a successful venture alive takes energy and knowing what to say and how to say it, along with an ability to transition to new levels. Most people don't prioritize, specialize, or focus. They simply drift from project to project. The specialist who becomes entrenched in her industry and knows what she is talking about will attract the people she needs."

GET CONNECTED!

It is your responsibility to make the most of structured events that pull together people who share interests, backgrounds, or professions. The benefits you get from attending conferences and meetings are directly connected to the effort you are willing to put into making introductions pay off.

No one can do your networking for you. This is not something you can delegate. Sending a representative from your office or a friend to gather material is not going to bring the results that actually being there would generate. The greatest benefit of personally meeting new people is the sense of immediate connection that occurs as soon as you shake hands. This personal encounter raises expectations, creating a sense of anticipation that a mutually beneficial relationship will develop. Even if your conversations are brief, the knowledge that you have had a face-to-face, one-on-one conversation imparts a sense of accomplishment and strengthens your commitment to stay in touch.

Sarah Wong St. John says that her mother, who came to America as a war bride, always encouraged her daughter to do whatever she wanted. "My parents were both born in China and are very old-fashioned," says Sarah, a ten-year veteran in the field of radio promotion. "When growing up, if I spoke up or spoke out, it was construed as being smart-alecky, impolite, not respecting of my elders. I know these were the old-fashioned values designed to keep women in their place, but luckily my mother was a bit of a risk taker. She never made me believe that anything would be held back from me because of my race or heritage. She said, 'If you want to do that, you go ahead, and if you don't succeed it will not be because of how you look or who you are.'"

As Sarah moved ahead in the communications field, she became very socially active, joining a variety of professional organizations to further her career. "Often I was the only

Chinese person in the club or the organization, but that never bothered me. Here is my plan. It worked for me and I want to pass these tips on to those who join organizations in order to boost visibility.

"After joining a professional association, I immediately volunteer to be on the hospitality committee. This way I get to meet the members when they show up and I circulate among the group, helping members get to know each other. The next year, I will volunteer to be program chairperson. In that position, I know I will be able to stand before the group and introduce the speaker, getting everyone's undivided attention. From those positions, the presidency is next, and I have to say that I became the president of every organization I ever joined."

In addition to her radio career, Sarah is an actress who performs regularly in community theater, and she currently serves as the commercial director for Country Playhouse Theater in Houston. She does admit that her Chinese heritage—the strict training in self-restraint and modesty—makes it difficult for her to tell people about her acting and to encourage them to come out and see her perform. However, she is learning how to do it without sounding self-conscious or conceited, a tricky balance that keeps her very conscious of the manner in which she actively promotes the theater as well as her part in the production.

COURT THE CONTACTS YOU NEED

Networking within specific target groups can be both challenging and exciting. Across the country, expos, seminars, and conferences and reunions are held that are designed especially for African-Americans, Hispanics, Asians, gays and lesbians, Baptists, and other ethnic, religious, or cultural groups in specific industries or fields.

Use creative and fun ways to seek out the famous, high-profile, or inspirational people who will fuel you with energy to press on with your journey. Write to them and introduce yourself, then go to their book signings, speeches, or seminars and meet them. Previous correspondence gives you a starting point to engage the person in conversation. I have been in crowded rooms where a high-profile person whom I wanted to meet is surrounded by a crush of people. I have found it pays off to be patient and observant and to take advantage of opportunities to introduce yourself when the hoopla dies down. I have to admit that the ladies' room or standing in a corridor waiting for an elevator or in front of a hotel waiting for valet parking has provided opportune moments for me to engage a high-profile person in conversation when I have a better chance of holding the person's attention and of being remembered.

Joanne Harris, editor of *American Visions* magazine, was able to snag an interview with a very high-profile television personality because she was willing to take a big risk.

"While attending a conference in Florida," she says, "I noticed Bryant Gumbel getting into a golf cart, starting out onto the course to play. I had been trying, with no success, to get to him because I wanted to do an in-depth piece on him for the magazine. I knew I had to take a chance and approach him at that moment. I commandeered a golf cart and followed him out onto the green, praying he would not think I was some crazed fan who was stalking him. At an appropriate moment, I got out of the cart, walked over to him, and introduced myself. After I stated my request, he was very congenial and somewhat amused. I think he was impressed that I had taken such initiative to speak directly to him. He took my card, immediately agreeing to do the piece. He kept his promise and delivered when I contacted him later. I have to admit that I was very relieved and happy that everything worked out as I had hoped."

I am continually amazed and pleased at how accessible and polite the majority of "important" people can be. When I began my research for this book, I went through issues of *Essence, Black Enterprise, Today's Black Woman, Jet, Ebony, Emerge*, and other publications looking for stories about sisters who were steppin' out. I sent them letters, congratulating them on having been profiled in the magazines, introduced myself, and invited them to share. Many of the stories you have read here came from ladies I had never met, but they accepted my invitation to make a contribution.

In the early 1980s I read in the local paper that my idol, the author Alex Haley, was coming to Houston for a very high-powered social event that few outsiders could get into. The announcement also stated that he would hold a news conference to talk about his book *Roots*, for the media only, at a major hotel downtown. I wanted so badly just to meet him, shake his hand, and let him know how much I admired him! What to do?

I hurriedly used my typewriter to construct what I hoped looked like an official press pass, along with credentials to back them up. This was desperation in action! I drove to the hotel, strode importantly across the lobby, flashed my home-made ID at the concierge, and was directed into the press room. Terrified, I sat in the first row with my back to the TV cameras and the reporters. When Mr. Haley finished talking and asked for questions, I could hardly believe I had the nerve to ask about his writing schedule. He was happy to answer. I asked more questions about the life of an author. He was gracious, charming, and inspiring.

When the press briefing ended, he walked over to me and invited me to accompany him to the elevator. He asked, "Are you an aspiring writer? You sounded like one." I confessed my ruse. He laughed and shook my hand, inviting me to stay in touch. That began a correspondence that was very special to me. I have one of his letters framed and hanging on the wall of my office.

THE TEN COMMANDMENTS OF NETWORKING

In her book, *About My Sister's Business: The Black Woman's Road Map to Successful Entrepreneurship* (Simon & Schuster/Fireside, 1996), Fran Harris gives her sisters excellent advice on how to successfully make contact with individuals who can help raise visibility and meet objectives. Here are Fran's ten commandments of networking:

1. Thou shalt have specific networking goals in mind before the event.
2. Thou shalt carry business cards everywhere you go.
3. Thou shalt not spend more than five minutes with one person or group.
4. Thou shalt describe your business in thirty seconds or less.
5. Thou shalt be well groomed.
6. Thou shalt appear as eager to give a referral as to receive one.
7. Thou shalt act like you're the hostess, not the guest.
8. Thou shalt write comments on the business cards you collect.
9. Thou shalt ask questions and listen intently.
10. Thou shalt follow up and follow through.

Keep Track of Your Contacts

Acquiring contacts to add to your networking circle is a futile exercise unless you develop and maintain a tracking system that allows you to access them as needed. I maintain two Rolodex files. One is personal, which also includes professionals whom I call on a Regular basis, like my agent, editor, and fellow authors. The second Rolodex is for industry and media contacts (newspaper, TV, radio and special publications) whom I know will take my calls immediately. This includes those who help sell and promote books: booksellers, graphic designers, members of writers' organizations, libraries, museums, sisters' reading clubs, cultural organizations, etc.

Computerize Your Contacts

In addition to my Rolodexes, I maintain several computerized databases of media people and other individuals who belong to or serve my target audience. These are contacts I make to promote an event, launch a new title, or solicit speaking engagements.

When I sat down for my first book signing, nine years ago,

I had the foresight to place a notepad on the table and invite those who bought my book to become a part of my mailing list. I also photocopied every check I was given, even if it came by mail. Every sister who has requested a copy of my newsletter, *Sisters of the Word,* has been added to my list, and that practice continues to this day. Wherever I go, I make sure I bring home new names to add to my lists. The result is a database of fans that is edging close to four thousand— names of people across the country who make up my target audience. By mailing to everyone at least once a year I am able to maintain fairly clean lists that are extremely valuable when a new book comes out.

After attending an event where I've smiled and chatted for hours, I enjoy going through the many business cards that I collect, making annotations on the back. Something as simple as "black dress, mayor's office" or "has contacts with the Artists' Collective" will prompt my memory about whom I've met and what new resources I have acquired. This is a habit I stick to, even if it is late at night. If I wait until the next day, I may lose a valuable contact. These names go directly into my database.

I consider a computerized database of contacts an indispensable vehicle for developing relationships that go a long way toward increasing visibility. Using the computer for online discussions in chat rooms, on message boards, and other interactive sites will also give you access to networking twenty-four hours a day. Cruising the information superhighway is a popular way of making valuable connections that reach across the globe. Accessing some hook-ups will require subscription fees, while others, like *Net Noir* and *Prodigy's Black Experience Bulletin Boards,* can be accessed via your service provider.

Find an easy way to keep on top of the results of your networking efforts. It will pay off over and over.

Stay Informed

If you plan to do active networking you must be able to enter a circle of conversation and make a valid contribution. If you lack background knowledge or experience in the subject under discussion, you may feel somewhat timid about speaking up. Don't let information paralysis keep your mouth shut. Get busy and broaden your scope of knowledge.

Action Steps

1. Subscribe to (or go to the library each month and read) the leading African-American, Hispanic, Asian, or special-interest publications.
2. Get up-to-date on relevant "hot" topics that are currently in the mainstream news.
3. Know what's going on within your community/target audience that would interest someone from outside.
4. Decide where you stand on controversial issues that might be discussed among colleagues. Examples are affirmative action, pending legislation affecting illegal immigrants, abortion rights.
5. Understand your industry, as well as its competition.
6. Join volunteer organizations where you can serve as well as learn.

Start with your local library to find leads to source information that will help you stay well informed. R. R. Bowker publishes *American Library Directory*, a volume that can help you access specialty libraries across the country. Talk with your librarian to find other ways to get the information you want. My visit turned up these titles.

Need information about the federal government? Try the following:

Who Knows: A Guide to Washington Experts
Washington Researchers
2612 P Street NW
Washington, DC 20007

Need to access an information service? This will lead you to services that collect statistics and information.

Information Sources
Information Industry Associations
555 New Jersey Avenue
Washington, DC 20001

Want to access a database that contains names you need?

Directory of On-line Databases
Gale Research
835 Penobscott Building
Detroit, MI 48226

Looking for a publication that addresses a specific topic? Try this directory:

The Standard Periodical Directory
Oxbridge Communications
150 Fifth Avenue, Suite 236
New York, NY 10011

By making it a priority to continue to gather resources and names of people to add to my network, I have managed to put together a valuable tool. I utilize and guard my lists just as any corporation would, but I also share my resources when appropriate, too.

14

The Glare of the Spotlight

Attitude Focus: Attracting Media Attention
The media are big business. Television and radio stations are
not in the business of making you successful, but of making
their companies successful. First and foremost, they respond to
ringing cash registers.

CATHY HUGHES, CEO, RADIO ONE, INC.

"*T*he biggest misconception black women have about media is that it is there to help them," says the media mogul Cathy Hughes. "Yes, the station managers are out to help—help themselves. The media is not going to come running to your door to make you a success. What's in it for them? Sisters must understand the nature of the beast. The bottom line is, you get what you pay for. The surest way to promote your business is to buy advertising time. This allows you to present your own interpretation of who you are and what your company is about. You have control and it opens doors for your target audience to view you as a professional, even if you only spent a small amount for your promotion. Media is protective of its client base, it needs to be to survive, so when you place an ad, you also acquire an advocate. My feeling is, you can't afford *not* to advertise your service, product, etc."

However, if the funds just aren't there to buy time, Cathy advises sisters to cultivate the media. Get it down to an art form. Don't sit in your store and expect to hear from the media. Get out and connect. You can support organizations, associations, pay membership dues, and make valuable connections.

"Once a month I do a free two-hour block of commercial time for small businesses on my AM station," says Cathy. "People call in and I give them ninety seconds to talk about their businesses. This is my way of thanking the Lord that I was able to grow from an itsy-bitsy AM radio station to where I am today. I am probably the only AM station in the country that does this."

ATTITUDE ADJUSTMENT TIP #1

Join forces.

Jackie Richmond had been working for the University of Maryland for an adult education think tank, when she created a newsletter called *Serendipity*. When a colleague of Jackie's asked if she could pass Jackie's résumé along to the president of a consulting agency, Jackie agreed.

"At that time, I didn't even know what a consulting agency was," Jackie admits. "When my friend came back, she informed me that the president of the agency was interested in talking to me and was going to call me that night. I didn't think anything about it, but he did call and said he had an opening for a writer for a high-blood-pressure project. I was shocked but pleased. When I began working for the consulting firm, I didn't know anything, but I was open to learning. That's how I got into the field of health-care services."

Jackie, who now works for an international public relations firm in Washington, D.C., does social marketing, target-ing health messages to specific audiences. She feels that her best asset, besides her writing talent, is her ability to pay attention to what the situation is and figure out the best way to approach the problem, often, she admits, from a common-sense perspective. "You must know what people are seeing and hearing through the media," she says. "Being able to lis-ten, having a certain amount of sensitivity to the issue, and remaining open to normal media outlets is important. I ask myself, 'What are the people taking away from what is already out there?' Sometimes you have to insinuate yourself into an already cluttered field, so I try to find a niche and fill in a gap. To do this I may have to use a spokesperson nobody else has used."

When a local group did a public service announcement (PSA) for breast cancer and mammography awareness with Angela Bassett as the spokesperson, Jackie's firm took notice. "Our company had already developed a general-audience PSA with a breast cancer awareness message. The local group didn't have enough funding to really promote their PSA, and it was getting limited exposure. My firm decided to work with this local group to expand the promotion of the piece with Ms. Bassett. Our goal was to get more air time, especially since she was in *Waiting to Exhale* and it was hot, and since our message was targeted to the African-American community. We felt Angela Bassett was a critical spokesperson, and if she was on TV, people would stop and listen. By taking advantage of something that already existed and joining forces with another group, we were successful. We also made copies available for showing during the Black Caucus Weekend, held in D.C., and got even more exposure."

ADVERTISING

It is best to use the services of a professional advertising agency if you plan to do commercial advertising on television. Even if you are going to make your own commercial for a local cable program, it is wise to consult a professional to keep your commercial from sounding and looking cheap and unprofessional. Lighting, sound, and set design are important factors in creating the type of message that reflects your business or product. Shop around. Ask colleagues who have used professionals for references. Because of the expenses you will incur, you want to make sure your message is properly formatted and will make a positive impact on the audience you have targeted. Advertising professionals can provide high-quality technical support in the creation of your product, demographic data to shape your message, and marketing input to help you get the most from your money.

Reaching the middle-income African-American consumer is the full-time job of Janis P. Thomas, executive vice president of brand marketing and licensing for Black Entertainment Holdings, Inc. (BET). In her high-profile position with the only black-owned and -operated publicly traded company on the New York Stock Exchange, Janis is at the center of one of the fastest-growing media-entertainment companies in the United States.

"This middle-income black consumer has been underrepresented and undertargeted by mainstream marketers," she says. "BET set out to change this. As the chief marketing officer for branded products, I am responsible for merchandising development and sales in BET's theme restaurants, called BET Soundstage, as well as overseeing the BET Design Studio to produce a branded line of retail clothing. We know our target audience very well and are reaching out to that consumer with disposable income who purchases branded products."

During her fourteen years with Black Entertainment Television, Janis has helped the company grow into the giant entertainment entity it is today. "I started out at WRC-TV and WTTG-TV in Washington, D.C., doing on-air work. I soon found that I wanted to be behind the scenes, making things happen." With her master's degree in mass communications from Howard University, Janis was well equipped to become a part of the original BET staff. "When the company was small, I had room to make mistakes and grow," says Janis.

"These were really opportunities to learn. I always went about my job with the attitude that I was ready and willing to do my part, no matter what job I was given."

If the idea of approaching a TV producer makes you nervous, remember, your community cable and/or university-based stations, as well as the local affiliates, are required to do a certain amount of community programming and are anxious to spotlight local talent, if you have something interesting and newsworthy to talk about. Creative strategies abound to access your target audience, whether you initiate the coverage or the television producers contact you. Here are various ways of getting television coverage:

- Breaking news coverage. You may be the center of a hot news item covered by a TV station (not arranged in advance).

- A televised press conference. If your or your company's news is worthy of coverage, an advance notice to the media will bring them out to hear what you have to say.

- A televised debate. If you are on a panel or team that is debating a controversial topic, your debate may get media coverage, especially on local cable stations. Universities, religious institutions, and high-profile nonprofit agencies often hold such debates.

- An arranged interview.

- A woman-on-the-street opinion survey.

- An instructional program.

- An infomercial.

- A video news release.

- A paid commercial.

- A public service announcement.

- A feature or special-interest story.

TWELVE STEPS TO GETTING ON TV . . . AND GETTING INVITED BACK

Denise Y. Bunkley (my sister-in-law), a twenty-year veteran of broadcast production, is currently the producer-writer for an entertainment and talk program on the CBS affiliate in Dallas, Texas. Her experience as a producer, media relations counselor, and event planner has provided her with the opportunity to spotlight and interact with a wide variety of successful people.

"Landing a television appearance is one of the most effective marketing opportunities available," says Denise. "The key is to offer a product that is informative and interesting and distinguishes itself from the hundreds of other letters and press kits television producers routinely receive. Your job is to present a package that attracts the attention of the show's booker or producer."

As you prepare to promote your product or event, consider these suggestions from Denise:

1. Know the target audience of the show on which you want to appear. If the show's target audience is broad and diverse, promote your product, service, or event as one with broad appeal to a spectrum of viewers. If the target audience is more narrow, tailor your message to fit the group you want to reach.

2. First, call ahead to identify the name of the person who is responsible for scheduling guests—usually a producer, talent coordinator, or show booker. Then send a well-written, concise cover letter with a press kit four to six weeks before you would like to appear. The press kit should include a press release, clippings if applicable, photo, fact sheet, sample questions, and tour schedule. Include a copy of your book, CD, or product.

3. A follow-up call should be made within days of the anticipated arrival of your correspondence at the studio. Your goal in the telephone call is to "book" or schedule the appearance. Take air time into consideration when making *all* telephone calls. By this, I mean make calls to morn-

ing shows in the afternoon, and afternoon shows in the morning. Don't forget to check time zones. If you are rejected because of a schedule conflict, inquire about alternative dates. If you are turned down, try again in about three months.

4. If you are scheduled for an appearance, call your contact one week before the interview to confirm it. Ask any questions at that time. The day of your appearance, the producers and staff are very busy and will appreciate it if your questions are limited to those that are truly important and related to that day's program. If additional information is required, send it immediately. Return all calls from your contact immediately.

You should ALWAYS get copies of your interviews to use for additional promotion. Ask about the procedure before the day of your appearance. You may need to provide a blank tape or pay a fee. If the station does not provide this service, you can always set your VCR or get a friend to tape the show for you.

5. Solid-colored dresses, suits, or slacks with a jacket are the best attire. Prints can detract from your message. Stay away from white and light colors. Jewelry should be conservative. Simple and classy always works.

6. Arrive promptly at the scheduled time. Time controls the television business. If you are running late, call and inform your contact. Tardiness complicates the timing of a television show and is a big NO-NO.

7. Let the producer know in advance if you will be bringing props. Television is a visual medium. It is good to have books, CD's, artwork, samples, etc. Make sure information submitted for graphics (e.g., telephone numbers, addresses, dates, etc.) is correct.

8. Do not travel with an entourage. If others do accompany you, immediately ask where they may wait for you.

9. You must be credible. Be prepared. Be informed. Stay focused on your message. Know your product and value the opportunity to share your story. Identify your goals and commit to accomplishing them. Keep answers con-

cise and to the point. Stick with what you agreed to do on the show, because it has been written and planned on the basis of that agreement.

10. Be friendly and smile when appropriate. If the audience likes you, there is a better chance that they'll like your product, too.

11. Look at the host when answering questions. Do not look at the camera unless directed to do so.

12. Thank your host before you leave. Follow up with a short thank-you note to the host, contact, and producer. Include a business card.

"Remember, a good show and a good reception can mean a repeat appearance," Denise advises. "Staff members change positions and stations. If one of your contacts leaves, they may think of you for their next program."

In addition to the tips given by Denise, I urge my sisters to continually research opportunities to be interviewed. Watch TV and listen to radio stations in other cities when you travel. What programs suit your promotional needs? How? Where might your story fit in?

Make a phone call to find out who the producer is, what the length of the show is, whether it is live or taped, what topics they are looking for, and how the station accepts communication. Usually, a recorded message will instruct you how to mail, fax, or e-mail your story idea. Producers' needs vary, and the format may include talk shows, community debate, cooking/crafts/arts programs, and the regular evening news. Strategize on how you can meet their needs.

If you can include an interesting local angle, it will give your story a good chance of getting picked up.

If you get an invitation to go on the air, take it, even if it means rearranging your schedule. As you can imagine, getting a spot on national television is difficult, but not impossible. Competition is fierce for a chance to be on the popular talk shows and news magazine programs, but exposure on shows like *Oprah* or *Prime Time Live* can bring instant recognition and near-celebrity status.

When word got out that a camera crew from the national newsmagazine show *48 Hours* planned to film authors at the 1995 American Booksellers Association meeting in Chicago, everyone, including me, wanted to be on television. My publicist was leery of my prospects and offered little encouragement. After all, I was an unknown entity and Dan Rather was busy fielding questions about Connie Chung's recent firing.

But since Dan Rather, the show's host, had been kind enough to give me a fabulous quote for the cover of my novel *Black Gold,* I decided to go for it and immediately faxed my appearance schedule to the producer, referring to Mr. Rather's endorsement of my work. The results? In a small booth in the mammoth convention hall of forty thousand–plus attendees, a camera crew zoomed in on me and began filming. I started talking. I spoke about my books for only about twenty seconds, but wherever I go, people say, "Didn't I see you on *48 Hours*?" I just smile and answer, "Yes."

This was spontaneous coverage, but I was prepared. I was not about to leave this opportunity to chance and I am so glad I didn't blow it. When you get a few seconds to toot your horn on television, you'd better be ready.

THE INTERVIEW

ATTITUDE ADJUSTMENT TIP #2

Enjoy your opportunity to shine.

Participating in an arranged interview on radio or television provides optimum opportunity to shine. The first few seconds of an interview are crucial, especially if you only have a few minutes. But even if you have been allotted a fifteen-to-thirty-minute segment, what you say in the opening will determine whether the listener or viewer sticks with you or zaps the remote to find something more interesting on another channel. Plan to grab the audience with an interesting opening or risk wasting an opportunity to make yourself memorable.

Anticipate the kinds of questions that would be asked in an interview, and decide how you would answer. Gather key facts to back up the data you plan to share. Center your discussion on three or four main points to avoid rambling away from the subject at hand. What do you want people to know about you, your service, your product? Create a mini-agenda in your mind to tick off as the interview progresses.

Don't put yourself on the spot. It is perfectly okay to decline, in a professional manner, any question that you feel is too personal or offensive or is not related to the topic at hand. Hidden agendas are real. These traps catch you off guard and make you feel compelled to respond. Use tact in circumventing an issue that could spell disaster for you or your company. You may have to rehearse such delicate replies in advance. On more than one occasion I have simply stated, "I prefer not to comment on that." Case closed.

Be relaxed and personable. Strive to establish a sense of rapport with the interviewer before and during the program. Once you are miked and on the set, ignore the cameras, and talk to the host, not the audience. Conversation should be natural, so talk to the person interviewing you as if you were chatting one-on-one in your kitchen. If for some reason there is tension between you and the host, don't let it show. If you do, the audience will think you are the one with the problem, not the on-air personality they are used to watching.

Give informative, but not lengthy, answers. Timing is important in TV, so watch your host for subtle cues as to whether you are expected to expand on or curtail what you are saying. The more interviews I do, the more comfortable I become with judging the length of my responses.

If, at the end of an interview, you are asked if there is anything else you'd like to say, jump in and finish your agenda. This is an opportune moment to expound on a point or reiterate your objectives, leaving the viewers with the heart of your message fresh in their minds. Having a polished finish makes you come off as a professional who is in control. If you have a service motto or slogan that makes a catchy ending, now is the time to use it. You may be pleased to see your words turn up later as a published quote. Reporters actually like it when you come off as a well-prepared guest, providing vital information they may have overlooked.

Dressing Down

Unless your service or profession requires a unique type of clothing that helps communicate your message, it is best to opt for conservative clothing if you are going on the air. Try to dress as you would for a regular business day in your profession. Don't suddenly get a new hairdo or change your style just because you will be on TV. You will probably feel uncomfortable in your new look and this uneasiness will be reflected in the way you sit and move on camera.

As mentioned before, solid colors are best, especially in blues, grays, and browns. Black can wipe some people out, yet look fine on others. I like myself in red and often wear it on TV, though some professionals say that it does not photograph well. Look at photos of yourself in a variety of colors. Pay attention to what the various shades and patterns do for or to your complexion. Consult a stylist or professional shopper for advice.

I watch the female newscasters and newsmagazine show hosts to analyze what they are wearing and how it looks. Tailored jackets with collars generally look better than jewel necklines. A V-shaped neckline makes a woman's face appear slimmer. Oversized shiny jewelry is not a good idea, as it can reflect light and draw attention away from your face.

Celebrities and models with bodies that scream to be noticed can opt for short, tight skirts. That's great for them. But if you do wear short skirts, be very careful about how you sit and cross your legs. Generally, I prefer to wear classic, tailored pantsuits, so I don't have to worry if too much thigh is hanging out.

Unless you are a professional television personality and have your own makeup artist, it is best to arrive with your street makeup on and let the studio makeup artists touch up your eyes and lips, or powder down the shiny areas just before air time. The same applies to hair.

The Big Day

Give yourself plenty of time to get to the studio, and plan to arrive about fifteen minutes early. This allows for traffic, parking, and unexpected delays. It also gives you time to get acclimated and to relax before the show. Make sure you know your contact's name and bring along any written correspondence concerning your appearance. Because of security concerns, your word may not be good enough to get you into the studio. This can be frustrating, especially if the taping is after-hours or at a small station where there is not a lot of personnel on duty. On more than one occasion I have had to produce my letter of invitation before I was granted permission to enter the studio.

Don't expect the host to have copies of your book, CD, or product on hand, even if they were sent ahead. Many, many times I have been told that the advance copy of the book disappeared somewhere between the mail room and the producer's desk. Also, cable and community TV hosts often give extra copies of books to those who produce the show—their way of "paying" their technicians and support staff. But it may mean that your book is nowhere to be seen on interview day. To be sure, bring a copy with you.

When arrangements were set for me to do the *Connie Martensen Talks Books* show in Los Angeles, five copies of my new book, *Starlight Passage,* were requested. My publicist assured me they would be sent ahead, so to keep my luggage light. I arrived with only one copy. To my horror, the advance copies had not arrived, and they were absolutely necessary for the camera angles Connie used in her show. The appearance was about to be canceled when I remembered I did have extra covers. We wrapped the covers around other authors' books and the taping proceeded, though her technicians were very disappointed not to get signed copies of my novel. I took their names and promised to send personally autographed copies to each one. As soon as I got back to Houston I did just that, and never again was I caught without my books.

GETTING COVERAGE FOR A SPECIAL PROJECT

Action Steps

1. Start organizing your event or project early enough to get press materials out in a timely manner. Generally, lead time for print is longer than for television or radio.
2. Develop a theme or title that is catchy and appropriate to the project.
3. Create a time line in which you outline each stage of the plan, including the names of those who will be assisting you.
4. Appoint a person or committee to be solely responsible for publicity.
5. Have this person contact the community relations people at the local radio and TV stations and the newspapers to get coverage for your event. In a corporate setting utilize the internal newsletter or company publications.
6. Involve high-profile sponsors.
7. Tap into your social and community organizations via their newsletters, visits to chapter meetings, and targeted letters to solicit assistance in spreading the word.
8. Think and speak on a grand scale when developing the campaign for your project. Don't start from a position of what you *can't* do. Maintain a positive, go-for-it attitude.
9. Analyze the competition and opposition.
10. If you've done this project before, review what worked and didn't work in the past. Be willing to change traditional methods of operation.

Example of a special project: The historic Black Expo has folded its tent after seventeen years of touring the country. It was designed to spotlight black artists and entrepreneurs and to help small businesses reach a target audience. It is discouraging to realize the expo is gone, but I also view this turn of events as an opportunity to fill a void and serve the public. When my chapter of the Coalition of 100 Black Women wanted to host a book signing with a local author as one of its annual fund-raisers, I suggested that we expand our efforts and invite every published African-American author in the city who had a current book out to participate in the book-signing as part of a fall 1998 expo highlighting black businesses related to the arts. This event will attract much more media attention than any of our previous projects, and the public will be excited about meeting and supporting its own talent while helping the coalition make more money than it could have by spotlighting only one author.

15
Embrace the Applause

Attitude Focus: Humility and Gratitude
> Come center stage
> take the spotlight
> do not hesitate to
> walk from beneath the shadows.
> You are not designed to be
> a wallflower to
> success
> change
> empowerment
> or
> self-confidence.

RAMONA SUSANE NICHOLAS

ATTITUDE ADJUSTMENT TIP #1

Focus on others.

"*I* was such an avid reader when I was young, I used to get in trouble in school for reading," says Faye Childs, founder of Blackboard: African American Bestseller List.

After graduating from Capital University in Columbus, Ohio, with a degree in communications, Faye started writing her first novel while doing advertising and promotional work for concerts, special attractions, and even boxing matches. She discovered that she loved this type of work. It was stimulating and she thrived on the get-up-and-go atmosphere where she was talking to vendors, sponsors, people who rented halls, artists, and performers.

PERSISTENCE PAYS

"When I finished my manuscript," says Faye, "I began to think about how my book would be promoted if it ever got published. I decided to do some research on how books by African-American authors were being promoted. This is when the bottom fell out of my dream. It was 1990, and I was shocked to find that only three black authors were being promoted: Alice Walker, Toni Morrison, and Alex Haley. I kept on researching, finding very little about new black authors. I asked myself how I found out about new titles and authors. I realized that I usually turned to the *New York Times* best-seller list for information. After talking to friends, who agreed that word-of-mouth and the *New York Times* list were their most common sources of information, I went to the library to do some more research. Still, there were few books by black authors there. I had to dig through a lot of research to find out how many stores contributed to the *New York Times* list. It soon became my personal mission to decipher what, exactly, a best-seller list *was*: How was it compiled and what were the benefits for the authors who made it? How successful were they? How much did being declared a best-selling author increase book sales? It became clear that making the list was very important."

Using general information from her research, Faye decided to start her own best-seller list for African-American authors. She went to the library and checked phone directories for thirty-two cities, then picked three bookstores from each city, both mainstream stores and those serving the black community. She wrote letters to the booksellers, telling them about her project and asking them to help her by sending her their monthly sales figures for black-authored books.

"Ninety percent of those contacted agreed to participate," says Faye. "This effort was totally self-funded, and my first best-seller list debuted on August 19, 1991, in the *Columbus Dispatch*."

Launching the list was just the start. Faye knew that she needed an endorsement by a credible institution or organization if she wanted the list to be taken seriously. Her goal was to attract national attention and become accepted in the publishing industry as the source for reporting the standards of excellence in black writing. Faye telephoned George Meyers, the book editor at the *Columbus Dispatch*. He advised her to contact the American Booksellers Association (ABA). When Faye called ABA headquarters in New York, she was told not to bother because they were already planning to do such a list. Faye panicked and seriously thought about giving up, but she didn't. Her instincts told her to press on. She cut out the first Blackboard: African American Bestseller List from the *Columbus Dispatch* and mailed it to the director of the ABA with this note: "I don't know if you've done it, yet—but I already have." They quickly backed down, telling Faye there was no need for them to reinvent the wheel and inviting her to New York. She went to the headquarters of the ABA, got the organization's endorsement, and benefited greatly from the media blitz they orchestrated.

Faye says, "The response was overwhelming. My story was covered on the front page of the *Wall Street Journal*. *Emerge* was the first magazine to pick it up, then *Essence* followed. The official African American Best-seller List was launched! When I think about how naïve I was when starting out, I am sure I would be too intimidated to do it now."

Tenacity and persistence paid off for Faye, who has watched the list grow in importance and value over the years.

An example of the importance of tenacity occurred in 1997, when several publishers pulled out of ABA/Book Expo America. Faye stood to lose important underwriters and support for the annual reception she holds to announce the African American Bookseller of the Year.

"I help sell millions of dollars' worth of books for publishers each year through my list," Faye says. "I got angry when the support was not there, so I just got on the phone, called the publishers, and told them how much I needed their support. I got the sponsors, but if I hadn't taken a personal approach, Blackboard might not have been represented at the reception that gives African-American authors and booksellers exposure to more than twenty-five hundred people in the publishing and bookselling industry. That was and continues to be my primary goal: to ensure that authors and booksellers who target the black community get the attention they deserve. When I focus on what I want, I go after it."

> A personal marketing campaign must be thought of as a sincere effort to serve and share—not as a vehicle to make you rich.

Every contact you make helps shape the impression you create, defining who you are. As you build professional and personal relationships, concentrate on building your reputation. Demonstrate your interest in others by sending personal notes of congratulations or sharing articles of mutual interest. Remain accessible to those who can learn from your experiences, and strive to be known as a reliable person of integrity who genuinely cares about others. This is the greatest compliment you can receive.

ATTITUDE ADJUSTMENT TIP #2

Share.

"My mission statement is *'noblesse oblige,'*" says Dr. Elaine P. Adams, vice chancellor of the Houston Community

College System. This motto means "Of him or her to whom much is given, much is expected." For Elaine Adams, who has been honored by leading educational institutions across the country for her dedication and service, this mission statement has served as an important guidepost during the evolution of her ground-breaking career in higher education. "To me those words mean that I have been very fortunate in life, and that good fortune must be shared with others for it to be meaningful to me."

Elaine was educated and started her teaching career in schools located in the poverty-stricken areas of New Orleans that are now referred to as the M Zone—the Murder Zone. There, she says, the nuns and her first principal encouraged her to believe that there were people whose lives would improve as a result of her intervention. Knowing that there were people whom she could assist boosted her own self-esteem and moved her focus from herself to others. It was an important lesson for her to learn.

This successful administrator in higher education believes that her most important asset is her perseverance. "I am hard to kill," Elaine says. "The odds may be stacked against me, but I stick with a problem until I reach a reasonable solution. This perseverance has helped increase my recognition factor. Colleagues gained confidence in me. If there was a difficult task or a tough assignment, I could be relied on not to shirk it, although it may involve hard work or unpleasantness. However, this can be a negative side for African-American women who are often stereotyped into this role. In other words—call *us* if something needs fixin', but save the plum assignments for others. There should be a balance in the distribution of assignments, with rewards for those who persevere and are successful in the critical, unwanted assignments."

Elaine goes to great lengths to do what she can to find solutions to problems. When the Houston Community College System was mulling over the idea of establishing a campus in a shopping mall in an area of town that was in transition, there was much concern about safety. Would students feel comfortable enrolling in a college located in a mall tainted with a reputation for being violent and unsafe?

While vacationing in Los Angeles, Elaine learned that some malls in Los Angeles with negative images had undertaken changes to turn things around. They were able to increase security and communicate safety messages to the public. Armed with a camera and a notepad, Elaine set out to visit these revitalized malls in Los Angeles in order to document their effective practices. Back home, these notes and photos were critical in helping the regents of HCC decide to open what is now the largest community college operation in an active mall in the nation. Guess who was named as founding president of that campus? Dr. Elaine P. Adams!

This active educator spends a lot of time talking to students. She says, "The students are generally eager to hear from a woman of color who has experienced some success. I try to be very realistic in the information I provide. In communicating with students, I also clarify my own life patterns."

ATTITUDE ADJUSTMENT TIP #3

Celebrate success.

As months pass by and your promotional campaign begins to produce the results you dreamed of, it is important to take the time to celebrate your successes, even if they seem small. Progress toward goals comes in uneven spurts, with highs and lows, twists and turns, that often disguise the achievements and benchmarks we have set for ourselves. When you reach a turning point in your plan, step off the road for a few minutes and celebrate where you are, then move on up to the next level, ready to accept a new challenge.

When sisters reach a certain level of competence and expertise in their fields, they are quite often pulled in two different directions. As they rise in the corporate arena, they may feel pressure to hold on to what is familiar. Often there is an element of guilt about moving on and moving up.

"Success pulls you away from some people and closer to others," says Jackie Richmond, vice president for health-care practices for an international public relations firm. In her position, she specializes in social marketing, which means using public relations approaches and strategies to sell health-care messages—lifestyle changes people can take to live longer and better-quality lives. She oversees government contracts her company has with agencies like the National Institutes of Health.

With a master's in public administration and twenty years of experience in health communications, she has achieved a high level of success in her field. "I do feel isolated at times, being the only black VP in my company," she admits. "When I go somewhere, the first identification with me is that I am an African-American woman. A certain responsibility comes with that. As I have matured, I realize that this responsibility has taken on a different complexion. I want to be better and better at what I do in the health communications arena—get better at my craft as I identify appropriate channels and tailor messages to a particular audience. If I am in a meeting with a representative from an African-American organization or community group, I sometimes feel that I am on the wrong side of the table. I identify with the issues they are bringing to the table, and from my position, I often have to make the decision whether or not my company will be able to do pro bono work for them. I empathize with my brothers and sisters, but I can't do everything. There is a fine line I have to walk. I have to have a foot on both sides. I can't forget that I am African-American first, but I am also a professional who has a job to do. If I turn the group down, I can sense what they are thinking: 'Hey, what is wrong with this sister? She could come to our office from six to ten in the evening to help us out.' But when my day is over, I need to get my own brain cells replenished. I am constantly trying to figure out how to keep my feet in both worlds."

Our desire to give back to our communities, still do our work, and have a good life takes careful balance. "It is not

quantity but quality," Jackie observes. "I had to make a decision to give myself a break. We sisters must decide how we
are going to use our time and talent to give back, without
depleting ourselves I use my writing talent to compose my
church newsletter. It may not be a lot, but it is what I feel I
can do. African-American women can feel so guilty, they end
up running everywhere, exhausting themselves. But in the
name of what? Our first priority needs to be our homes.
Sisters carry too much baggage and a lot of it is self-imposed.

"I am okay saying that I deserve the best and can afford it.
Life is about choices and being able to live with the consequences of those choices. Good and bad. I have paid my dues.
I don't apologize for where I am. I am comfortable, and
intend to go further. Everything is in order, but there is more
to come. We don't have to settle."

Jackie gives this advice to her sisters: "Do not be afraid to
look into the mirror. We walk by mirrors and check the
makeup, but we don't check the person. Look in that mirror
and say, 'I am okay. I have this under control. I am doing well,
making a contribution to the world.' Don't be afraid of doing
self-examination and finding yourself doing very well. Too
many times when we do self-examination, we look for the
negatives instead of recognizing all the things that are good.
If we can learn to celebrate ourselves, this can be an infectious and positive thing. Don't be afraid to be smart. Don't
look for approval from outside of ourselves. Too often, we are
afraid of owning up to how great we are."

I think it is valuable to start new traditions and establish
celebratory rituals that involve family, coworkers, colleagues,
or employees. I look forward to participating in special
moments that document my journey with lasting memories.
As we rush from deadline to deadline, with one eye on the
next project, the next promotion, the next media appearance,
we keep the other eye on our competition. It is easy to miss
opportunities to congratulate ourselves *and each other* for
having made it as far as we have. Simple activities such as
treating colleagues to lunch or sharing a glass of champagne
with a special person can serve as a rite of passage in your

adventure. This provides a time to demonstrate the affection and gratitude you feel for those who helped you step out to shape and develop the mission that is yours.

Setbacks and disappointments can be hurtful, valid reasons to cry and complain. But soon, time eases the pain of failure and you can look back, even laugh at your mistakes, and forgive the stumbling efforts you made in the early part of your journey. Concentrate on being thankful for the inner fire that compelled you to embrace your dream. *You* were the one who moved beyond the prospect of a life without passion and decided to transform routine into riches. Doing so, you used the wealth of talent God gave to you and created a life of purpose.

By remaining poised for success and *sharing* who you are, you can reinforce your decision to sell your dream while making a difference in someone else's life. Embrace the good points, the high points, and follow this advice to keep things in perspective.

Action Steps

1. Always deliver your message with professional and personal style as well as a great deal of sincerity.
2. Be humble with your thanks and show appreciation for others' interest.
3. Establish and maintain strong rapport with your target audience.
4. Keep your spiritual connections strong.
5. Smile. Often.
6. Stay fresh and forward-looking by paying attention to the young people in your life. They can provide inspiration, hope, and balance.

You will be graced with support and financial gain if you sell your dream with passion. People love to be attached to a winner and those who demonstrate an attitude of gratitude will keep their message strong and alive long after its delivery. I had not been back to my alma mater, Mount Union

College, for almost thirty years. When I moved away from Ohio and settled in Houston, I lost contact with the school. Last fall the director of multicultural affairs called to ask whether I would return to the campus to spend time with the African-American students. I didn't hesitate. You see, when I was attending that college, I was the only black female on campus. It was a lonely, isolating experience, but that loneliness was a worthwhile sacrifice to make in order to receive a first-rate education at a prestigious private college.

I was eager to visit with the sixty-one black students currently in attendance and to do anything I could to encourage them to stay there and succeed. The weeklong visit was an emotional reunion and an uplifting experience that I will never forget. I was so glad I decided to interrupt my rigid writing schedule to spend time with the bright, talented young people who graciously welcomed me. When the multicultural affairs director took me to the airport after my visit was over, she handed me an envelope that contained a very generous check. I was shocked! I had not come expecting anything. I had come to serve.

Part III Worksheet

Assessment Questions

1. Do you feel as if you are in control of things? _____

2. Do you usually prefer to follow rather than lead? _____

3. Why? _____

   _____

4. Would you go to an event alone if you didn't know any-body there? _____

5. When unexpected problems or changes arise, do your spirits sink? Do you panic? _____

6. Are you comfortable dealing with financial matters? _____

7. Are you comfortable with your physical appearance? _____

8. Does the thought of speaking before a large group or appearing on TV excite or frighten you? _____

9. Have you recently extended a hand to a sister in your field? _____

10. Has a sister extended a hand to you? _____

11. Do you believe that you have something of importance to say? _____

12. Why should anyone listen to you?_____

_____

Action Steps

1. Take inventory. What equipment/materials/tools do you need to get organized, updated, and in control? _____

_____

2. Focus on a current problem. Break it down into small achievable steps. _____

_____

_____

3. Examine your budget. Are your financial resources being properly allocated? _____

4. Identify one source for free publicity/assistance and use it.

_____

5. Write a letter of introduction to someone you would like to bring into your network. Do this once a week.

6. Look in the mirror. Commit to changing whatever bothers you most.

7. Clean your closet. Toss outdated, ill-fitting clothes and begin creating the image you visualize.

8. Practice, practice, practice your speech, sales pitch, presentation, etc. in front of a large mirror or with someone you trust and respect.

9. Perfect your delivery until it is clear, comfortable, and natural.

10. Send a message of encouragement to a sister.

11. Gather family, friends, and your support team together to celebrate your decision to *Step Out with Attitude* and *Sell Your Dream*.

Recommended Reading and Resources

*T*here is a vast amount of information available that in various ways addresses attitude, positive thinking, marketing, and promotion. The materials vary in scope and focus, and in relationship to the needs of women of different races and ethnic backgrounds. Here is a selection of information sources to explore as you create your personal promotional campaign.

BOOKS

Professional and Personal Development

Abarbanel, Karen. *How to Succeed on Your Own.* New York: Henry Holt, 1994.

Benoit, Pamela J. *Telling the Success Story.* New York: State University of New York, 1997.

Bixler, Susan. *Professional Presence.* New York: Putnam's, 1991.

Boyd, Julia. *In the Company of My Sisters: Black Women and Self Esteem.* New York: Dutton, 1993

Brown, Les. *Live Your Dreams.* New York: Avon Books, 1992.

Browne, D. Anne. *You Can Get There from Here: Life Lessons on*

Growth and Self Discovery for the Black Woman. Bryant & Dillon, 1995.

Caple, John. *Finding the Hat That Fits.* New York: Plume, 1993.

Covey, Stephen R. *The Seven Habits of Highly Effective People.* New York: Simon & Schuster/Fireside Books, 1990.

Garvin, Andrew P. *The Art of Being Well Informed.* New York: Avery Publishing Group, 1993.

Jones, Laurie Beth. *The Path: Creating Your Mission Statement for Work and Life.* New York: Simon & Schuster, 1996.

Kimbro, Dennis, and Napoleon Hill. *Think and Grow Rich: A Black Choice.* New York: Ballantine Books, 1991.

Mindell, Phyllis. *A Woman's Guide to the Language of Success.* Englewood Cilffs, N.J.: Prentice Hall, 1995.

Reid-Merritt, Patricia. *Sister Power: How Phenomenal Black Women Are Rising to the Top.* New York: John Wiley, 1996.

Segal, Jeanne. *Raising Your Emotional Intelligence.* New York: Henry Holt, 1997.

Sherman, Stephanie. *Make Yourself Memorable.* New York: American Management Association, 1996.

Shields, Carol. *Work Sister Work: Why Black Women Can't Get Ahead and What They Can Do About It.* New York: Carol Publications, 1993.

Spicer, Christopher. *Organizational Public Relations.* Mahwah, N.J.: Lawrence Erlbaum Associates, 1997.

Taylor, Susan. *Lessons in Living.* New York: HarperPerennial, 1995.

Toogood, Granville N. *The Articulate Executive: Learn to Look, Act, and Sound like a Leader.* New York: McGraw-Hill, 1997.

Vanzant, Iyanla. *The Value in the Valley: A Black Woman's Guide Through Life's Dilemmas.* New York: Simon & Schuster/Fireside, 1997.

Williams, Terrie. *The Personal Touch.* New York: Warner Books, 1994.

Entrepreneurship

Abrams, Rhonda M. *The Successful Business Plan: Secrets and Strategies.* Grants Pass, Or.: Oasis Press, 1993.

Boston, Kevin. *Smart Money Moves for African Americans.* New York: Putnam's, 1997.

Broussard, Cheryl. *Sister CEO: The Black Woman's Guide to Starting a Business*. New York: Viking, 1997.

Covello, Joseph, and Brian J. Hazelgreen. *The Complete Book of Business Plans: Simple Steps to Writing a Powerful Business Plan*. Naperville, Ill.: Sourcebooks, 1994.

Goldstein, Arnold. *Starting on a Shoestring: Building a Business Without a Bankroll*. New York: John Wiley, 1995.

Graves, Earl. *How to Succeed in Business Without Being White*. New York: HarperBusiness, 1997.

Harris, Fran. *About My Sister's Business: The Black Woman's Road Map to Successful Entrepreneurship*. New York: Simon & Schuster/Fireside, 1996.

Wittig, Susan. *Work of Her Own: How Women Create Success and Fulfillment off the Traditional Career Track*. New York: Putnam's, 1995.

Networking

Bunkley, Crawford. B. *The African American Network*. New York: Plume, 1996.

Fraser, George. *Success Runs in Our Race: The Complete Guide to Effective Networking in the African American Community*. New York: William Morrow, 1994.

Public Relations/Publicity

Banner & Greif, Ltd. *That Extra Push: A Guide to Publicity at Trade Shows and Industry Expositions*. New York. Banner & Greif.

Dobmeyer, Doug. *Competing Successfully for Media Coverage: A Guide to Getting Media Coverage for Non-profit and Community Organizations*. Chicago: Dobmeyer Communications.

Hahn, Fred, and Kenneth Mangun. *Do-It-Yourself Advertising and Promotion*. New York: John Wiley, 1997.

Wade, John. *Dealing Effectively with the Media: What You Need to Know About Print, Radio, and Television Interviews*. Mediability, Inc.

WEB SITES AND INTERNET ADDRESSES

African American Biographical Database
http://aada.chadwyck.com

Biographical stories provide awareness and insight into the black experience.

Business Wire
http://www.businesswire.com

Interactive, personalized services related to doing business on-line.

Electra
www.electra.com

A gathering place for women, offering information on a wide range of subjects.

Entreprenet
http://www.enterprise.org

A small business guide library.

FinanceHub.Com
http://www.finance-hub.com

A directory of topics related to venture capital.

Tracey L. Minor, author of *Power Moves for People of Color*
tminor@mail10.voivenet.com

A free electronic calendar of conferences, workshops, and events of importance to people of color.

Multicultural Advantage, an executive-search firm that specializes in the placement of people of color in middle- and senior-level positions
multinet@aol.com

Women's Wire
www.women.com

Umbrella site offering a variety of topics of interest to women.

World Association of Small Business Electronic Commerce
http://www.wasbec.uca.edu

A small-business resource guide.

World Class Speakers
http://www.speak.com

A guide to locate professional speakers on a variety of topics.

Prodigy: Black Experience Bulletin Boards
www.blackexperience.com

America On-line: Net Noir

www.netnoir.com

Compuserve: AVS On-line
http://americanvisions.com

ASSOCIATIONS AND ORGANIZATIONS

African American Women's Network, 605 East Berry Street, #900, Ft. Worth, TX 76110. Dedicated to women interested in mentoring.

Association of Black Women Entrepreneurs, Inc., 213–624–8639.

Black Public Relations Society of America, New York: 212–614–4599; Los Angeles: 213–962–8051.

Business and Professional Women/USA, 202–293–1100.

Corporate Women's Network, 2350 Seventh Avenue, New York, NY 10030.

The Encyclopedia of Associations, published by Gale Research, Inc.

Hispanic Public Relations Society of America, 212–614–5024.

National Association of Black Journalists, 703–648–1270.

National Association of Black Women Entrepreneurs, 313–871–4660.

National Association for Female Executives, 800–634–6233.

National Coalition of 100 Black Women, 212–947–2196.

National Council of Negro Women, 202–737–1020.

National MBA Association, 312–236–2622.

National Society of Black Engineers, 703-549–2207.

National Trade and Professional Associations of the United States, Professional Secretaries International, 816–891–6600.

Professional Women of Color, 510 East Thirty-eighth Street, Brooklyn, NY 11203.

Public Relations Society of America, 212–228–7228.

9 to 5: National Association of Working Women, 800–522–0925.

SPECIAL-INTEREST CONFERENCES

The Black Enterprise Entrepreneurs Conference, 130 Fifth Avenue, New York, NY 10011. Sponsored by *Black Enterprise* magazine.

African American Women on Tour, 3914 Murphy Canyon Road, Suite 216, San Diego, CA 92123–4493. A national empowerment conference for black women that travels to major cities each year.

Direct Marketing to MultiCultural Markets. Sponsored by Multicultural Marketing Resources, Inc., 212–242–3351.

National Professional Network Cruise, 800–340–1965. African-Americans sail the Caribbean in style to attend workshops, see live stage shows, and make new friends.

Web Search Engines

Yahoo!: http://www.yahoo.com/

Lycos: http://www.lycos.com/

infoSeek: http://www.infoseek.com/

WebCrawler: http://www.webcrawler.com/

Alta Vista: http://altavista.digital.com/

Excite!: http://www.excite.com/

Magellan: http://www.mckinley.com/

Savvy Search: http://savvy.cs.colostate.edu:2000/

All4One Search Machine: http://easypage.com/all4one/

Index